" THE MILITANT DEMOCRACY"

JOSEPH COWEN AND VICTORIAN RADICALISM

Nigel Todd

BEWICK PRESS   **TYNE AND WEAR**

© 1991 Nigel Todd

First published in Great Britain by
Bewick Press
132 Claremont Road
Whitley Bay
Tyne and Wear
NE26 3TX

ISBN 0-9516056-3-1

Printed and bound in Great Britain by
Billings and Sons Limited Worcester.

CONTENTS

ACKNOWLEDGEMENTS:

A great many people have helped in the research, discussion and publication of this book. I would like to pay a particular tribute to the following: Mrs. M. Harris for allowing me to read the papers of the late Keith Harris; Raymond and Mabel Challinor; Bill Lancaster; Maureen Callcott; Royden Harrison; Joan Hugman; Stafford Linsley; Jean Lunn; E.D. Spraggon; Andy McSmith; Archie Potts; Owen R. Ashton; M.L. Jones (Blaydon); the staffs of the Newcastle upon Tyne and Gateshead Public Libraries, the Newcastle upon Tyne Literary and Philosophical Society, the Tyne and Wear County Records Office, the Bishopsgate Institute, the Co-operative Union Library and the British Museum; and the students of the "People Make History" courses at the University of Newcastle upon Tyne's Centre for Continuing Education for their interest in Joseph Cowen. Any errors are my responsibility.

Thanks are due, also, for the generous assistance of Northern Arts, the Lipman Trust, the Joseph Cowen Society, Wallsend People's Centre, Eileen Raby (editing), Allison Barrett (cover), Brenda Kelly-Dodds and Graham Stevenson (technical).

Finally, a very special thanks to Ruth and Selina for their considerable patience and understanding over a long period of time.

Nigel Todd
Newcastle upon Tyne, July 1991

Yours truly
Jos: Cowen

1

CHAPTER ONE : WHO WAS JOSEPH COWEN?

This is a story of rediscovery. For much of the Victorian era the name of Joseph Cowen was familiar - sometimes famous, sometimes notorious - in Britain, Europe and occasionally beyond. And then Cowen was quite literally extinguished from memory. English Liberalism regarded Cowen as a pariah and excluded him from its history. Separated by his own brand of Radicalism from wholehearted involvement with the emergent Socialists of the 1880s and 1890s, and withdrawing from politics too soon to be claimed as a pioneer of the modern Labour Movement, Cowen was overlooked by most labour historians. There was nobody to speak on his behalf. Consequently, Cowen became a marginal figure for later generations, a sort of mystery man. Joseph Cowen and mystery were often inseparable. Large areas of his life were constructed deliberately to defy the best efforts of biographers (and secret policemen) at unravelling the exact part he played in some spectacular nineteenth-century dramas, including at least one assassination attempt and a string of insurrections around the more despotic reaches of Europe. He gently but firmly resisted any probing investigations into his life-story and the one apparently "original" biography, written by Evan Rowland Jones in 1885, was drafted and tightly controlled by Cowen. In private and public Cowen drew a veil over certain details of his life, modestly claiming that these could not be of any real interest. But he did erect definite barriers, arguing that it would be "indiscreet" to publish too much because of "unpleasant consequences" for people still facing political risks. (1) Nevertheless, his reputation was sufficiently well-known for the *New York Times* to describe him as "one of the most extraordinary men in Europe ... the friend of every conspirator from Moscow to Madrid." Or, in the words of the *Daily Telegraph*, he was "more splendid, and generous and daring and enthusiastic than any private Englishman of his time" in promoting European revolutions. (2)

Alongside a protective confidentiality Cowen remained an exceptionally public figure. From the late-1840s to the mid-1880s he was prominent in all manner of campaigns, reform movements, support committees for overseas revolutionaries and exiles, co-operatives and trade unionism, the theatre, newspaper publishing

and between 1874-86 he held a national platform as a Radical
Member of Parliament for Newcastle upon Tyne. His public
meetings attracted great audiences, consolidating a position of
immense political influence. Over the middle of the nineteenth
century, Cowen was held to be "the life and soul of every advanced
movement in the North of England." (3) Keith Harris, who wrote
one of the best short summaries of the range of Cowen's
involvements, argued that in "home affairs Cowen was to establish
a Newcastle school of radicalism" enjoying national pre-eminence.
(4) Contemporaries of Cowen were convinced that his political
conquest of Northumberland and Durham rivalled, if not exceeded,
Joseph Chamberlain's significance in Birmingham and the Midlands
by the 1870s (5) and the "reputation for radicalism tinged with
republicanism" acquired by the north east of England was
"especially" due to Joseph Cowen. (6)

To be an enigma and a noted politician at one and the same time
was a tortuous exercise. So what was he really about, this
"remarkable and perplexing character"? (7) The answer always
brought mixed reviews but Cowen's chief opponents for much of his
life were usually unequivocal. "Like all the "radical" reformers we
have met with, he is a born despot" said one Tory newspaper editor
criticising Cowen's Northern Reform Union in 1862. (8) "Arrogant
domination" was the term used by the journalist W.T. Stead who
clashed sharply with Cowen's anti-Czarist views. (9) And marching
at the head of a labour procession through Newcastle upon Tyne in
1873 Cowen heard vehement calls for his hanging from shopkeepers
and merchants. (10) Shortly afterwards, standing for election to
Parliament for the first time, Cowen was castigated by the Tories as
"a Communist, a Revolutionist, a Republican, and an Atheist." (11)
He was additionally denounced on the grounds that "his speeches
were violent; his company was doubtful; he was an advocate of
extreme, and often of revolutionary measures" (12) and he "seemed
uncouth" to other Members of Parliament. (13) There was a lot
more where that came from, but Cowen took it in his stride,
believing: "A Tory, to my mind, is the embodiment of all that is
objectionable." (14) For other people, Cowen's political behaviour
could be explained merely in terms of a personality quirk or even
defect. Critics, who in some cases doubled as allies, regarded him
variously as "terribly self-centred" (15), "a conspirator to the tips of
his fingers" (16), "emotional" and a "crank" (17), or stricken by

"vanity". (18) A more recent study of Cowen's parliamentary relationships concluded that he had "no scruple, no notion of right and wrong when it came to a matter of his own advancement" and was affected by his European connections to the extent that "conspiracy became part of his character." (19) Joseph Cowen was always the object of vitriolic denigration and lavish praise. But assessing whether the attacks were deserved requires an acknowledgement of three considerations. Firstly, and obviously, it has to be borne in mind that Cowen's critics generally had their own axes to grind. Secondly, there is the problem of identifying Cowen's own intentions at any given moment and this is not easy in a context of occasional secrecy. But finally, and perhaps most significantly in judging Cowen's role in history, it is necessary to grasp the meaning of his huge popularity.

When Joseph Cowen died in 1900, at the age of 71, the attendance at his funeral was "vast" and drawn mainly from the "workpeople" of Tyneside. (20) The "multitude of mourners" included:

> "miners' representatives, a lieutenant from the Garibaldian army
> ... a delegation from the Irish Nationalist Party, whose telegram
> of condolance was the first to reach Newcastle after his death,
> delegates from the various Co-operative Societies, Mechanics'
> Institutes and Temperance Organisations"

as well as "labour leaders ... and strong Radicals." (21) It was an impressive tribute to a rich man who had left public life fourteen years previously and one echoed in some interesting quarters. Cowen had never been a Socialist, preferring his own brand of ultra-Radicalism, but among the obituaries was a glowing note in *Justice*, the newspaper of the Marxist Social-Democratic Federation: "Revolutionists of all countries will join with us in mourning the death of Joseph Cowen ...the sturdy champion of oppressed peoples everywhere." (22) A few years earlier Frederick Engels had hoped that a new "proletarian-radical" party might be launched and led by Joseph Cowen "an old Chartist, half, if not a whole Communist, and a very fine fellow", (23) and the Socialist William Morris regarded Cowen as "very friendly and nice." (24) From an opposite corner of the Labour Movement to the Marxists, Thomas Burt, the Northumberland miners' MP, recounted with sincere feelings: "I knew Mr. Cowen intimately; I admired and loved him." (25)

Indisputably, Cowen had been widely liked and "at miners'
demonstrations in Tyneside valleys" his portrait had adorned "the
silken banners of colliery unions as they marched in procession."
(26) People even dedicated books to Cowen. The journalist, W.E.
Adams, was moved to dedicate his autobiography to "the memory of
Joseph Cowen, M.P., whose influence in journalism, courage in
politics and commanding eloquence in the tribunes of the people,
will ever be numbered among the inspiring traditions of Northern
England." (27) Reverend Joseph Parker, who published a little book
of Tyneside stories in 1896, decided to "honour my book" by
recognising Cowen as "the most brilliant Tynesider I have ever
known." (28) And the major history of the Tyneside Irish published
in 1917 was also dedicated to an Englishman, Joseph Cowen. (29)

Cowen had a genuine talent for "the common touch". One
parliamentary commentator recorded that when Cowen arrived at
Westminster he "looked like a rural Nonconformist Minister
entering the solemn conclave of mitred and robed prelates." (30)
Although Cowen was wealthy through his brick-making and gas-pipe
manufacturing businesses, his acquaintances noted that "no man
cared less for money than he did." (31) His clothes were "not made
by a fashionable tailor", and never looked new. (32) Dressing like "a
workman, with a black comforter around his neck", Cowen wore "the
only wide-awake hat at that time known in the House of Commons."
(33) The hat became a Cowen trademark, causing a "sensation" (34)
by breaking strict parliamentary conventions on headgear long
before Keir Hardie appeared with his famous cloth cap. The hat -
popularly known as "a Joe Cowen" (35) - was chosen by Cowen
partly because hard hats irritated his skin but also as a political
gesture encouraged by the Hungarian nationalist, Louis Kossuth,
whom Cowen knew well and who inspired young radicals to abandon
the social convention of wearing "stove pipe" hats. (36) An
"under-sized man" walking with "a slight stoop", (37) in a "slouching,
ungraceful" manner, and wearing "his hair long", (38) Cowen
integrated himself fully into the folk-imagery of nineteenth century
Tyneside. W.E. Adams noted:

> "the characteristics, the ideas, the idiosyncrasies, even the
> prejudices of the people among whom he had been born and
> bred, were more truely represented by him than were those of
> any other district by any other prominent figure in public life."
> (39)

He "talked the Tyneside tongue", (40) which the House of Commons had difficulty in understanding, (41) but Cowen "clung to it as one of the most precious of his possessions", (42) finding that it "added to his majority" at election times. (43) Despite rigidly shunning alcohol and smoking, Cowen shared other popular enthusiasms such as horseracing. (44) And he had an "extraordinary interest" in people, seeking out the "comparatively obscure." (45) Even some of Cowen's enemies were moved to describe him "as the most amiable" Radical that they had come across, (46) and his love of children could find him on all-fours giving "horse-rides" whilst waiting to address public meetings. (47) He was considered:

> "the most gentle and genial, and exquisitely courteous of men ... shy of smart people ... hated smart talk ... delighted in deep and serious conversation ...[and] would go out of his way to avoid title and fashion, the prouder and more glittering, the more he shunned it." (48)

A "man of fascinating personality", (49) Cowen could captivate people with his "peculiarly beautiful, lustrous and expressive eyes" (50) and his renowned oratory. The ability to speak well and hold the attention of an audience whether in the open-air or inside a large hall was a vital political skill and one which Cowen worked hard to develop. He prepared his speeches in advance believing that "preparation was the best compliment a speaker could pay to an audience." (51) At meetings of miners in Northumberland and Durham, Cowen could talk:

> "with an intonation that they understood, in a garb differing not greatly from their own "Sunday best", and in words so idiomatic that they could be understood without mental worry." (52)

He was considered "unsurpassed" as a parliamentary speaker, (53) and "one of those rare orators of whom there are not more two or three in a century." (54) By the early 1880s, Cowen was described by the historian Justin McCarthy as:

> "the foremost of all the younger generation of Parliamentary orators...After Mr. Gladstone and Mr. Bright comes Mr. Cowen...The music of his phrases, the passion of his language, the grace and beauty of his sentences, and the honourable independence of thought which inspired all his utterances never failed to make the majority of his hearers forget for the moment not merely the rough northern accent of the speaker, but the unpopularity of the opinions which he was expressing. It has

been Mr. Cowen's fortune generally to support, in the House of
Commons, causes unpopular to the majority of the House." (55)

In pointing to Cowen's advocacy of supposedly "unpopular causes",
McCarthy indicated a source of Cowen's popular appeal outside
Westminster. Cowen could employ "style" and communicate
brilliantly but without resorting to empty rhetoric. He drew on a
rich body of opinions constantly informed by an astonishing capacity
to devour books, pamphlets, newspapers and information. According
to the journalist Henry Lucy, Cowen's "splendid intellectual gifts
were trained by constant study. Endowed with a far-reaching and
tenacious memory, he remembered most things he read, and he read
everything." (56) The point was substantiated by Cowen's friend,
Jessie White Mario, a veteran of Garibaldi's Italian campaigns, who
wrote that Cowen "had every book, newspaper and pamphlet relating
to all Liberal movements in England and abroad from his earliest
boyhood." (57) Cowen's Blaydon home, Stella Hall, was crammed
with books and pamphlets and his London address in the 1880s was
filled with "the most recent productions of the Democratic Press."
(58) McCarthy further explained the basis of Cowen's substance on
another occasion:

> "Had Cowen been an ambitious man, or had he been formed
> by nature to be a serviceable Party man, he would undoubtedly
> have taken a high place in some Liberal Administration. But
> Cowen was emphatically not a Party man. He was emotional, he
> was sensitive, he was filled with an almost fierce spirit of
> independence. He would not follow any leader one step along
> any path farther than his full convictions and his whole
> conscience would allow him to go." (59)

This impression of a man with deeply-rooted convictions was
confirmed by Cowen's close collaborators such as Thomas Burt:

> "If I were asked to characterise Mr. Cowen in a word, I should
> say he intensely loved liberty. To that he rendered no mere
> lip-service; he devoted his life to it. Not only did he love liberty
> but he hated slavery ... Mr. Cowen was a good hater, but he
> never hated his fellow men. He was one of the most tolerant of
> men, but he was ever intolerant of shams, of injustice, of wrong,
> and of tyranny. Those he hated with a perfect hatred." (60)

That "love of liberty" nourished Cowen's enormous interest in
Irish nationalism which, through the 1870s and 1880s, progressively

formed a complex and gripping story, packed full of intrigue, flamboyant public stands and extremely bitter conflict, winning Cowen a good deal of Irish admiration. T.P. O'Connor, a prominent Irish Home Ruler who believed Cowen had the potential to have been "the first democratic Prime Minister of England", spoke for many of his colleagues when he wrote:

> "There was at that time literally not one Englishman - with, perhaps, the exception of a few Positivist leaders, like Frederick Harrison and Professor Beesley - who was ready to say a word for the Irish Cause. Only the insight of political genius, and the reckless courage of a man who cared only for principle and for liberty could bring forth a man who would step out of the ranks of his countrymen and advocate a Cause that was regarded as disloyal, impractical, visionary and perilous." (61)

Cowen therefore became one of the infinitesimal number of English MPs to stand out against the full might of the British state and its coercive policy towards Ireland in the early 1880s. In doing so he had also to confront the deep and emotive reserves of anti-Irish feeling in England. It was an unquestionably "perilous" course.

But all these complications lay far in the future on the night when Joseph Cowen's friends bombed the Paris Opera ......

CHAPTER TWO : THE EXCURSIONISTS

When the Paris Opera House was ripped apart by bombs on the night of 14 January 1858, six people died and over one hundred were injured. But the intended victim, the French Emperor and dictator Louis Napoleon, escaped unharmed. Shortly afterwards the Parisian police arrested the leader of the assassins, an Italian revolutionary named Felice Orsini, who confirmed the attack had been politically-motivated. Louis Napoleon was held responsible by Orsini for hindering the achievement of Italian independence from the Austrian Empire. The Opera Plot brought serious international repercussions. France and Britain came "within a measurable distance of war" (1) as it emerged the conspiracy had been hatched just across the Channel. The French government alleged the bombs had been made in Britain and several people living in London were implicated. This accusation soon escalated into a demand that a French Communist exile, Dr. Simon Francis Bernard, should be deported from England to face charges in France. The British government under Lord Palmerston responded not only by putting Bernard on trial at the Old Bailey but also by introducing a Conspiracy to Murder Bill into Parliament with the object of tightening control over the activities of foreign refugees. It was an inept move. Radical opinion in Britain, outraged by the government's "appeasement" of Louis Napoleon, denounced Palmerston's "French Colonel's Bill" (2) and unleashed a wave of protest throughout the country. By the middle of February the government had been defeated on the Bill in Parliament, and Palmerston's ministry resigned.

An assassination attempt, fear of war and the fall of a government was drama by any standard, and somewhere in the midst of it all stood Joseph Cowen. In common with most Radicals, Cowen firmly supported Italian independence. And it was in this context that Cowen and Orsini became closely associated, especially during the autumn of 1856 when Orsini stayed with Cowen while lecturing to public audiences on "Austrian and Papal Despotism in Italy." A close friendship was forged with Orsini describing Cowen as "an excellent friend, a good father to his family and a true lover of liberty devoted to the Italian Cause." (3) Cowen's wife, Jane, "spent hours" correcting the English in Orsini's speeches and in return he taught her French. But Orsini very nearly came to grief at Stella Hall. After he complained of headaches in the mornings, a maid discovered he was leaving gas jets open at night in his room believing the way to turn off the gas lights was to blow out the flames. (4) As a mark of the friendship, Orsini's portrait was later installed at Stella Hall alongside those of other prominent revolutionaries and radicals. The public purpose of Orsini's visit to Tyneside in October 1856 was to cultivate support for the Italians. Orsini recalled the north of England "was a good school for me. I found a free and most intelligent population." (5) At Blaydon, a noted centre of working-class radicalism, the local mechanics' institute conferred honorary membership on him, a tribute previously extended only to Louis Kossuth the Hungarian nationalist. Meanwhile, Cowen and Orsini were engrossed in "repeated conversations ... about tyrannicide - a matter in which [Orsini] seemed interested." (6) From here Cowen's exact involvement with Orsini becomes blurred, not least because Cowen "destroyed most letters from ... European revolutionists he received before 1860", (7) and subsequently insisted "there were matters in connection with Orsini's attempt ... that it would be very indiscreet to publish." (8)

Other people were anything but discreet. The French and Austrian governments were known to be suspicious of Cowen whose father - Joseph Cowen, snr - was mistakenly rumoured to have been detained in France under the impression that he was really Joseph Cowen, jnr. Cowen's father was at one point refused a passport and investigated by the Austrian and French consulates in London and "another gentleman" named Cowen was "detained on the French frontiers under suspicion of being a friend and emissary of Mazzini" the Italian nationalist and revolutionary. (9) Tory newspapers on Tyneside claimed Cowen was "in the confidence of conspirators" and called for his prosecution for "conspiracy to murder." (10) Cowen's allies replied by labelling the Tory journalists as "the Newcastle agents of the French Police." (11) As late as 1891 an anonymous critic claimed that "Orsini, the day before he left England to make his attempt on the life of Napoleon III, had a solemn discussion with Joseph Cowen ... on the justice of tyrannicide." (12) Cowen denied that he had spoken to Orsini "for some weeks before he went to France", (13) but the journalist, Wemyss Reid, who knew Cowen quite well, maintained that Cowen provided "the funds for carrying out Orsini's plot." (14)

Apart from Joseph Cowen's personal connections with Orsini, there were further intriguing links with the Opera Plot. In the official indictment of the conspirators, published in Paris, the bomb-casings were described as "part of a newly-invented gas apparatus." (15) And "it was commonly known that the explosives had been exported from England by a well-known industrial firm." (16) By a coincidence, the Cowen family business was one of the leading manufacturers and exporters of gas-retorts in Britain, and Cowen's use of these and other products to conceal consignments of revolutionary literature had for a long time "effectually baffled the most vigilant espionage of the despotic powers" of Europe. (17) Additionally, the French government's demand for the return of Simon Bernard offered another clue to Cowen's awareness of the plot. Bernard, it later emerged, had approached Thomas Allsop, an ex-Chartist and Owenite, and George Jacob Holyoake, a Co-operator and Radical - and close friend of Cowen - for help in planning the assassination. Holyoake was persuaded to test prototypes of the bombs and made a nightmare journey to Sheffield, carrying explosives in a bag on a shaking 'train, then detonating a bomb in a disused quarry. He also tried out two more bombs at Allsop's house in Devon. (18) The names of Allsop, Holyoake and Cowen featured prominently in the frantic aftermath of Orsini's arrest and execution. Allsop published a pamphlet in defence of tyrannicide written by W.E. Adams, a former compositor who had indirect associations with Cowen a few years earlier through a republican group based at Brantwood, a large house owned by the Cowens (later sold to John Ruskin) near Coniston in the Lake District. The British government prosecuted Allsop for the pamphlet in 1858 but succeeded only in supplying the Radicals, including John Stuart Mill and Joseph Cowen, with a fresh platform. Both Cowen and Holyoake spent considerable amounts of time at the Bernard trial as well as organising public meetings protesting against the prosecution. When the government's case collapsed, Cowen invited Bernard to recuperate at Stella Hall, (19) and whilst on Tyneside Bernard spoke at a large public meeting in Newcastle. (20) On another occasion Cowen saved Bernard from a hostile crowd in Hyde Park: the exile had been mistaken for a French government spy when, in reality, he was on his way to act as guest speaker at a protest rally. (21) Without doubt, Cowen was deeply involved with the central figures of the Opera Plot. He was greatly distressed by Orsini's execution, writing to Holyoake:

> "Poor Orsini - I suppose he would die yesterday. Poor fellow, I have never had him out of my thoughts for some weeks past"

and had told a friend on hearing of Orsini's arrest: "What a pity this last attempt did not succeed." (22) Late in life Cowen is believed to have claimed that he helped to "fill the bombs which Orsini threw at Napoleon." Cowen was almost certainly the mystery participant believed by the historian of the Plot "so carefully protected by the rest that all trace is lost to history." (23)

Cowen, Allsop, Holyoake and Bernard were extremely lucky to escape the retribution following the outrages at the Paris Opera. That they were able to do so owed as much to the political climate of the time as to their conspiratorial skills. At the English end of the affair Cowen and the others were not behaving as isolated terrorists but could draw on a balance of popular sympathy. A lot of people hated Napoleon III. *Louis Napoleon!* the man who in exile had served as a special constable against the London Chartists and in France had buried the hopes of the democratic revolution of 1848 in the brutal murder and imprisonment of thousands of working men and women. To Holyoake, Louis Napoleon was "the assassin of French liberty...whose career is one of the infamies of Imperialism." (24) For W.E. Adams, the French dictator's *coup d'etat* had been corrupt and grotesque and he had seized power by "wading through blood." (25) Joseph Cowen shared the same sentiments, perhaps even more strongly, (26) telling a Newcastle meeting in mid-February 1858:

> "Louis Napoleon rose to his bad eminence by a combination of the greatest cunning, cruelty, and perfidy: but the English people had got rid of their dictator [Palmerston] and he hoped that their French friends would speedily get rid of theirs (Great applause)." (27)

Thirteen years later, when Louis Napoleon had at last been forced to abdicate, Cowen would still describe him as "one of the most relentless aggressors or oppressors in Europe, a man who was the manifestation and the living incarnation of despotism." (28) These views were widely shared and the Radicals were therefore able to portray Orsini as a hero, notably on Tyneside. Orsini's name was greeted with "vehement applause" at a Newcastle public meeting addressed by Holyoake and chaired by Cowen in late-March 1858, (29) and with "rapturous applause" at Blaydon mechanics' institute in May. (30) Over a year later, in September 1859, Cowen was cheered at the same institute when he insisted that "the attempt of poor Orsini, although not in Italy, was for her benefit." (31)

How did Joseph Cowen come to take an immense risk with his own life and liberty? What was the attraction of the Italian struggle, a conflict in a country Cowen had never visited but which drew him towards such extreme measures? Firstly, there was a fear that the kind of despotism rampant in France, Italy, and central and eastern Europe might be imported into Britain. This was, after all, an era characterised by a refusal to extend the right to vote even to all men let alone women, the "stamped" press laws had inhibited the circulation of newspapers among the working-classes, and draconian action was often taken against trade unionism. Whigs and Tories competed with each other in Parliament to suppress demands for greater freedom, and Radicals were always alarmed by legislation of the "French Colonel's Bill" variety. There was a related belief, too, that failure to help people fighting for freedom in Europe "would encourage the spread of tyranny and might eventually involve the loss of British liberties", and it has been argued this was "the chief driving force" behind Joseph Cowen's interest in the Italian Question. (32) Undoubtedly, Cowen took on board the Radicals' commitment to "fraternity" with European revolutionaries. Another important point to recognise is that Cowen also forged real personal relationships with Italian freedom-fighters and these exercised a powerful influence on his outlook. It was this mixture of strong political ideals and intense friendships - a recurring facet of Cowen's life - that singled out Cowen as possibly "the outstanding Englishman of his day in supporting foreign revolutionaries." (33)

Cowen's initial step along the road of "fraternity" was taken in 1844 when a wave of indignation arose over revelations that the Home Secretary, Sir James Graham, had authorised the opening of private letters passing through the postal system. It was believed that confidential information contained in correspondence from an Italian nationalist, Joseph Mazzini, had been passed by Sir James Graham to the Austrian government, leading to the arrest and execution of two Italian insurrectionists known as the Bandiera brothers. Possibly, the Austrians acted against the Bandieras for other reasons, (34) but the British government was seen to be culpable and admitted interfering with the mail. The ensuing protests sparked the growth of interest in Italy, (35) and as people marked their letters "Not to be Grahamed", (36) a sixteen-years old Joseph Cowen then chairing the Eclectic Debating Society at Edinburgh University mounted a public attack on the Home Secretary. It was an onslaught Cowen sustained for many years. As late as 1859 he was still winning rounds of applause in Blaydon by referring to the Bandiera brothers: "They were shot...and their blood lies on the head of the Member for Carlisle [Graham]." (37) The long-term significance of the Bandiera affair for Cowen was a friendship with Joseph Mazzini. Cowen wrote to Mazzini, seemingly inspired by a realisation that "events of great importance were transpiring. There was an underground discontent throughout all Europe [and] mutterings of revolution all over." According to Cowen, this realisation, coupled with the Bandieras' execution, "led to an acquaintance with the Italian patriot which ripened into a friendship...and largely influenced my political course." (38) Further contacts with Mazzini brought about what Cowen saw as "the crowning friendship of his youth." (39) The association was very strong in both personal and political terms, as Cowen's daughter, Jane, recalled in an unfinished biography of her father: "If I were asked who was the man that my father ever held in the deepest reverence, I should unhesitatingly answer - Joseph Mazzini." (40) Justin McCarthy argued that Cowen's political distinctiveness owed much to Mazzini. (41) And the Socialist, H.M. Hyndman, felt that Cowen was one of Mazzini's "most earnest and devoted supporters" and the two friends had run "risks...in the matter of supplying arms to the revolutionaries and giving aid to their plots." Hyndman also wrote that Cowen had confided about Mazzini: "When I think of the things I did at the instance of that man my hair almost stands on end." (42)

Joseph Mazzini was one of the seminal personalities in the long struggle for Italian independence. As early as 1831 he formed a "Young Italy" movement devoted to achieving an independent Italy united under "a Rome of the People" - a republic. During the shortlived republic of 1849 Mazzini (together with Orsini) organised the defence of Rome, working from a small office rather than lavish state apartments, was accessible to all callers, and ate each day at a cheap restaurant. The death penalty was abolished, the tax burden on the lower classes reduced and the right to vote was extended along with freedom of the press. Mazzini was one of the first to connect the rights of "the people" with the resurgence of Italy as a nation. Though never a Marxist, he did advocate a popular "socialism" envisaging the growth of industry and towns controlled by state-owned public services and co-operatives. As "an internationalist" as well as a fervent Italian nationalist, Mazzini looked forward to "a federation of the world" in which free peoples would abolish war by eliminating "cosmopolitan kings who used their subjects for their own ends." (43) Mazzini was consequently more than willing to make common cause with radicals and revolutionaries in other countries, particularly if this brought extra assistance for his constant promotion of plots and risings in Italy. With this colourful background Mazzini became an exceptionally attractive "hero" in British Radical circles inclined towards romantic notions of adventurous "individualism". The young Joseph Cowen along with many others of his generation fell under Mazzini's spell. But the personal affinity between the two men was especially intense as Mazzini once indicated when he complained to Cowen that in a letter to a friend "you did not send one single friendly word. Do you resent my long silence?" (44) And in an obituary for the *Newcastle Daily Chronicle*, authorised by Cowen, Mazzini was seen as:

> "a talisman in quarters where men are least disposed to bow to authority. Those who were fortunate enough to enjoy the privilege of his friendship dwell with peculiar tenderness upon the fascination which his character exerted. It would be difficult to describe the secret of this superb attraction." (45)

Within the framework of a shared politics and friendship, Cowen and Mazzini took the arts of secrecy and conspiracy to new heights. Prior to meeting Joseph Cowen, Mazzini had found ways of smuggling political pamphlets into Italy with the help of sympathetic seafarers. (46) Now with Cowen's enthusiastic aid Mazzini was able to expand the smuggling operation. Around 1850 Cowen told Mazzini that "he had discovered means by which he could send his [Mazzini's] publications to Italy and proposed doing so." There was then a lengthy period in which Cowen "succeeded in smuggling parcels of revolutionary literature into the Italian ports along with bricks, [gas] retorts and other fire-clay goods ...How it was exactly accomplished was never divulged." (47) Cowen became "a frequent visitor at Mazzini's quiet lodgings in London" where the landlady "knew by sight the spies who were dogging" the exiled Italian. A "constant correspondence" was kept up between the two conspirators (48) with chemicals used sometimes to conceal handwritten messages. (49) But meetings were preferred because of "the extreme caution and secrecy that had to be observed." (50) Cowen's visits to London ultimately awoke the suspicions of the "despotic governments". His movements were watched - "spies were stationed at Newcastle" (51) - and "for several years, there were countries which it was not advisable for [Cowen] to set foot in." (52) The enhanced need to avoid detection meant that Cowen and Mazzini sometimes met at Newark and York rather than London, (53) or "to throw the Police off the scent" they went to Doncaster. (54) Mazzini never visited Cowen's home although a false newspaper report was once published to disguise his whereabouts. In August 1859, the *Newcastle Daily Chronicle*, in which Cowen was acquiring the dominant interest, announced: "Sig. Mazzini is at present staying at Stella for recuperation." (55) Holyoake was later told the misleading report was considered essential because some indiscreet hints made about Mazzini's travel intentions

> "might have had very bad results - you know how - and we set to work to counteract them. The report answered most admirably and not a single soul about these quarters had the least suspicion that he was not here. Enquirers at Stella House were told he was at Blaydon Burn for quietness. The people at Blaydon Burn thought he was here. Now the affair is over not a single word must be spoken upon it." (56)

Through Mazzini, Cowen spent more time campaigning publicly for the Italian cause. Mazzini created a People's International League to stimulate interest in Italy and Cowen had connections with the League from 1847. (57) In 1851, the PIL was superseded by the Society of the Friends of Italy. Again the inspiration stemned mainly from Mazzini and Cowen became the youngest member of the Society's management committee, working with Holyoake. (58) It was an activity that continued throughout the 1850s under one guise or another. Joseph Cowen could be found in 1856, for example, as "a very active member of the committee" of the Emancipation of Italy Fund, addressing "large gatherings of working-men" at Blaydon and elsewhere, and raising contributions from "miners, potters, ropemakers, bakers, tailors, druggists, printers and stationers" as well as shopkeepers, often by selling portraits of Mazzini (twenty-three were sold in Newcastle in one month). (59) A small printing press, based at Stella Hall, produced "much revolutionary literature" including Mazzini's 1858 pamphlet, *The Late Genoese Insurrection Defended*, containing a preface in the form of a letter from Mazzini to Cowen. (60)

By participating so deeply in Mazzini's projects Cowen's own range of contacts widened considerably. He met other Radicals such as Holyoake, Peter Taylor and William Ashurst, (61) and found the succession of "solidarity committees" had the effect of identifying like-minded people "by bringing together most of the earnest men ...into closer communion." (62) This by-product of the Italian struggle was to have profound implications for Cowen, stretching into other parts of Europe and not least into issues of political and social reform at home. Yet for the moment the Italian story had a fair distance to travel and not just in the company of "earnest men". There was certainly at least one earnest woman who made a tremendous impression on Joseph Cowen - Jessie White. In an age when women were pressured to remain in the background, Jessie White broke most of the prevailing conventions and worked as a female war correspondent in Italy for both the London *Daily News* and the *New York Times*. Arrested more than once for subversion in Italy, Jessie White married a Garibaldian, Alfredo Mario - but kept her own name - served as a medical officer with Garibaldi's army, lectured in the United States during the period of Garibaldian exile in the early 1850s, and ended the wars for Italian independence as a major. Jessie White had also been won to the cause by Mazzini and with Cowen's help she challenged the male dominated world of Tyneside public meetings, demanding that "every Englishman" should dig into his pockets for money to "send men, ships and arms" against tyranny in Italy. (63) Cowen, believing Italy's "only hope ... was in revolution", invariably organised and chaired Jessie White's meetings. (64) Jane Cowen recollected "it was then a rare thing for a woman to address a public meeting" but "when she spoke drew great audiences." (65) Dressed in a Garibaldian jacket Jessie White spoke in tones that sounding "like a bell" to Joseph Cowen and the pair became life-long friends. (66) Over 1857-58, she undertook extensive speaking tours, attracting keen support in the towns around Newcastle and "by her enthusiasm and eloquence she worked

up the Tyneside democrats to an extraordinary state of excitement."
(67) During her March and May visits in 1857 extra meetings had to
be arranged to accommodate the large numbers who flocked to hear
her, and she was received "amid renewed cheering" at Newcastle's
principal Radical meeting place, the Nelson Street Lecture Room.
(68) In May of the following year she spoke on Italy at Hexham, on
Orsini and Louis Napoleon at Blaydon and - to "loud and
long-continued cheers" (69) - she defended Orsini at South Shields.
The series of meetings amounted to a *tour-de-force* consolidating
Radical Tyneside, serving to blunt the shock-waves of Orsini's
assassination bid, and preparing the ground for the area's direct
military involvement in the next phase of Italian unification -
Garibaldi's Sicilian Rising of 1860.

Guisseppe Garibaldi was already a Tyneside hero and a friend of
Joseph Cowen long before 1860. The "liberator of Italy" visited the
Tyne in March-April 1854 when in charge of an American clipper
ship, *The Commonwealth*. On learning Garibaldi was coming to
Tyneside, Cowen offered to arrange a public demonstration.
Garibaldi, prefering a more private itinerary, simply stayed with the
Cowens and visited the Blaydon mechanics' institute. (70) But there
was one public ceremony aboard the *Commonwealth*. Cowen, several
Polish exiles and a group of working-men, representing the local
branch of the Society of the Friends of European Freedom, gave
Garibaldi a telescope and sword - bought with money raised from
penny-collections around the factories - together with a glowing
Address (written by Cowen). (71) Garibaldi then sailed away, leaving
behind a lasting impression assiduously cultivated by the Radicals.
Cowen, for instance, organised a pro-Garibaldi public meeting at the
Blaydon mechanics' institute in September 1859 and delivered a long
speech on the situation in Italy, ending on a message of
encouragement to Garibaldi "carried with three cheers". (72) By now
Joseph Cowen was virtually in control of the *Newcastle Daily
Chronicle* and, abandoning its previous condemnation of Mazzini and
Jessie White Mario, (73) transformed the paper into an "almost
unique" Mazzinian newspaper, (74) carrying "the fullest accounts ...of
what was happening in Southern Italy, and actively propagandising
for Garibaldi." (75) In November 1859 Cowen advertised the
Chronicle editorial office as a depository for financial contributions
to buy arms for Garibaldi. (76) Behind the scenes the smuggling
firm of Mazzini-Cowen was "actively engaged in collecting and

sending out arms to the Garibaldians", (77) and Cowen was readily responding to Mazzini's requests for more weapons. (78) Telegraphing Cowen from Genoa, under the code-name "Seloa", Mazzini asked for a ship to be bought to carry "any Armstrong guns" and 600 men to Italy. Cowen bought a vessel named *City of Exeter* and sent it to Antwerp for diversion to Italy. Within weeks, Cowen met another of Mazzini's demands: "Is there a steamer to be hired for one month? The thing to be done would be this, to take some 5000 muskets we have in London, with some other materials of war, cartridges, etc., to some part of our shore, where there is no risk." (79) Two months later, in July 1860, Richard Reed, Cowen's manager at the *Chronicle*, was writing confidentially to Holyoake with details of arms supplies *en route* from Sheffield to Mazzinians bound for Italy: Cowen had again made the purchase arrangements. (80) Meanwhile, the *Chronicle* went on publishing appeals for money and reporting meetings from Berwick to Darlington and day-trips along the Tyne all held to raise funds. (81)

This underground military exercise burst out into the open on 13 August 1860 when the *Chronicle* published a leading article titled: "WHO WILL FIGHT FOR GARIBALDI?" The article reported that Holyoake's London Garibaldi Committee was recruiting volunteers to join Garibaldi's Sicilian campaign:

> "Our readers will have seen the gallant part played by the small band of Englishmen who fought with Garibaldi at Melazzo...Enlistment of Englishmen to serve with Garibaldi is illegal...But there is no law that can prevent any man from voluntarily going to Italy and placing his services at the disposal of General Garibaldi."

Two days later the *Chronicle* printed a London address to which volunteers could apply for places on what Holyoake circumspectly termed "Excursions to Sicily and Naples" particularly for "Members of Volunteer Rifle Corps." (82) Using the *Chronicle* to recruit for a military expedition imbued with Radical politics, and directed against governments with which Britain was at peace, was a high risk strategy. Not surprisingly, those who had suspected Cowen of clandestine intrigues stretching from Paris to Naples were quick to sieze their chance. The principal figure in the reaction was George Crawshay, a local iron-master and mayor of Gateshead. Ironically, Crawshay had once supported Mazzini but gradually turned against the Italian Risorgimento, strangely convinced it was really a Russian scheme to enlarge the Czar's influence in Europe. To attack Mazzini on Tyneside inevitably meant a collison with Joseph Cowen. Crawshay fired the first shot in the autumn of 1859 when he accused Cowen of corrupting the minds and hearts of the people of Blaydon with the ideas of Mazzini. (83) Crawshay challenged recruitment for Holyoake's "British Legion" (as the "Excursion" was to become) in order to keep Cowen "out of mischief", (84) and in mid-August 1860 he appeared at the Newcastle police court requesting a warrant for the arrest of the *Chronicle*'s editor, John Baxter Langley.

The *Chronicle*, accused of breaching clauses of the Foreign Enlistment Act prohibiting recruitment for foreign armies, faced a potentially important test-case which could have severely obstructed the despatch of the British Legion to Sicily. Yet the "Orsini factor" arose again, demonstrating that a political climate favouring the Garibaldians could strongly influence the administration of English law. The *Chronicle*, meanwhile, had a field day at Crawshay's expense, comparing him with Don Quixote and setting the scene for the police court hearing:

> "We anticipate that a hearty guffaw will be elicited by the announcement that the worthy and generous but eccentric Chief Magistrate of Gateshead, Mr. George Crawshay, has given us notice of his intention to apply for a summons against us for a breach of the Foreign Enlistment Act. We suspect that the scene which is promised for performance in the Police court on Monday will be amusing, if not profitable....Admission free!"

Monday came, and so for the *Chronicle* did the entertainment:

> "The performance of burlesque which we promised to the public came off in the Police Court... The Mayor looked portentious and solemn, as if a charge of murder was about to be tried..... The Officers of the court made grimaces in the desperate effort to look grave; whilst the reporters in their private box, put no such restraint upon their mirth. So the farce began..."

Every so often John Baxter Langley interrupted the "prosecution" to suggest George Crawshay should really cast himself as a government informer rather than an advocate, and Crawshay's own presentation suffered from "the peculiar intonation of voice, and the awkwardness of emphasis he placed upon certain extracts [which] excited considerable amusement in the Court." (85) The magistrates

took just five minutes to dismiss Crawshay's application for a
summons against the *Chronicle* and, to cheering in court, told him
to apply instead to the Court of Queen's Bench. Crawshay did, in
fact, take the case to the higher court but too late to prevent the
Legion's departure. In any event, the case was a failure because the
judges ruled that only the government and not individuals could
prosecute for breaches of the Act. It hardly helped when Crawshay's
own barrister declared his support for Garibaldi. Crawshay and his
allies were furious at the outcome, issuing a special broadsheet
attacking "this notorious and open violation of the law", (86) but
Cowen, Holyoake and the *Chronicle* had got clean away, claiming a
victory for press freedom. (87)

The way was now clear for the British Legion to leave for Sicily
but the project had encountered its own problems. Lacking
experience of military "excursions" and suffering organisational
delays, the Garibaldi Committee was also plagued by an expert
confidence trickster named "Capt. E. Styles". Styles impressed the
Committee. He wore a flamboyant Garibaldian uniform and traded
on the "romanticism" of the Italian adventure. Holyoake, after the
event, said it was assumed Styles "had been in Italy and in some
army...His influence grew by not being questioned. Without our
knowledge and without any authority, he invented and secretly sold
commissions, retaining the proceeds for his own use." (88) Through
the Committee, Styles approached Joseph Cowen in Newcastle
offering free passage, rations, uniforms, arms and pay to anyone
volunteering for the Legion, (89) and the *Chronicle* duly publicised
Styles as a contact for the "Excursions". At length, again according
to Holyoake, the Committee took control of the situation and sent
several hundred men to Italy. "No more was heard of Styles", wrote
Holyoake. (90) More active "Excursionists", as will be seen, took a
different view of Styles, and Holyoake's relating of the incident may
well have been prejudiced by constant in-fighting within the
Garibaldi Committee. Unfortunately, the British Legion still awaits
a history of its own as Holyoake's more detailed account was lost in
Italy. (91) Other references to the Legion are sparse and tend to
downgrade its role (92) although it was composed largely of
politically committed Radicals who volunteered because they
believed in the Italian cause, and together with similar contingents
from various parts of Europe took the form of an "International
Brigade". Thanks to the efforts of Cowen and his *Chronicle*, and the

work put in by Jessie White Mario and Felice Orsini over the previous few years, part of the Legion was drawn from Tyneside. Almost thirty years later one of these Newcastle volunteers - John Eyre Macklin - wrote a lively series of articles about the Legion for the *Newcastle Weekly Chronicle*, stressing the *Chronicle*'s connection with the "Excursion":

> "With many Novocastrians, I volunteered for the Garibaldian expedition, and left...for London. Previous to my departure I had a friendly interview with some gentlemen belonging to the **Chronicle** staff." (93)

The "interview" was part of the recruitment process.

Macklin had been a non-commissioned officer in the Royal Artillery and he could also speak Italian. He joined one of the two ships, full of volunteers, which sailed from England to the Bay of Naples in September 1860. Together with Macklin there were about eigthteen men from Newcastle, Gateshead and Shields. (94) The Legion saw fierce action at Capua from 18th October where they marched to the battlefield accompanied by a band playing the "British Grenadiers". Casualties were quickly sustained, dispelling any lingering romantic illusions about the nature of war, but the comparatively inexperienced force held their ground under repeated attack. Macklin's own contribution was marked in a field promotion to lieutenant authorised by Garibaldi. The General was particularly impressed by a bridge-building success on the Volturo when Macklin managed to build a bridge at a key point. When looking after the wounded during the battle, Macklin met the superintendent of hospitals who turned out to be none other than Jessie White Mario - "the Florence Nightingale of the Garibaldian army." Jessie White asked Mácklin to convey greetings to Joseph Cowen, whose name, Macklin believed, was "almost as familiar in Italy as it is on Tyneside." Cowen, as it happened, was thwarted from going to Italy due to business pressures and family illness. (95)

Returning to Naples after the victory at Capua, Macklin found captain - now major - Styles under house-arrest. Styles, it emerged, had not vanished but had joined the Legion in Italy where he was a popular officer. Col. Peard (the Legion's commanding officer) and his senior officers had arrested Styles for reasons of their own and Macklin was given charge of the guard. It was a duty that neither

Macklin nor his sentries relished and one volunteer, Tom Donnison from Gateshead, conspired with a woman friend of Styles to help the major escape. Peard then put Donnison under arrest, sentencing him to be shot. The execution was never carried out because Macklin smuggled Donnison out of prison and back into the army. John Macklin temporarily remained in Italy after the departure of most of the Legion, missing the heroes' reception given to the Tyneside volunteers when they arrived home in January 1861. Towards the end of the month Cowen organised a splendid "Welcome Home" supper at Newcastle's Neville Hotel with John Baxter Langley in the chair. (96)

The dinner at the Neville Hotel by no means ended Cowen's interest in Italy. There would be more excitements in the future. But until the early 1860s he was indisputably engaged in conspiracies, plots, gun-running, and arguably flouting the law. In this heady torrent Cowen also forged lasting friendships with the principal revolutionaries and radicals of the period. However, a combination of careful secrecy and a location 270 miles distant from London enabled Cowen's activities to remain relatively discreet despite the suspicions of numbers of European secret agents. On the home front, some of those who could not be bothered to enquire too deeply about the rustlings in the Tyneside undergrowth were only later to realise their mistake.

CHAPTER THREE : A CHARTIST AND SOMETHING MORE

What made Joseph Cowen go further than most Radicals in supporting Garibaldi and Mazzini? One easy answer might focus on Cowen's apparent martial adventurism. Thomas Burt remarked that Cowen "liked to hear the bugle note" when reading poetry. (1) And in 1852 Cowen stated:

> "there are some people so dead to all sense of honour, righteousness, & of truth that the only way of reaching their consciences is through **their hides or their stomachs**," [Cowen's emphasis]

meaning that appeals for justice addressed to European tyrants had to be backed "by a party of well-armed soldiers." (2) It sounded blood-curdling, yet should be qualified. Cowen was defending the Society of Friends of European Freedom, linking overseas refugees with their British sympathisers, against an accusation of being too "warlike". By insisting that "something more forceful than Peace Tracts" was needed to secure justice "from the Continental Despots", Cowen was simply making the point that solidarity campaigns should recognise the actual circumstances faced by exiles rather than imposing values forged in the more placid British environment. Behind Cowen's seemingly extravagent choice of language rested a principle of respect or empathy for the experiences and opinions of those to whom he lent assistance. It was a principle adopted by Cowen in his youth and guided many of his political relationships later in life, (3) largely explaining why Cowen could travel to the farthest lengths in helping other people's causes.

Many influences shaped Cowen's principles and attitudes during his youth and some of these are now almost impossible to identify with precision. Outsiders saw the Cowen family as "a very nest of revolutionary Radicalism", (4) although the reality was more complex. Cowen's mother, Mary, came from a poor family near Blaydon and together with her shoe-maker brother, Joseph Newton, she took an active part in the reform movements of the early nineteenth century. She read political tracts avidly, leading a group of "Female Reformers" connected with the Northern Political Union in 1819. (5) Following a "shotgun" marriage in 1822 to Cowen's father - also named Joseph (6) - Mary played a pronounced role in developing the family brickworks. Joseph Cowen, snr, had also participated in radical politics. Coming from a family of blacksmiths in the Winlaton area, he acted as secretary to one of the Winlaton "classes", or "branches" of the Northern Political Union, and was a marshal for the huge 1819 demonstration held on Newcastle's Town Moor in protest at the Peterloo Massacre. (7) From 1831, however, the Cowens' business success, gradually encompassing the brickworks, a colliery and land ownership, a small railway line and coal staithes, was matched by entry into the local Whig oligarchy signifying acceptance into "County society". Cowen, snr, accordingly adjusted his politics to embrace Whig politicians, the middle class Anti-Corn Law League and even the New Poor Law. Interestingly, as Cowen's father engaged in a little social climbing, Mary Cowen avoided the exclusive balls, dinners and social occasions attended by her husband. (8) Quite possibly the young Joseph Cowen's life-long distaste for "society" and his belief in women's entitlement to political rights owed a good deal to his mother and other female relatives (the first woman whom Cowen heard speak in public was his aunt, Bessy Newton, at a Primitive Methodist "camp meeting" on Tyneside in 1850). (9) Mary and Joseph Cowen, snr, had six children between 1822 and 1835 with the young Joseph born at Blaydon Burn on 9 July 1829. Cowen, jnr, was the only one of the two sisters and four brothers to develop an interest in politics. The others were absorbed into the comfortable life-styles typical of families enjoying the Cowens' social and business status. One brother even enrolled as a special constable during the Chartist demonstrations of 1848. (10) It is probably futile to try to explain why the young Joseph Cowen's attitudes differed from those of his brothers and sisters by delving into personal and family psychologies. There is insufficient information to sustain any sensible judgement. In any event, raging and organised radicalism was commonplace throughout Cowen's boyhood and teenage years. For many people, trying to change the world was a necessity, and Joseph Cowen, jnr, readily acquired an affinity with these community concerns.

Winlaton, where Cowen grew up, was a fascinating place. The village was relatively isolated from Tyneside geographically and had a distinctive history. Very rapidly between 1816 and 1821 Winlaton was transformed from "a Tory village to a stronghold of radicalism." (11) The sea-change was brought about by a sharp economic dislocation when the Crowley family's iron works, which had dominated the area for over a century, closed under the impact of the post-Napoleonic War depression and the onslaught of stronger competitors. Not only were most jobs lost but an elaborate system of social welfare also vanished. The Crowleys' paternalism had contrasted sharply with the labour practices of other employers and extended to the provision of "superannuation, sickness and death benefits and widows' pensions. Schools were built for the children of employees and a special court was instituted to settle disputes." (12) This "greatest cordiality between the masters and men" (13) was reflected, too, in a shared High-Tory politics. (14) But the collapse of the iron works unleashed an era of bitter class conflict as new employers imposed the dictates of market forces on their workers. *Tory Winlaton became Revolutionary Winlaton!* Fired by a sense of "betrayal" when the "new masters" failed to continue the old social relationships, (15) Winlaton swept into the most advanced radicalism available. The village won a reputation for favouring "physical force" to achieve political rights and in 1819 the mayor of Newcastle warned the government that 700 demonstrators, concealing arms made at Winlaton, had taken part in the local protests against the Peterloo Massacre. (16) The next ten years saw Winlaton as a bastion of revolutionary politics on Tyneside. This tendency reached its highest expression through Chartism in 1838-39 when Winlaton acted as a lynchpin of the movement. (17) Winlaton Chartism keenly involved women (18) and mobilised around the "physical force" party. Julian Harney, then a leading figure on the revolutionary wing of Chartism, used Winlaton as his base and Chartists from the village took part in a pitched battle with the police and army for control of Newcastle's streets in July 1839. (19) During the abortive Chartist general strike the following month, Winlaton held a one-week strike and nightly parades around the village. When rumours spread that a troop of dragoons had been despatched from Newcastle to search for arms - a roaring illicit trade in arms sales to other Chartist centres was conducted from Winlaton (sometimes with profit margins of 600 per cent!) (20) - the villagers were well-prepared: "Previous to this startling anouncement, large quantities of hand-granades, pikes, spears and caltrops had been made." Guards were posted to sound the alarm if soldiers appeared, and even a cannon was found for use in the defence. (21)

Joseph Cowen was ten years old when the Chartists virtually ruled

Winlaton. As a boy mixing freely with other local children and playing around the various workplaces, (22) Cowen was fully exposed to the atmosphere of the times, an atmosphere stimulating a good deal of political discussion at home. Nor did this social education end in 1839. Keith Harris made the important point that later industrial disturbances, especially the locally traumatic 1844 miners' strike, strongly influenced Cowen as well. (23) Cowen's formal education also had unusual features. He attended a school at Ryton conducted by Richard Weeks whose advanced teaching methods introduced pupils to complex literature such as Scott's novels and encouraged group discussion. Cowen left the Ryton school at the age of 15 years having enjoyed the experience and as an admirer of Weeks. (24) But a year spent at Edinburgh university had a profound impact. Prevented from attending an English university because of discrimination against "Dissenters" - Cowen was baptised a Methodist although he carefully avoided identifying with any religious sect - the young Cowen was sent to Scotland in November 1845. At Edinburgh he was considerably impressed by his tutor, Rev. John Ritchie, a determined Chartist and "fearless Radical and popular platform speaker." (25) Ritchie was a dynamic person-ality in an Edinburgh alive with political and religious ferment and his chapel served as a venue for Chartist meetings. (26) Cowen quickly noted his tutor's influence: "It is to him that I am indebted for seeing many things in a different light than before." (27) Edinburgh sharpened Cowen's views and he threw himself into the major causes of the day, collecting anti-slavery tracts, for example. (28) He became president of the university debating society, subscribed to radical journals, and studied science, literature and philosophy (but did not seek a degree). An emerging interest in "ultra-Radicalism" was not welcomed, however, by Mary and Joseph Cowen with the result that a widowed aunt was engaged to act as a chaperon to divert Cowen, jnr, from politics. The ploy failed - it was said that the aunt also "entered with great zest into the theological warfare" of Edinburgh (29) - but it left Cowen complaining of "petty persecution" and of being

> "hampered in by people who profess and I doubt not take a great interest in my welfare, but who are bound up with such narrow minded prejudiced notions." (30)

By the beginning of 1847 Cowen had left university and was back at Blaydon.

He joined Joseph Cowen and Company at a time of dramatic expansion. Bricks were in demand and a technical breakthrough in producing fireclays, achieved by Cowen, snr, in 1844, brought enormous sales opportunities for the firm at home and abroad. The pressures on Cowen, jnr, were substantial - it became "customary" to spend twelve hours a day at the office (31) - particularly when he was left in sole charge of the brickworks during his father's absences. At first, Cowen found these pressures frustrating:

> "Mingling here in all the bustle of a business life, I find I can only devote a little time now and then to the improvement of my mental faculties. And even the few moments I have to spare from the regular pursuits of life are generally taken in planning and concocting other plans for the next day & I am so tired I often fall asleep over my books. But knowing the benefit that will result from devoting a few hours a week to study I intend in the future to do so." (32)

The pace of Cowen's life rarely eased and in 1855 he could tell Holyoake: "I have a dozen keelmen boring me with all sorts of questions while I write." (33) Determined to keep up his political and other interests Cowen became a life-long workaholic.

On returning from Edinburgh, Cowen was so anxious to take his political ideas to "the people" he would ride "a pony and harangue men who were working by the roadside." (34) But he soon turned to a more imaginative scheme. Inspired by articles in the *Peoples Journal*, Cowen and "one or two more young men" founded a Winlaton literary and mechanics' institute early in 1847. (35) The aim was popular education accessible to women and men, social and political as well as technical and scientific and rooted in a democratic philosophy. The traditional role of mechanics' institutes as tools of factory and mill owners, intended to instruct male workers in a limited range of skills, was overthrown at Winlaton just prior to the 1849-50 revival of the institutes. From the start, Cowen argued that women, who had supported the foundation of the Winlaton institute, should be "admitted to all the rights of membership." (36) The institute was certainly "open to all" by 1850 (37) and probably from the beginning judging by resolutions approved at the opening of the nearby Blaydon and Stella mechanics' institute stipulating that "every male and female (be they ever so poor) shall have a sound and rational education." (38) Similarly, there were no restrictions on subjects at the Winlaton and

Blaydon institutes. Winlaton pioneered the way according to the *Peoples Journal* because it did not "prohibit discussions on politics and religion" and neither was there a ban on "political and controversial works" in the institute library. (39) Blaydon followed suit and "exceptionally" among mechanics' institutes provided "political, social and theological lectures." (40) By 1848, Winlaton had a programme of lectures on history, astronomy and moral philosophy, chemistry and natural history. (41) Cowen's involvement with the institutes in the late-1840s enabled him to experiment with new approaches to adult education. He introduced the lecture-series, anticipating the work of the University Extension Movement. (42) Participatory learning was encouraged, too, through a discussion society at which members of the Winlaton institute delivered their own lectures. (43) Cowen sensed that people had to be persuaded of the value of education and this required an active promotion of the work of the institutes: "If they [working men] will not come to the institution, the managers of the institution should go to them." (44) Education therefore had to be seen as attractive and enjoyable and Cowen's chief public relations vehicle for conveying this message was the "soiree" based on "factory festivals" devised by employers such as Peter Taylor. The first soiree at Winlaton took place on 29 June 1847 when 230 women and men had a tea. They listened to speeches and the Winlaton violin band, and contributed to the funds of the institute library. The event was followed in August by a musical river excursion. (45)

Cowen remained secretary of the Blaydon and Stella mechanics' institute for twelve years after 1847, devoting substantial time and money to adult education. He often gave lectures on everything from English history to Co-operation, "The Power of the People to Improve their own Character and Condition" (46) and sympathetic assessments of Robespierre. (47) Those who remembered Cowen's enthusiasm for popular education in the 1840s and 1850s believed that "at his own expense, [he] provided ... books and everything necessary, as well as paid the salaries of the teachers" for mathematics, reading and writing and drawing, being "pre-eminent as an educationalist." (48) In 1859 Cowen became secretary of the Northern Union of Mechanics' Institutes but the Blaydon and Winlaton institutes now had a history difficult to match elsewhere in the absence of intimate support from someone like Cowen. The Blaydon institute's 1859 soiree, for example, demonstrated just how far the movement had developed. Held in a field owned by Cowen's father, the event attracted 1500 people to tea in a marquee. It was enlivened by "a cannon fired at intervals" and boats took parties on trips along the Tyne. The venue was decorated with wreaths bearing the names of Robert Owen, Milton, Oliver Cromwell, Shakespeare, George Stephenson, Louis Kossuth, Garibaldi and Mazzini. (49)

For Cowen, education and politics went hand-in-hand. After a brief youthful attachment to the notion that the middle classes might help the working classes, Cowen concluded that working class self-emancipation was the key to radical change: "If [the people] are to be elevated, mentally, morally, physically and socially, they must accomplish the task themselves." (50) Education was central to this process and, so far as Cowen was concerned, working people were perfectly able to appreciate learning: "some people thought because the people had dirty hands they had dirty minds. That was not only an error, but a lie." (51) Cowen openly admitted that education should be a training ground for reformers. It was a perspective underlined heavily by the Winlaton and Blaydon institutes' keenness to invite Chartist lecturers, sponsor demands for the abolition of the death penalty, and host meetings for black American fugitive slaves including William Wells Brown who was cheered rapturously at Blaydon in 1850. (52) Of course, this mixture of popular education, radicalism and working class emancipation caused alarm in more conservative quarters and "hostility" from county "influentials" lay behind an attempt to curb Cowen as early as May 1848. The Winlaton institute tried to raise funds by auctioning old newspapers but an anonymous informant complained to the excise board that the stamp tax was being flouted by the sale. Cowen and another official of the institute were fined a staggering £100 each, although the fine was later withdrawn in favour of a stern warning. (53) The most sustained opposition emerged in 1856 over the issue of "free thought" and secularism. Cowen's belief that the institutes should encourage discussion on all subjects - a principle implemented avidly by the Blaydon and Stella institute - infuriated local Primitive Methodists who wanted a strict prohibition on lectures and literature which questioned the existence of God. The Blaydon institute also ran into trouble with religious groups because its newsroom opened on Sundays "when it could be of most service to the working class." (54) Christian fundamentalists reacted by opening a rival, the Blaydon news room and literary society, and according to Cowen "the Incumbent (or Incumbrance) of Stella...commanded or requested (which is the same thing) those under his influence to leave" the mechanics' institute. (55) The affair briefly caught the attention of the national press when the Earl of Ravensworth congratulated the break-away group for banning "irreligious or ... immoral" books and lecturers who "impugn the authority of the Holy scriptures." Cowen replied with a letter to *The Times*. (56) Back in Blaydon, the mechanics' institute vigorously denounced its competitor for having no working class support (57) and, as Cowen gleefully recounted to Holyoake:

> "Our fight with the Parson goes on famously. This great scripture reader has "bolted" leaving numberless debts unpaid and a young woman in the family way to him! Altho' he is a married man with 6 or 7 children. He has deserted wife and family as well."
> (58)

This was not quite the end of the battle. A revival of secularism in 1859 caused the Blaydon institute to invite Charles Bradlaugh to speak. This provoked uproar in Blaydon with religious sects calling for a ban on the meeting. Cowen (who was now financing Holyoake's secularist propaganda and encouraging secularism in Blaydon) and the institute were castigated as "infidels" but were equally adamant in refusing to bow to their critics. Bradlaugh did speak at the institute hall which was filled to capacity by a friendly audience. (59)

Within education and politics may be found a further important inspiration for the young Cowen of the late 1840s: Chartism. Cowen would have known about the Chartists as a child and he mixed with supporters of the People's Charter at Edinburgh. Although in decline the Chartist organisation was still perceived as significant in the 1847-50 period, not least in the Newcastle area where radical working class activism revolved around the Charter and the movement retained an unusual degree of strength. The Chartists formed the leadership of democratic politics on Tyneside and it was not surprising, in view of Winlaton's traditions and reputation, that Cowen should seek a connection with Chartism. The movement's public meetings continued to attract large numbers at Newcastle - 1500 stood "in the rain" on the Town Moor in April 1848 to hear Chartist speakers and voted against a time limit on speeches so that all the speakers might be heard "in full" (60) - yet it was now more common for the meetings to feature recriminations between leaders of the fading movement rather than credible guidance on the way forward. Although the national structure of Chartism may have been disintegrating, the universe it constituted allowed the forging of new relationships. This was Joseph Cowen's point of entry into the movement and on 29 October 1849 he told a Newcastle Chartist audience that "he must avow himself a Chartist. He knew the Chartists had committed excesses, but that did not affect the justice of their claim. He was for universal suffrage" (which, in this period, meant universal male suffrage). (61) Cowen's approach to Chartism resolved the "physical" versus "moral" force division besetting the movement by arguing that both options for achieving change were tenable depending on the circumstances: "I do not share in the silly horror some entertain towards revolutionaries...physical force is often, but not necessarily the opposite of moral force, and by such services [can] become moral and justifiable." (62)

Cowen identified politically with the working classes whilst accepting that he was far from being a "working man". This was a serious commitment extending beyond speeches and even the promotion of a new type of mechanics' institute. Cowen searched for real insights into working class life and "lived for some time in the colliery villages." (63) Mingling with north eastern industrial communities in the late-1840s, Cowen met not only a developed class consciousness (64) but also evidence of an alert interest in knowledge that made one Newcastle bookseller observe the "pitmen were by far his best customers" especially for books on mathematics, Greek, Spanish and similar exotic subjects. (65) This environment impressed Cowen just as he was becoming extremely critical of the middle classes. By 1850 Cowen had virtually written-off the middle classes, telling the Winlaton institute: I have little hope of any material asistance [for reform] being derived from higher or aristocratic ranks and I have less of obtaining any help from the so-called middle-classes." (66)

If Joseph Cowen appeared disposed towards radicalism, he was acutely aware of the fragmentation afflicting Chartism and the necessity of opening new avenues for reform, inevitably in alliance with elements of the middle classes. In 1849 he advocated support for limited measures of reform as "an instalment of their rights in order to move a step forward." (67) The following year he said of middle class reformers: "He would go with them as far as [they] went, and when they had got thus far, he would go much further." (68) This view differed from those who called for the People's Charter or nothing, but reflected the post-1848 reality. Chartism had been defeated and was falling apart, visibly so in the north east where unemployment and emigration weakened the movement's ranks. (69) Confusion reigned and was illustrated graphically at a Newcastle meeting in October 1850. Cowen proposed a motion in support of seeking limited measures of reform, seconded by John Kane, an active Chartist and trade unionist, who stressed the importance of universal suffrage as an ultimate objective. The motion was attacked by James Watson, who often represented Newcastle at Chartist National Conventions, on the grounds that the interests of the working and middle clases were fundamentally divergent. Two other Chartists, McIntosh and A. Gunn, put forward an amendment demanding universal suffrage to be won by physical force. Cowen responded with an impassioned appeal restating "his sincerity as a friend of the Charter" and cautioning against divisive personality squabbles. The meeting carried the motion and the amendment with "many persons voting for both." (70)

Among the remaining Chartists there were several who came to the conclusion the movement had neglected to educate its members with the result that opportunities for real social reforms had been lost. Chartists had not given sufficient thought to the implications of economic and social changes underway in society and Chartism, it was argued, had failed to link demands for constitutional reform with a clear set of proposals for meeting the social needs of the working classes. As new possibilities for addressing those needs came within reach, the movement was missing a chance to make the right connections in its own philosophy and practice. Cowen shared this standpoint, suggesting that lack of education had been "one reason why they had been sixteen years agitating for the Charter in vain" and were now discovering the mass of the movement's supporters felt nothing more could be done. (71) Whilst Holyoake optimistically noted in 1850 that there "is more public life and intellectual activity in Newcastle than in any other two towns" (72), the more perceptive Harney commented that "a too large proportion of the people are completely sunk in apathy." (73) During the middle of 1850, Cowen, echoing other Chartists, warned that the People's Charter by itself would not end poverty. (74) In the autumn, he declared that he was "a Chartist and something more." (75) Nationally, the rump of the once powerful movement also started to call for social reforms including help for the unemployed, old age pensions, and universal education. But the age of the Chartists had passed and survivors were already rowing towards fresh shores. "The 19th Century" as Joseph Cowen wrote, "is not the time to be going back." (76)

CHAPTER FOUR : THE VOYAGE OF THE *KILINSKI*

The *Princess* was a British steamship apparently on an ordinary merchant voyage when, in February 1864, she was arrested at the Spanish port of Malaga. According to one story, the port officials believed the ship was carrying arms for Garibaldi to use against the Italian Papal States and, on the pretext of the captain's non-payment of harbour dues, the *Princess* was impounded. (1) Another rumour suggested the Spaniards were prepared to overlook their suspicions and allow time for the ship to leave but the captain and crew got drunk and missed their opportunity. (2) Whatever the truth, one point was clear: the *Princess* was not an innocent cargo carrier but a warship in disguise *en route* to the Black Sea to harass Russian shipping. The actual name of the *Princess* was the *Kilinski* and she was the flagship - in fact the only ship - of the Polish National Navy. And the *Kilinski* had been fitted out on the Tyne by Joseph Cowen largely "at his own expense." (3)

The plan to launch a Polish National Navy was a daring appendix to a tragic and heroic chapter in Poland's history - the 1863-64 uprising to free Poland from Czarist rule and create an independent Polish state. It was a cause attracting Cowen's full support. His *Chronicle* newspapers gave detailed reports on the insurrection and advocated the supply of arms to the Polish nationalists:

> "We assemble in our meetings to denounce Russia and praise Poland; we grow eloquent and enthusiastic; we cheer and clap our hands, and then we go home ... We have done little to aid them ... The Poles are fighting without arms, using implements of husbandry in default of weapons of war ... They have told us themselves that all they wanted of us is arms ... so apparent is this to every one of us that predictions of failure depend upon the failure of supplies. All the elements of success exist in Poland, save the elements of war." (4)

The Polish cause was cheered at meetings in Newcastle in 1862 and 1863 and in other old Chartist centres of the midlands and the north of England. (5) Cowen went further by providing practical assistance for the Poles. Secrecy was essential with lives at risk and explains why "little trace of Cowen's contribution has survived." (6) But sufficient evidence exists to confirm that Cowen employed his practised skills in conspiracy and smuggling. At one stage "he had a wonderful box constructed and well-lined with banknotes suitable for issue by the Secret Committee of Government in Poland, although the agent carrying the box was discovered and arrested in France." (7) Urged on by Mazzini, (8) Cowen used his commercial connections for cloak-and-dagger exploits in response to Polish requests:

> "On Wednesday next we are sending an agent to Galatz - he has a passport as a Swiss - in the capacity of waiter in the saloon on steamboats. Could you send him a recommendation to your Company? ... Garibaldi has desired me to send one hundred revolvers to Galatz. Could you kindly let me know if in a fortnight you should be able to send these arms from Vienna by the Danube to Galatz through your people, or from England direct to Constantinople." (9)

Cowen met all requests and to ease the process he even acquired a business interest in steamers plying the Danube. (10)

The *Kilinski* was probably the most audacious scheme in Cowen's partnership with the Poles. It was suggested by Konstanty Lekawski who, in confidential correspondence, claimed credit for proposing "to hoist a Polish flag in the Black Sea" and who looked to Cowen for "a Captain and a boat." (11) Unfortunately for Lekawski, based at Constantinople, the Polish government-in-exile firstly rejected his idea but then decided to go ahead without his knowledge: "I have been particularly excluded ... and did not know ... they were fitting out a steamer." (12) Meanwhile, the Polish leaders approached Cowen for a ship. Details of the vessel's departure reached Lekawski only after she had left England and he then had to race across the Mediterranean to make contact. Lekawski went to Messina in Italy where he found not the ship but a Polish agent on the same mission. From Messina he travelled to Leghorn and then on to Genoa and from there to Marseilles. Eventually, Lekawski met another secret agent at Alicante who told him the ship was in Malaga. "Full of disappointment" (13) Lekawski collected the *Kilinski* and returned to England where he learned that the Czar had brutally crushed the rising inside Poland.

The *Kilinski* affair poses questions about the complexity of Joseph Cowen. On the one hand, here was a man deeply committed to education and democracy in the pursuit of peaceful social reform.

Yet in sharp contrast the same Joseph Cowen could associate with Italian and Polish insurrectionists and assassins and go so far as to declare war on the Czar. As a result, Cowen's professed belief in peaceful reform was treated with scepticism in some quarters. However, as with Chartism, Cowen embraced both "moral" and "physical" force. His behaviour was governed by an assessment of what was needed in a given situation to achieve those principles of liberty and justice which he regarded as universally relevant. At home, Cowen judged that popular pressure could win extensions of liberty. Abroad, he deliberately relied on the advice of people whom he came to respect and trust by virtue of their own courage and experience. Mazzini was one such person and Lekawski was another. Just as Mazzini profoundly influenced Cowen's contribution to Italian independence, so Lekawski acted "in effect as Cowen's adviser on East European affairs." (14) By coincidence, "the burden of the [requests] of Mazzini and Lekawski was - money, arms, ammunition, ships - & leaving it to him [Cowen] to find a way through." (15)

Poland entered Cowen's life long before the *Kilinski* episode. Numbers of Polish refugees arrived in England after the failure of their 1848-49 revolution. Because these refugees were radical democrats, Cowen, through his Chartist and Italian contacts, helped set up a Polish refugees committee in Newcastle. As secretary and treasurer of the committee, Cowen organised public meetings, fund raising concerts, collections, clothing, accommodation and jobs for the Poles. Money "was forthcoming from the less wealthy sections of the community" (16) but Cowen personally met a large proportion of the costs of resettling the refugees. He donated "all the money" he had "to spare" and then paid a £40 debt left behind when the committee "separated leaving a big balance which I have had to pay." (17) At some point in 1851-52 Cowen got to know Konstanty Lekawski who had come to Newcastle as a refugee. The two men soon became friends with Lekawski giving lectures in French and German at the Blaydon mechanics' institute and joining Cowen in the presentation to Garibaldi on the Tyne in 1854. Lekawski also put Cowen in touch with the Polish Democratic Society for which services of a conspiratorial character were performed. Cowen arranged for "parcels ... containing propaganda materials, arms or secret instructions" to be delivered in eastern Europe, and a "secret correspondence ... written in invisible ink" was conducted between Cowen and Lekawski. Agents of the Democratic Society went east on "sacred missions" in the guise of "commercial travellers" representing Joseph Cowen and Co. (18) Not all of Cowen's engagement with the Poles was clandestine. The Polish case for national independence was also promoted in a flamboyant manner during the mid-1850s by means of public meetings and manifestos. In this respect, Newcastle already offered a rich experience to draw upon.

Cowen was not slow to utilise local traditions and resourcefulness. The middle classes, represented by the town's anti-Chartist former mayor, Sir John Fife, and the industrialist Charles Crawshay had convened public meetings for Italian and Hungarian freedom in 1849. (19) In 1851, the Chartist James Watson either arranged or requisitioned the mayor to hold public meetings for Poland and Hungary. (20) The South Shields Chartists, indeed, had raffled a portrait of the Hungarian nationalist Louis Kossuth in May 1850 to aid emigre funds. (21) A fresh opportunity to raise the Polish claims arose in 1854 when the British government went to war with Russia in the Crimea. Cowen, Harney and Lekawski tried to exploit the situation by forming a Newcastle upon Tyne Foreign Affairs Committee - possibly "the first attempt at setting up a definitively pro-Polish organisation in the country" - with the aim of turning the Crimean War into a war for Polish independence. A public meeting was held on 29 November 1854 when Cowen, who was secretary of the Committee, and Harney proposed a message of solidarity with the Poles and called for revolution to overthrow the empires in central and eastern Europe. By December the Newcastle Committee was linked with similar groups in other towns. The movement enjoyed initial success, uniting Chartists and ex-Chartists with middle class representatives, and in May 1856 Cowen and the Foreign Affairs Committee held two tumultuous public rallies welcoming Louis Kossuth to Tyneside. But the principal objective was never realised due to the British and French governments' refusal to assist the Poles. There were problems, too, as a virulent anti-Russian sentiment diverted attention away from Poland despite Harney's success in detaching the Newcastle Committee from Russophobia. (22) Interest in Poland waned after 1855 but Cowen continued his contacts with Lekawski and in 1863 joined the central committee of the Friends of Poland whose members included Peter Taylor, John Stuart Mill and W.E. Adams. As a sidelight on history, it was this organisation that played a small part in the creation of the

International Working Men's Association or First International in
1864. (23) Cowen, meanwhile, was more preoccupied with the
Kilinski scheme having paid an emotional farewell to Lekawski. Jane
Cowen recalled her father summoning the children "to come and say
Good-by to Mr Lekawski - he is going away. He [Lekawski] tenderly
embraced us - we ran back to our nursery & we never saw him
more." (24) Konstanty Lekawski died in a still unfree Poland in
1872.

There had been a further interesting connection between Cowen
and Lekawski in the early 'fifties. Refugees from the collapse of
Chartism and radical exiles from the European empires both
advocated model democratic states, namely republics. Lekawski, like
Mazzini, was a republican and the notion of a form of government
unfettered by aristocratic privilege and open to popular direction
had a natural appeal to fragments of Chartism. The result was an
emergence of republican groups inspired by W.J. Linton's journal
The English Republic. Joseph Cowen happily embraced republicanism
and was instrumental in founding a National Republican
Brotherhood at Newcastle in January 1855, grafting republican ideas
"on to the usual Chartist programme" centred around the right to
vote. (25) The purpose of this Brotherhood, in which Lekawski also
participated, was defined by Cowen at a Newcastle dinner in January
1856 when he condemned "the incompetence and incapability of the
classes who now governed this country" as well as the "stolid
indifference on the part of the masses" in relation to the
government's poor conduct of the Crimean War. He further
conceded that the prospects for social reform were bleak as "all the
old landmarks [Chartism] had been broken up." Nevertheless, there
was a crying need for "new life" in politics and for this reason the
"Republican flag had been unfurled." (26) These Newcastle
republicans did not have a lot of success. The array of former
Chartists who resurfaced as republicans (Harney became secretary
of the Brotherhood) had reputations which could hardly soothe
middle class fears. As if to emphasise the point, Cowen delivered a
favourable lecture on the French revolutionary Robespierre at the
Blaydon mechanics' institute in May 1855, (27) and Richard Reed
proposed an "enthusiastic" toast at a Brotherhood dinner to "the
glorious time when kings and oppressors shall be overthrown and
the republic established - democratic and universal." (28) Cowen,
Reed and Harney had tempered their republicanism to emulate the

United States but their republican concept was still cloaked in the European imagery of barricades, mobs and guillotines. In later years, Cowen played down his republicanism probably because it tended to make him a target for crude Tory carping, yet a republican strand remained "an integral part of his philosophy." (29)

One function of the Republican Brotherhood, more by accident than design, was to hold together a group of Tyneside Radicals gathered around Cowen. Brotherhood meetings considered the prospects for reform in Britain and the organisation attempted to present its political ideas to a wider audience through a magazine, The *Northern Tribune*. During a short life-span (1854-55), the *Tribune's* pages were filled with a blend of republican ideals, articles sympathising with European nationalism, Chartist comment and occasional proposals for a renewed campaign for manhood suffrage embracing "men who can forget their differences." Cowen, or his father, carried the costs of the *Tribune* and employed Julian Harney as editor. Printing was undertaken at Brantwood in the Lake District by W.E. Adams and W.J. Linton. As a first venture into publishing, Cowen learned a great deal from the *Northern Tribune*, eventually realising that the age of the monthly political journal was ending. Developments in electric telegraphy meant that news could be circulated faster and a daily press became viable (especially with the repeal of the stamp tax in June 1855). Cowen accurately foresaw in March 1855 that the abolition of the tax "will cause a revolution in journalist literature ... for political periodicals there will be no place. They must become newspapers or nothing." He therefore announced the disposal of the *Northern Tribune* "to Holyoake, who is going to incorporate it with *The Reasoner* and bring out the two as a newspaper (unstamped) at 2d. I am going to start a local newspaper." Although the Brotherhood continued to publish a newsletter in 1855, *The Republican Record*, Cowen took an active interest in the *Newcastle Chronicle*, while Julian Harney left for Jersey on behalf of the Newcastle Foreign Affairs Committee to help Louis Blanc and other French political refugees. (30)

By the close of 1855, Joseph Cowen was 26 years old and had moved to Stella Hall, Blaydon. He had married Jane Thompson, daughter of a Durham coalowner, in 1854 and the couple would have two children, also named Jane and Joseph. The highly profitable family business placed large amounts of money at Cowen's disposal, sustaining a very comfortable life-style as well as subsidies to radical movements. He was now well known among revolutionaries from Italy to Poland and his friends and acquaintances at home ranged through the Chartist and Radical litanies. On Tyneside, Cowen's reputation for collaborating with the working classes was established. He was pouring vast quantities of energy and time into aiding exiles, mechanics' institutes and republicanism. It was all hard work not least since the eclipse of Chartism had left Cowen and his circle on the very margins of political society. The 1850s were years for making money rather than reforms. This was the epoch of Victorian prosperity built on an unparalleled expansion of shipbuilding, armaments, coal-mining, railways, engineering and construction. True, the fruits of this industry were inequitably divided between the social classes of the country but enough of the benefits trickled down to key sectors of labour to generate an awareness of economic improvement. One historian has aptly observed:

> "After about 1850 ... the pace of expansion in the North East was to show a spectacular acceleration, making the region one of the principal growth areas of late Victorian Britain ... During the second half of the nineteenth century, North East England was a principal beneficiary of a remarkable increase in economic activity on a national and international scale." (31)

The post-1850 Tyneside economy was rapidly restructured by several of the major industrial magnates of the nineteenth century. In 1852 Charles Palmer's shipyard at Jarrow launched an iron-built screw propelled vessel, the *John Bowes*, which became the prototype of modern cargo ships. Thereafter, Palmer's business boomed and, at the dawn of the twentieth century, a quarter of the world's entire new shipping tonnage was being built on the Tyne and the Wear. Similarly, William Armstrong used the Crimean War to extend from engineering into armaments, establishing his Elswick works as a fountainhead of arms supplies for international customers over the next few decades. Consequent on this astonishing economic growth came sizeable increases in population. Armstrong and two other engineering employers in west Newcastle employed nearly 20,000 men by the 1880s - "creating the most important centre in the world for the manufacture of ships, armaments and locomotives" - and stimulated a process of "massive change that was to enlarge the small central nucleus of Newcastle and its adjoining villages into a major industrial city." (32)

The ostensibly boundless horizons enjoyed by business were matched by Britain's enhanced imperial role highlighted at this time in two ways. Firstly, there was the Crimean War of 1854-56. Despite inept and incompetent military leadership, the war aroused zeal even among Radicals due to the extreme unpopularity of the Czar. It was soon apparent that the British and French governments were fighting the war for reasons of Great Power rivalry and had no intention of pressing for Polish independence. Joseph Cowen and his friends equally soon discovered to their cost that patriotic and jingoistic sentiments pushed Radical hopes to the sidelines. This emergence of imperial attitudes also informed the second signifiant flexing of British strength. The year 1857 witnessed the "Indian Mutiny", regarded by Indians as an important chapter in their long struggle for national independence. Newspapers in Britain, with a few exceptions, portrayed the uprising in grisly and lurid detail from the standpoint of the British colonial and military authorities. The impact was overwhelming. Tyneside Radicals generally vociferous in their complaints about foreign policy fell silent over the government's behaviour in India, only raising criticisms of army brutality long after the defeat of the "rebels". Joseph Cowen was no exception to this rule.

With much popular attention captivated by war overseas and a rampant capitalism at home the 1850s might be seen as bleak for Cowen's political concerns (the family business, on the other hand, did quite well). His recorded statements on the situation in Britain do suggest a critique of the effects of the new wealth. Cowen denigrated the middle classes for betraying reform, telling a public meeting at Winlaton mechanics' institute in 1850 that he detected "little nobility and but small chivalry" among the middle classes whose "great attempt is repression on the one side and pitiful servility [towards the aristocracy] on the other." (33) Two years later, speaking at the Chartists' Newcastle Democratic Reading Room, Cowen called for "the just and equitable distribution of wealth" because "wherever we see some men very rich we always find close alongside many who were poor." (34) During this period Cowen experienced an "intense feeling of resentment of the privileged classes and their supporters." (35) Whilst he welcomed social and economic advances - "notwithstanding all the shortcomings of

modern society, there is a vast improvement upon the ages which
have preceeded it" (36) - he also roundly rejected "that old heartless
indifferentism so prevalent in our age and country ... These sordid
and degenerate days of money-hunting and mammon-worshipping ...
of the laissez-faire men." (37) In adapting to the new capitalism,
Cowen completely despised the "Manchester School" of liberalism
and held that there were higher values than unfettered
commercialism. His assessments of Victorian society strongly hint at
a search for a humanistic social order responsive to democratic
influence rather than shaped by aristocratic or financial imperatives.
At a later date the search was to lead Cowen towards a more
tangible alternative vision.

Little could be done to redress the inequities of Victorian Britain
in the absence of either a vibrant working class movement or the
goodwill of those who possessed economic and political power, the
middle classes. This was why the vexed question of co-operation with
middle class reformers was a recurring topic at Chartist meetings in
1849-51 and subsequently in journals like the *Northern Tribune*. But
lack of interest on the part of the middle classes kept the question
of alliances at the level of academic debate. To an extent Cowen's
preoccupation with European adventures may have been a diversion
forced by the obstacles confronting domestic reform. Having noted
the point, though, it is important to underscore Joseph Cowen's
exceptional attachment to the exiles' causes. And towards the close
of the decade, almost out of the blue, the internationalist dimension
suddenly uncovered an opening for the renewal of the reform
movement. Jessie White's speaking tours of Tyneside in 1857
produced meetings packed to capacity. Working class Tynesiders
cheered for Garibaldi and Italian liberty yet their responsiveness
indicated, too, a reviving interest in reform. At a parliamentary level
there was further talk of promoting a new Reform Bill as legislative
shortcomings on matters of direct concern to working class
communities - legal protection for co-operative and friendly societies
and safety in the mines, for example - added weight to the case for
labour representation. It was against this background that the
periodic calls to launch a campaign for manhood suffrage made by
Cowen and others since 1852 began to gather support at meetings
in Carlisle and Newcastle during 1857. (38) As the year ended, and
with the Indian excitement receding, Cowen spearheaded the
formation of a new movement, the Northern Reform Union. The

Union was set up at two public meetings in January 1858, the first taking place at Newcastle's Chartist Institute on 2 January. These meetings were planned carefully to position the NRU as the heir to the Chartist crown yet distanced from Chartism in order to cultivate the middle classes. Cowen announced the Union would press for three principles derived from the People's Charter - manhood suffrage, vote by ballot and abolition of the property qualification required by MPs - and stated "the Chartists made this proposal." He was followed as a speaker by Thomas Thompson, "a delegate from the Chartist Association", who spoke in favour of the three principles after "some lengthy remarks on the blood-sucking propensities of the aristocracy." (39) The Chartist participation was nevertheless presented in terms of "rational Chartists" and "new men" unconnected with the old Chartism. (40) "Physical force" was apparently rejected at the first public meeting. (41)

The three principles advanced by the Union inevitably provoked arguments, especially over "manhood suffrage" articulated by Cowen as "a vote for every man ... because he was a man, because it was his right." (42) By emphasising votes for men only, the NRU drew a fierce response from some women. Francis Gill wrote to the Union's secretary, Richard Reed:

> "I can deplore that such an association actually places itself in the rear of public opinion instead of constituting itself the guide and educator of the public mind," (43)

and Jeanette Natham told Reed:

> "At present I do not feel inclined to become a member of any society which as a society is purely selfish in its objects and does not recognise the principles of justice and rights for all mankind." (44)

Gill and Natham may have reminded Cowen of his own attachment to women's rights but the NRU accepted the marginality of women, settling for the Chartist compromise of enfranchising men first and women later. For his own part, Joseph Cowen could rationalise the position by defining any reform as simply an "instalment" on greater prizes, insisting he was "always willing to take what you can get, refusing no step in the right direction." (45) Within the NRU there was also a secondary debate centred on the leadership's assumption that paupers as well as criminals and the insane should be excluded from an enlarged franchise. Other NRU activists condemned the idea on the grounds that poverty was not a crime. The proposal was not adequately thought out and probably indicated a desire to appear "responsible". (46) Though the definition of "manhood suffrage" was too conservative for some, it was considered dangerously "advanced" by many middle class reformers. The sanctity of property ownership still coloured the thinking of reform lobbies whose generally preferred option was one of extending the vote only to male householders. (47) Even people who endorsed European revolutionaries "shrank from Mr. Cowen's views on home policies." (48) Yet this did not stop the NRU advising its branches to involve the middle classes (49) as well as issuing public appeals to "Middle Class Reformers". (50)

Apart from revamping the Chartist programme, Cowen made a new departure by organising the NRU along professional lines. The Union was located in Newcastle's imposing Grainger Street at smart offices "beautifully lighted by pane and gas, and as handsomely and completely fitted up as a merchant's office in Manchester." The London press favourably contrasted the NRU with the metropolitan-based Parliamentary Reform Committee which had offices "three stories higher and ... six degrees meaner." (51) Cowen also ensured that his close friend from the Winlaton mechanics' institute and the Republican Brotherhood, Richard Reed, was appointed full-time secretary of the Union. Under Reed's efficient secretaryship and with Cowen as treasurer the NRU embarked on a dynamic series of meetings and petitions aimed at encouraging the popular groundswell for reform. The NRU's public meetings were scheduled to coincide with parliamentary sessions so as to sharpen their influence. By May 1858 at least 17 meetings had taken place, often with Cowen and Reed as the main speakers. A further cycle of meetings was then organised for the summer months. Cowen and Reed spoke at Blyth on 7 July, at a "crowded" meeting in Crook, Co. Durham, on 20 July and shortly afterwards at a memorable meeting in a field near the Tyneside village of Windy Nook where "the inhabitants ... are all active politicians, who cherish as a relic of glorious times the flag under which they marched during the agitation for the [1832] Reform Bill." (52) The meetings rolled on into August taking in Hexham, Blaydon and Darlington, and at an NRU social and tea held in Newcastle on 8 September it was reported that 30 public meetings had now taken place and local organisers (or "superintendents") had been appointed. September saw further rallies at Swalwell, Winlaton, North and South Shields, Gateshead, Middlesbrough and "nearly all of the large colliery and manufacturing villages" of Northumberland and Durham. Twenty-four petitions were collected and sent to Parliament in support of the NRU's three principles. (53)

With enthusiasm for reform bubbling throughout the north east of England, the NRU hoped to link with a wider movement. Cowen therefore visited York, Leeds, Rochdale, Bradford, Manchester, Liverpool, Sheffield and Birmingham together with Hawick and a few Scottish towns, and in October he addressed a Political Reform League soiree at Anderton's Hotel in London. The results of the "grand tour" were disappointing. Only Rochdale had an organised reform campaign and elsewhere there was either little popular activity or, as in London, divisions between "timid politicians of the Liberal School" and those who favoured manhood suffrage. (54) But the NRU bandwagon was not to be deflected and its crusade continued with more meetings at Newcastle, Shotley Bridge ("a large hall being completely filled") and Sunderland where Cowen was received with "loud and continued cheering, which did not subside for some time." (55) Renewed expectations of reform from Lord Derby's government brought a huge attendance at an NRU meeting on 29 November in Newcastle's Nelson Street Lecture Room with "hundreds unable to obtain admission". (56) By 21 December 1858, some 60 public meetings had delivered the Union's message to an estimated 40,000 people and the organisation had opened almost 40 local branches co-ordinated by a central council. (57) Cowen and Reed privately met John Bright who was heading the pressure for reform inside Parliament at Newcastle on 23 December. They apparently agreed to support Bright's more limited proposals for reform but this did not hinder the NRU's agitation for its own principles. (58) Consequently, the Union's programme of public meetings swept on through a "highwater mark" of activity during the first four months of 1859 including a demonstration at Newcastle's town hall on 8 February when a petition signed by 34,456 men was collated. Disregarding parliamentary set-backs, a wave of meetings criss-crossed Northumberland and Durham in the autumn of 1859 and Cowen once again canvassed other northern towns and cities (finding, as before, a less intense feeling for reform than in the north east). Over the two years from January 1858 the Northern

Reform Union organised 220 public meetings and Cowen and Reed fulfilled a punishing timetable to speak in fields, market squares and halls. (59)

Underlying the NRU was a single-mindedness of purpose. The Union concentrated solely on its own objectives, avoiding any other issue with the exception of a protest against the notorious game laws at Winlaton in November 1859. (60) The bulk of the NRU agitation was in meetings and petitions but the Union did attempt to expose the defects of the prevailing electoral system. Firstly, an attack was mounted on bribery at elections with "vigilence committees" formed to monitor local elections in the autumn of 1859. These committees were backed with an offer of a £10 reward for information about corrupt practices and the Union did try to prosecute for personation at a Gateshead election but was unsuccessful in court. A similar though more damaging fate met Richard Reed's bid to expose bribery at the Berwick-on-Tweed parliamentary election of 1859. Reed produced a detailed report alleging corruption and a meeting of 2000 people held at Berwick on 8 August demanded an inquiry into the election. The bribery petition received short shrift in court and the NRU suffered a humiliating public defeat. Years later Holyoake could still rail at the presiding judge, Baron Bramwell, "the Tory judge [who] sneered away all chance of a just verdict ... and aided and abetted the bribery and those who committed it." (61) Whatever the technicalities of the case, the outcome was a severe blow for the NRU's prestige.

The Union was equally unfortunate at the 1859 general election in Newcastle. For years, Cowen had been unimpressed with the Whig and Tory candidates. At the 1857 election he condemned all the Newcastle candidates at a protest meeting of "working men and democrats." (62) Originally, Cowen hoped the NRU would contest the 1859 election at Berwick, Newcastle, North Durham and Sunderland but in the event only Newcastle emerged as a serious prospect. Expecting to win middle class votes Cowen recommended the Leicester Radical, Peter Taylor, as a candidate and the Union invited him to stand "in the interests of radicalism." (63) Taylor played his role in projecting the NRU's "moderate" stance by urging an extension of the franchise as a way of preventing revolution. (64) Newcastle's middle classes were not so readily reassured. As soon as the NRU adopted Taylor there was a move to split the Radical vote by a significant local body of "moderate" Radicals grouped around a religious Dissenting position. Attempts to negotiate an agreement failed when the *Northern Daily Express* slated the Union's leaders as "Blaydon atheists". The 1859 election consequently turned into a dismal failure for the NRU. Taylor received only 463 votes whereas the Whig candidate, Headlam, was returned on 2687 votes compared with the Tories' 2680. Taylor, in consolation, did carry the show of hands at the pre-election "hustings" and again at a subsequent by-election caused by Headlam's appointment to a government post: "Twice I have been chosen as your representative in the House of Commons" wrote Taylor in a letter to the people of Newcastle. Nonetheless, the outcome of both the Berwick case and the 1859 election undermined the Northern Reform Union, and hostile London opinion rubbed salt into the wound by crowing about the NRU "sham". (65) The collapse of the appeal to the middle classes provoked bitterness. Cowen talked of compelling the government to extend the franchise, (66) and the Chartist James Watson even floated the idea of forming a "working-man's volunteer rifle corp" at a meeting of the Union's central council (possibly as part of the general enthusiasm for "volunteering" prompted by concern about French militarism, but the notion of "citizens in arms" had obvious domestic implications as well). (67) In any event, there was no turn to "physical force", and the NRU was clear about the obstacles it faced. Cowen pinpointed class interests as a major problem, blaming the "shopocracy" as a "selfish and unprincipled class", (68) opposed "to all real attempts to give the industrial classes political power. The election had proved this beyond dispute." (69)

This recognition of social and political realities is a more credible clue to the Northern Reform Union's eventual weakness than Cowen's supposed "incurable desire to be both Chief and Indians." (70) It is likely that Joseph Cowen was the driving force behind the Union and that he and Reed used the NRU central council "as a sounding board rather than as a policy making body." (71) The NRU was not, however, the compliant tool of one man. The Union acted through negotiation with people who were capable of objecting forcibly if they disagreed. NRU branches generally opened only after full discussions with local Radicals, Chartists and Secularists. (72) The Union's committed membership was experienced in co-operative benefit societies, teetotal societies, trade unions and mechanics' institutes (73) and therefore skilled in democratic politics. These people wanted the NRU to succeed although they had plenty of alternative commitments if progress could not be made immediately on the right to vote. Cowen's achievement was to temporarily weld this relatively sophisticated if diverse "movement" into an apparently powerful pressure group. It has been argued that the NRU and Cowen made misjudgements in aligning the campaign with Radicalism and treating "moderate" reform proposals lukewarmly. (74) Conversely, Cowen's meeting with John Bright, the visits to other towns and the Union's efforts to reach out to the middle classes reveal no lack of flexibility on questions of strategy or tactics. In the end, the dynamics of class politics meant that only the most "advanced" Radicals jointly with the remaining Chartists were likely to be seriously interested in building a movement around working class political rights, and this coalition was bound to alienate segments of the middle classes.

Towards the close of 1859, the steam went out of the NRU's reform campaign apart from a minor burst of activity in January 1862 when reform briefly looked promising at national level. Cowen spoke at a national reform conference and reported to the NRU that the chances of achieving manhood suffrage remained "dim" but he "would never be a party to abandoning their old flag." The NRU council agreed (75) and possibly shared his assessment that "the conventional parties in the state had abandoned the cause." (76) Yet the end of the NRU campaign had not brought the same fragmentation seen a decade earlier. By 1860, trade unionism and co-operatives were making headway and the NRU had aroused a new confidence among Radicals and working class reformers in Northumberland and Durham. Simultaneously, developments in Italy were again commanding Cowen's attention and the *Kilinski* would not be far behind. Richard Reed was also moving to a new job as manager of the *Newcastle Chronicle*. Joseph Cowen had at last achieved his ambition to own a real newspaper.

CHAPTER FIVE : "INTOLERANT AND INTOLERABLE CLIQUES"

Newcastle upon Tyne has long remembered Richard Grainger, the imaginative builder who reshaped the centre of the town in the 1830s. Grainger's stone-faced buildings, classical Theatre Royal and elegant streets gave Newcastle pride of place among nineteenth-century cities, evoking Gladstone's remark that one thoroughfare, Grey Street, "I think our best modern street." (1) "Ruthless determination" (2) as well as "all the craft and subtlety of the devil" combined with access to wealth and "an influence in society rarely possessed by one individual" enabled Grainger to "do things with impunity that would damm an ordinary man." (3) In a few short years, Richard Grainger completely transformed central Newcastle into "the first planned commercial centre in this country." (4) On his death in July 1861 a church bell tolled and shopkeepers closed their shops out of respect. Richard Grainger also left debts of almost £129,000. This fact had been carefully concealed by business and civic leaders for twenty years as had Grainger's flight to Liverpool in 1841 to escape arrest for debt. No effort was spared to ensure "neither the disgrace of bankruptcy nor indeed any public indignity [should be] suffered by the creator of the new Newcastle." (5)

Interestingly, the same sensitivity was missing in the treatment of John Brown whose name was fleetingly linked with Grainger in January 1861. John Brown was a "working man" who, too, engaged in "exertions, sacrifices and unwearied industry." (6) Brown also tried to build, in the parlance of the age, a new city. But John Brown's vision rested in the hearts, minds and liberties of the people, eventually leaving him as the very last "indefatigable secretary" of the Newcastle Chartists, and responsible for rent owed by the Chartist Institute, or meeting rooms, in Newcastle's Nun Street. With Grainger desperately searching for money-spinning ventures, the Chartists' Nun Street premises were unexpectedly "appropriated by Mr. Grainger for tenement buildings." For good measure, the luckless Brown's furniture was seized by bailiffs. (7) When the *Newcastle Daily Chronicle* drew attention to the affair in hardly complimentary terms, Grainger and his supporters seemed to have demanded a better press. The *Chronicle*, in fine irony, responded by noting "a more considerate landlord does not live than Mr. Grainger" and observing "the kindly manner in which his instructions are carried out." (8) Soon afterwards, the newspaper and a local co-operative literary society opened a public subscription to pay John Brown's debts. (9) These respective fates of Richard Grainger and John Brown said a great deal about Victorian values.

The closure of the Chartist Institute in a town where Chartism "lingered longest" (10) dealt the "mortal blow" (11) to a movement which once almost held Grainger's streets in its own hands. Now the old world of Chartism gave way to new landmarks. Under Joseph Cowen the *Newcastle Daily Chronicle* became one of the larger features of the new landscape. Cowen had steadily worked to gain control of the *Chronicle* since 1857 intending to "infuse new life into the concern." (12) He may have helped persuade Mark Lambert, the most active of the paper's three proprietors, to launch the *Newcastle Daily Chronicle* on 1 May 1858 as a "thoroughly liberal" daily. (13) Previously, the *Chronicle* (f.1764) had been a weekly. Lambert's Whig partners were certainly unwilling to see the *Chronicle* become a vehicle for the Northern Reform Union whose principles they opposed. (14) Cowen's tactic therefore was to ensnare the proprietors financially. Moving to daily publication necessitated expensive new printing presses and Cowen exploited the situation by lending money to Lambert. By 1859 Cowen's influence was evident when he arranged for J. Baxter Langley, treasurer of the London Political Reform League, to come north to edit the *Chronicle*. (15) Baxter Langley was able to shift the paper's editorial policy towards the NRU but he was still constrained by the Whig proprietors. Cowen then resolved to buy the newspaper and sought Holyoake's assistance. Holyoake, it seems, spent a week in Newcastle meeting the paper's staff and gathering information useful to Cowen. (16) At the end of 1859 Cowen had bought a half-share of the *Chronicle* for £1,150 and the other proprietors' financial problems soon afterwards enabled him to take sole ownership. (17)

The *Newcastle Daily Chronicle* became Joseph Cowen's consuming passion. One of his editors, Aaron Watson, noted Cowen was "first and foremost ... the owner of the *Newcastle Chronicle*. The paper meant much more to him than all his other interests combined." (18) He spared no effort for the newspaper, almost over-reaching his financial resources. In March 1860, Cowen confided to Holyoake that "the cash I have had to pay for the *Chronicle* ha(s) run me nearly ashore." (19) Holyoake later claimed Cowen put £40,000 into the paper before it began to pay, (20) probably around the early 1870s. (21) For many years, Cowen divided his time between mornings at the brickworks and afternoons and evenings at the *Chronicle* office. (22) The aim was "to make the *Newcastle Chronicle* the *Times* of the North" (23) but with a reforming edge. It was not uncommon for provincial newspapers of this period to be inspired by politics (24) and Cowen made no secret of his purpose. Speaking in March 1862, at the *Chronicle*'s 98th birthday party for staff and their families, he congratulated the paper on being "more radical than it was under the former management." (25) W.E. Adams, whom Cowen appointed as a columnist in 1863, confirmed in his autobiography that journalism and business were "merely a means to an end" for Cowen: the "press became the adjunct of the platform ... a regular channel for conveying his ideas to the public." (26)

Cowen took a close interest in editorial policy but in subtle ways. "I am not a journalist, but a brickmaker" Cowen would say, and according to Aaron Watson he wrote few articles for the *Chronicle*. (27) W.E. Adams, despite "friction" between himself and Cowen later in the century, (28) still regarded Cowen as having been "the ablest journalist of them all", (29) in a reference to his editorial judgement. Cowen naturally worked through his staff, selecting them for their political principles as well as journalistic abilities. *Chronicle* staff were recruited for their "unswerving devotion" to the paper's principles (30) and their "decided opinions, strong convictions." (31) But, at least during the 1860s, the journalists were not expected to "write anything that was contrary to [their] convictions" (32) or "which they did not strongly believe." (33) There was "always a choice between writers where any difficulty of conscience arose" (34) and staff were "given a free hand to get the best out of them." (35) Cowen's critics, on the other hand, were more sceptical about life on the *Chronicle*. W.T. Stead, editor of the rival *Northern Echo* once alleged the *Chronicle* "leader-writer, and even the editor ... [c]ould never altogether escape from the shadow of Joe Cowen." (36) This may have been coloured by Cowen's sacking of James Annand, the *Newcastle Daily Chronicle*'s one-time editor-in-chief, when proprietor and editor clashed in 1877 over aspects of Liberal Party policy.

Annand had axes to grind with his former employer but he left a valuable pen-portrait of the *Chronicle* at the end of the 1860s and early 1870s. Annand discovered a staff including:

> "One man who had taken part in the liberation of Italy, one gathered that tyrannicide was capable of justification, and it would have been possible to meet a quiet, white- haired, dignified gentleman who had carried over from London to Paris the pistols which played their part in one of the attempted assassinations of Napoleon III. Another member of the staff had edited a Republican journal. Another had played an active part in securing the escape of more than one patriot from the prisons of European despotisms. The Office was run on somewhat paternal principles. A room was set apart for social purposes. At five o'clock every afternoon the staff would assemble for tea, and again at ten o'clock in the evening. At these functions Mr Cowen himself was nearly always present. He used to lie on his back and join in the discussions which often ensued, either on general politics or on the subjects and line of treatment of leading articles for the following day." (37)

Aaron Watson has given a slightly different insight into the *Chronicle*, noting Cowen:

> "left everything to the editor and the staff. There was never any direct interference ... And always he would enter into a conversation, as if by way of passing the time, but invariably circling round the topic that was to be treated, and illuminating it so that only a very stupid writer could have treated it ineffectively."

But Watson observed there were unwritten rules governing the rights of conscience, preventing any journalist from:

> "either defiantly or carelessly, adventur[ing] on the expression of [his] own views when he knew that they were not those of the paper. That would have been something more than disloyalty when so much consideration had been shown to him as a "conscientious objector"." (38)

Cowen insisted his staff should not write articles contradictory to editorial policy. (39) He admitted as well that the press represented the views of proprietors and it was "a gross exaggeration to assume that [newspapers] express the opinion of the public." (40) Controversy over Cowen's exact involvement in determining the contents of the *Newcastle Daily Chronicle* raged for many years. In

1870, Holyoake actually described Cowen as editor of the newspaper, (41) and Richard Ruddock, who followed James Annand as editor-in-chief, was not given Annand's more extensive free rein. (42) Cowen's preferred practice of exercising a discreet "backroom" control over the paper could also infuriate critics:

> "Some whom [Cowen] pretended to regard as friends in public life found reason to regret that he owned the Chronicle, though when confronted with an injurious paragraph he would always disclaim responsibility." (43)

There was no denying that "in the last resort ... the power lay with Cowen" (44) although his degree of control varied depending on the subjects to be covered, levels of trust between owner and successive editors and the unavoidable pressures on Cowen's time from his other interests. In Cowen's hands the *Newcastle Daily Chronicle* grew through the 1860s and 1870s from a small scale Tyneside local newspaper into "one of the greatest provincial papers of the period" (45) and in Watson's words:

> "One of the most powerful newspapers in the Kingdom. In the counties of Northumberland and Durham its political influence was enormous. It had, besides, the reputation of being a "national" newspaper - that is to say, its influence was felt, and its views had their weight, in other newspaper offices and among politicians everywhere, not least in London, where it had an office of its own, and a London staff, of which George Jacob Holyoake was a principal member ... The "soul" of the Newcastle Chronicle was Joseph Cowen." (46)

Constant supervision of editorial policy was accompanied by a rigorous business discipline. Maurice Milne rightly emphasised that "Cowen never made the mistake of neglecting the commercial side" of the *Chronicle*. The paper was always meant to be successful "in its own right" and not "the expensive mouthpiece of a rich politician." Cowen applied "a tremendous business aptitude, great drive and resourcefulness." (47) The "bulk of his correspondence with the *Chronicle* reveals concerns no different from any other proprietors" (48) in relation to viability, and as a businessman Cowen firmly believed all his enterprises should be profitable. (49) There were even instances when paid advertising was allowed to take precedence over space for news reports. (50) Cowen was willing to invest in the latest printing machinery in order to produce the paper ahead of its rivals and to meet the demand of a rising circulation. New presses had to be installed to meet rising sales within a few months of Cowen's take-over, (51) and a thorough mechanisation was carried out between 1861-65. Inheriting a printing process based on one small hydraulic engine and a double-cylinder printing machine, Cowen introduced two steam engines and two four-feeder printing presses with a capacity for turning out 15,000 copies an hour, and further increased printing capacity to 40,000 copies by acquiring new American-built presses. (52) The *Chronicle* also moved to larger premises in Newcastle's Westgate Road. Typically, the grand new offices exhibited Cowen's predilection for brightness and "modernism", with "mahogany counters of elaborate and useful horseshoe design" and "replete in every respect, with departmental sections of glass, giving quiet and comparative privacy." (53) New printing technology was a hallmark of the *Chronicle* for the rest of the century and on the appearance of linotype Cowen swiftly became the first shareholder in the Linotype Company, placing an order for twenty machines backed by a cheque for £10,000 some eighteen months in advance of delivery. He was believed to have been "the first newspaper proprietor in England to introduce the rotary machine." (54) The *Chronicle* is also credited with being "the first English provincial newspaper" to install its own telegraph wire linking Newcastle with the paper's London office. Not surprisingly, the paper gained a reputation as "one of the most advanced newspaper printing centres in the country." (55)

Joseph Cowen was particularly fortunate in his choice of Richard Reed as the *Chronicle*'s general manager. Reed wrote a few leading articles in the early 1860s and edited the journal of his own trade union, the Chainmakers' Society. (56) He soon became completely absorbed, however, in managing the *Chronicle*'s transition to rapid production, overseeing the introduction of new presses and, sometimes, the recruitment of staff. (57) W.E. Adams considered Reed to be a "newspaper genius":

> "No shrewder intellect than his, I think, was ever connected with the press. If he did not write much himself, he knew how to instruct and inspire others to write. And his energy was amazing. Nothing in any department of the paper escaped his watchful eye. Added to his untiring zeal was a marvellous capacity for gauging the tastes and requirements of the reading public. Mr. Reed was a newspaper genius ... To him must be ascribed the credit of raising the press of the North of England from the parochialism of an earlier day..." (58)

Adams could call on the spectacular expansion of the *Chronicle* as evidence of Reed's contribution. When Cowen gained control of the paper it had a circulation of 2,500 copies a day. (59) By the mid-1860s Reed was organising the printing of 15,000 copies, and in 1868 the figure was up to 18,523 a day escalating to 28,539 by 1871. In 1873 the *Chronicle* claimed "the largest circulation of any provincial daily paper" at 35,534 copies. (60) Circulation figures of Victorian newspapers are difficult to estimate with accuracy and most statistics tend to reflect the numbers of copies printed rather than sold. It does appear, though, that the *Newcastle Daily Chronicle* could fairly claim to be among the front-runners compared with the performance of counterparts such as the *Manchester Guardian*, and it without doubt totally out-distanced its Tyneside competitors. (61)

The *Chronicle* was blessed with the advantages of Cowen's wealth and the keen commitment of proprietor, manager and staff. But these factors were not guarantees of success. What really gave the *Chronicle* a head-start was the combination of enterprise and politics encouraged by Joseph Cowen. Being first with the news was the essence of newspaper legend from the birth of the daily press and the *Chronicle* threw itself wholeheartedly into the game. Richard Reed's skilful management of printing and distribution enabled early and special editions to appear with unusual speed. Steam trains would be chartered to get news reports to Newcastle ahead of other local papers or deliver the *Chronicle* to northern towns such as Middlesbrough, Darlington and York ahead of the London papers. (62) Cowen also produced detailed reports and special supplements on any national conference held in Newcastle, deploying his large staff of reporters to cover these national events in depth. The 1863 conference of the British Association for the Advancement of Science - to which Cowen contributed a paper on fire-clays - was the prototype for treatment later accorded to co-operative and other congresses. (63) Additional reporting staff were engaged and extra copies of the *Chronicle*'s daily and weekly versions printed. Other newspapers were unable to match Cowen's resources and Wemyss Reid, then employed on the *Newcastle Journal*, physically collapsed in a vain attempt to compete with "a formidible rival possessing a staff three times as large" as his own. (64) One of the attractions of covering national conferences, it should be noted, was the potential for enhancing the *Chronicle*'s status among "influential" people, again cementing a reputation as a paper of "national" standing.

The *Chronicle* was adept at merging crusades for "liberty" with its own commercial self-interest. This was clear in Cowen and Reed's notable victory over W.H. Smith and Son who controlled important sales outlets at railway stations. In 1864, Smith tried to use his monopoly to squeeze a higher sales commission out of the Newcastle papers. When the proprietors refused Smith's terms, he banned their papers, including the *Chronicle*, from his station bookstalls. For his own reasons, Smith then bought copies of the *Journal* and the *Northern Daily Express* and displayed these for sale but excluded the *Chronicle*. Only Louis Napoleon annexing Tyneside would have been more likely to rouse Joseph Cowen to arms. Denouncing "News-agent despotism", the *Chronicle* went to war against the "would-be autocrat of the English press" and defiantly asserted:

> "We count the hostility of men like W.H. Smith and Son as an honour ... If a stop is not put to their grasping and greedy mode of management, they will very soon have the power of stopping the publication of any paper whose principles are offensive to them."

Chronicle "travelling vans" were put on the road selling the paper "opposite to all the large stations of the North Eastern Railway" to break "the over-reaching monopoly of such bumptious despots as W.H. Smith and Son." (65) And so the crusade continued. Labelling Smith's policy as "A NEW CENSORSHIP" the *Chronicle* relentlessly battered the "arrogant monopolists" and "autocrats of the Metropolis", promising neither "to break nor bend" in the fight to "safeguard public liberties":

> "We dare Messrs Smith and Son to do their worst. We rely in this struggle, as in all others, on the support and countenance of that public which has never yet failed us. Encouraged by that countenance and aided by that support, we mean to maintain against the assault of these haughty and avaricious hucksters the rights and liberties of the Newcastle press." (66)

Cowen won.

The fight with Smith illustrated something of the flavour of the *Chronicle* in the 1860s. The newspaper, like its owner, was greatly attached to causes. Cowen, for example, had publicly called for the abolition of capital punishment since 1849. (67) Under Cowen's influence, the *Chronicle* took up the issue from 1859 and in a typical commentary in May 1862 stated:-

> "Yet the scaffold will not stand for ever. For murder, as for robbery, we shall substitute other penalties than death; our lives will not be less safe." (68)

The paper was banned in France in October 1862 by Cowen's old enemy Louis Napoleon, (69) and it consistently echoed the demand made by generations of Radicals for the repeal of the game laws. (70)

Crucial to the projection of the *Chronicle* were the staff whom Cowen and Reed hired. These included, as James Annand noted, a coterie of experienced revolutionists and agitators. For over a decade after Cowen's take-over, the *Newcastle Daily Chronicle* carried a weekly "Local Gossip" column written under the pseudonym "Elfin". The author was Sidney Milnes Hawkes who combined a leisurely life-style - Aaron Watson described him as having "a most commanding natural indolence" - with an earlier career as a European revolutionary:

> "the gentlest and most tender-hearted of men [Hawkes] committed some desperate crimes in the cause of Italian liberty. He carried out to Paris the dagger and pistol with which Pianori was to assassinate the French Emperor; he forged passports for Italian refugees; frequently, at the risk of his life, he conveyed financial aid to both Mazzini and Garibaldi"

and eventually drifted into journalism "at Joseph Cowen's instigation." Hawkes also enlivened Cowen's Christmas staff soirees by singing *The Marseillaise* in French. (71) "Elfin's" column was sharp and critical and Hawkes used it for several campaigns. Its biting tone quickly drew enquires about the author's identity but Hawkes prefered to remain anonymous, writing mischievously in October 1862 that he could be found in:

> "news-rooms, in snug-parlours behind the bar, and at select parties... I know everybody, am familiar with everything ... in short, can get at secrets through stone walls, and render myself invisible at pleasure." (72)

Hawkes had exceptionally good luck in surviving libel actions although during a well-publicised exposure of prison flogging in

1870, he (together with Reed and Cowen) got away mainly on a legal technicality. (73)

Another of Cowen's successes was to pluck W.E. Adams from near-poverty in London and put him in charge of reviving the *Newcastle Weekly Chronicle*. Adams transformed the *Weekly Chronicle* from a "dull provincial paper of a kind published all round the country" merely rehashing old news items and from 1864 turned it into a magazine of "national reputation with a readership drawn from all over Britain." *The Weekly Chronicle* under Adams's 36-year editorship remains a gold mine of information about nineteenth century radical movements not least because Adams operated an imaginative features policy and, from the 1880s, went out of his way to persuade old Chartists and Radicals to write their reminiscences for the paper. A novel departure pioneered by Adams was the "Dicky Bird Society" which became a Tyneside institution. The Society was a children's club linked with a column in the *Weekly Chronicle* aimed at promoting the humane treatment of animals. (74) A by-product was the attraction of young readers to a quality Radical newspaper.

It would be mistaken to assume the *Chronicle* lived solely on a diet of politics and noble causes. The paper offered a broad appeal to its readers by detailing the activities of local churches, trade union branches, and other voluntary organisations, serialising books, reproducing snippets of odd pieces of news, social tittle-tattle, lurid crime reports, articles on history and economics, theatrical and literary reviews and, as another innovation, extensive sporting news. Cowen knew "a regular Party journal can never be an all-round success" - and argued the "only way to make a newspaper a success ... was to make it sufficiently interesting to make people buy it." (75) Aaron Watson noted:

> "...a fanatical politician, [Cowen] nevertheless perceived with incisive clearness that a newspaper is not made by its politics. The public must be attracted to it by other means, and, as the public of Tyneside was a sporting public, Mr. Cowen organised his sporting department on a scale and with a completeness up to that time unattempted by any other provincial journal." (76)

Even Holyoake was sent to cover boxing matches in 1863. (77) The decision to allocate space to sport startled proprietors of newspapers such as the *Manchester Guardian* and the *Leeds Mercury* who eventually sent a protest deputation to see Cowen. They complained that sports reporting lowered moral standards and were concerned that market pressures would force them to follow the *Chronicle's* lead. Cowen blandly told them: "I shall continue to conduct my newspaper in my own way." (78) Yet the last thing Cowen wanted was "lower standards". He geared the the *Chronicle* to raising standards in some important ways. The paper did not dismiss the sporting recreations of the working classes, although it condemned dog-baiting and activities which harmed animals. There was an educative ethos about the *Chronicle* conveying Cowen's own belief in the value of education for citizenship and reform. Furthermore, the ethos was neither pompous nor condescending but integrated into an attractive format resembling "a great American than an English journal." (79) This distinctive approach to popular journalism was also evident in the high quality of writing in the *Chronicle*. The paper even made a few concessions to poor eyesight by varying layout and print sizes slightly to move away from the Victorian printers' preoccupation with dense columns of print. Inevitably, mistakes were made. In May 1868 the *Newcastle Daily Chronicle* reported the death of the old Chartist Thomas Cooper and published appreciative obituaries. Fortunately for Cooper, the news was wrong (for the second time in a year). (80)

Cowen's formula was to connect the paper with the concerns and interests of the north east's burgeoning working classes, and Cowenism was astute at recognising the social and cultural changes of the 1860s. The role of the *Chronicle* was to champion those working classes and none less so than the miners in the huge coalfields of Northumberland and Durham. Coincidental with Cowen's growing influence over the *Chronicle*, the paper supported the miners' efforts to re-establish their trade unions which had been shattered by the 1844 defeat and had led a weak "guerrilla" existence ever since. (81) But two pit tragedies gave the movement an extra impetus - the Burradon colliery explosion in March 1860 and the Hartley pit disaster of January 1862. The *Chronicle* devoted a vast amount of attention to both events which together claimed over 270 lives. Special editions were issued updating readers on the scale of the accidents and the progress of the rescue attempts. At Hartley, the *Chronicle* reporter, finding his competitors had commandeered all the horse-drawn transport in the race to get stories back to their papers, flagged down a passing goods train by "leaping between the rails", persuading the driver to take him to Newcastle. He did get the report back ahead of his rivals only to find the engine powering the *Chronicle's* presses had broken down. The situation was saved by Cowen and Reed rolling up their sleeves and producing a special edition manually. (82) Cowen had a larger point to make by publicising conditions in the pits. The *Chronicle* used Burradon and Hartley to demand tighter safety regulations. Cowen agitated for a public inquiry into the Burradon explosion and with Baxter Langley's help engaged first-rate legal representation for the miners whilst the *Chronicle* raised funds for the victims' dependents. Writing to Holyoake, Cowen stated "all" my time was being spent on Burradon and he hoped to "raise a large sum of money" for the widows and children. By skillful lobbying and extensive publicity about the Burradon explosion, Cowen and the miners managed to secure some constructive amendments to the Mines Inspection Bill which became law in 1861. (83)

The *Chronicle* censured periodic evictions of miners and their families by pit owners, (84) especially the Cramlington evictions used to defeat a strike for higher pay in October 1865. Although deploring the Cramlington miners' resort to a "riot", the paper detailed the provocation engineered by the pit owners who called the police and "candymen" (bailiffs) to remove the miners from their homes. When the army was ordered into Cramlington to back the police, the *Chronicle* reported gleefully that the soldiers were "sarcastic" towards the police and the military band spent its evenings entertaining the village. (85) It was during the Cramlington strike that Joseph Cowen made another friend and ally, Thomas Burt, the youthful secretary of the Northumberland Miners' Association. Burt wrote a letter to the *Newcastle Daily Chronicle* arguing the miners' case and found himself invited to the *Chronicle* office where Cowen told him "the columns of the *Chronicle* were always open ... for the defence of the miners and their right to combine." (86) Cowen introduced Burt to the paper's staff as the "young pitman who had so effectively answered and silenced the coalowners." At a later stage, Cowen offered Burt a job as a journalist when it was erroneously rumoured that Burt had resigned from the secretaryship of the miners' union. (87) Gradually, the *Chronicle* built up a following in the mining districts, causing Aaron Watson to comment that the daily and weekly *Chronicles*, "one or other", found their way into "every miner's cottage" in the two counties. (88) This may have been an exaggeration but a more recent judgement has presented the *Chronicle* as "one notable exception" to a provincial press overwhelmingly hostile to trade unionism in the 1860s:

> "Owned by Joseph Cowen, the **Chronicle** had [become] ... one of the most influential and widely read of provincial newspapers. Its attitude to trade unionism was consistently one of support ... unlike other papers it actually encouraged the ... unions." (89)

Cowen's empathy with the miners and trade unionism had deep roots forged not only in the Northern Reform Union and Chartism but also through Cowen's involvement with education. When he came to shape the *Chronicle* Cowen was equipped with a respect not shared by middle class "society" for the abilities and tastes of the working classes. One result was a furore in the "boom" cultural arenas of Tyneside, theatre and music halls. On one level, the growth of interest in music halls and theatre in the early 1860s represented a move towards more organised and commercialised leisure and away from the relatively spontaneous popular culture of previous decades, but whether or to what extent this change entirely cramped and reshaped the cultural independence of the north east's working classes in the middle of the century is an unfinished debate. (90) In any event, the north east was nurturing "a very large supportive audience" for the theatre and in Newcastle "dramatic and musical taste seem[ed] to have been of exceptional standard." (91) The ramshackled Tyne Concert Hall in Newcastle's Neville Street emerged as the area's leading music hall under the management of George Stanley who had a lengthy theatrical background. Stanley wanted to stage plays and he applied to the town's magistrates for a licence to perform drama. The magistrates turned him down. In fact, the Newcastle bench rejected Stanley's applications for a drama licence no less than five times in 1861. What George Stanley discovered, or possibly already suspected, was that the principal magistrates enjoyed a close relationship with the town's Theatre Royal and the Theatre Royal, sanctioned by the bench, enjoyed a monopoly to show drama in Newcastle. Here was a scandal begging for exposure.

A *Chronicle* editorial in September 1861 thundered against the magistrates, accusing them of ignoring the public good because of "the private leaning of particular Justices to support the pecuniary interest" of the proprietors of the Theatre Royal. But it was Sidney Milnes Hawkes who really forced the pace in a crusade to destroy the licensing monopoly. Hawkes claimed in his "Elfin" column that certain magistrates had a financial interest in blocking George Stanley and one of them (an Alderman Dodds) had been heard to say in advance of hearing Stanley's application that the bench would not grant a licence. "If by some chance" a licence was conceded, according to Dodds, "the North Eastern Railway Company might be induced to pull down" the Tyne Concert Hall. (92) The argument now enlarged into a serious controversy both in Newcastle, where the *Chronicle* and the *Northern Daily Express* took opposing sides, and throughout the theatrical world. In November, as Stanley's fifth request for a drama licence was refused, the *Chronicle* citing the example of opposition to the stamp tax on newspapers, urged Stanley to break the law:

> "It is needless for Mr. Stanley to argue any more with such men. They are inaccessible to the aims of either reason or justice on this question ... The law is sacred only so long as it is not turned into an instrument of oppression and tyranny. When it is so perverted, there is only one remedy for it, and that is to BREAK IT ... Mr. Stanley will never get a theatrical licence till he takes the law into his own hands, plays in defiance of the magistrates and ... the Theatre Royal ... We strongly advise him to take this course." (93)

George Stanley did not take the *Chronicle's* advice but applied to the bench again in January 1862. He was again refused even though he presented two public petitions collected in his support. Stanley was fast becoming a popular hero, and he capitalised on this new status by advertising the Tyne Concert Hall as "Licensed by Public Opinion, But not by the Magistrates." (94) During the spring of 1862 George Stanley came close to flouting the magistrates by engaging the popular actress, Juliet Desborough, to give dramatic readings at the Concert Hall. The audience was delighted, partly because of the context. Desborough, in a letter to the *Newcastle Daily Chronicle*, had criticised the manager of the Theatre Royal, Edward Davis, for having her "forcibly removed" from the theatre in a dispute over casting. "Elfin" further alleged Davis had deprived Juliet Desborough of her fair share of the proceeds of her own benefit performance. The audiences at both the Theatre Royal and the Tyne Concert Hall sided with Desborough leaving Davis, who was heckled in his own theatre over the affair, to recall his earlier tongue-in-cheek observation that "Elfin" and "the proprietors of the *Newcastle Daily Chronicle* took the most unbiased, unprejudiced and unselfish interest in the welfare" of his theatre. (95) None of this impressed the bench. But after Stanley's seventh licensing application had been rejected in July 1862, "Elfin's" fury reached new heights. An extract from Hawkes's column is worth repeating at length as an example of how far Joseph Cowen was prepared to allow his newspaper to berate the local "establishment". Hawkes roundly chastised:

> "the injustice, arrogance and obstinacy of the Newcastle Bench ... Mr. Ralph Park Philipson, our municipal autocrat, has forbidden that another theatre be opened in Newcastle. He has a purpose to serve in keeping on good terms with the proprietors [of the Theatre Royal] ... To serve them, Mr. Philipson had undertaken to keep Mr. Stanley "out of the market", and his flunkies - Messrs. Dodds, Nichol and Co. - with becoming docility "register his decrees". Upwards of a year ago one of these sapient justices, with that arrogant vulgarity which is natural to him, declared that he and his colleagues could see "them d-d before they should have a licence." If these persons had conscientious objections on religious grounds I might deplore their illiberality, but I would write in terms of respect of their opposition to a second theatre. But to imagine that a man like Anthony Nichol, a keeper of race-horses, and a frequenter of betting rings and race courses; a scheming jesuitical lawyer like Ralph Park Philipson, or a vulgar man of the world like Ralph Dodds have any fine religious objection is simply ridiculous. The only course for Mr. Stanley to follow, if he wants to play dramatic pieces, is to take the law into his own hands, and perform in spite of the magistrates ... The intolerable despotism under which Newcastle labours must be broken ... In plain English, the intolerant and intolerable clique which dominates on the Bench and in the Council, and which holds the representation of the borough in its hands must be smashed."
> (96)

More followed, with a *Chronicle* leader the next day describing individual magistrates as "undignified and offensive", "coarse" and "illiterate" or, in one case, simply a Tory trying to obscure his humble origins. (97) At the end of 1862, the same magistrates hit back in a manner that hardly elevated their standing in the town. They refused George Stanley permission to hold a benefit performance at the Tyne Concert Hall in aid of the Lancashire Distress Fund set up to help textile workers laid idle by the American Civil War. (98) For most of 1863, the conflict between bench and theatre and press rumbled on but aside from some carping snobbery from magistrates about the working class nature of Stanley's audiences the bench was losing its will to carry on. In October, Stanley's eighth bid for a drama licence was declined but, significantly, the grounds for refusal concentrated only on the unsuitability of the Tyne Concert Hall building. The unmistakable implication was that a licence would be granted if more satisfactory premises could be found. That very evening George Stanley announced from the stage of the Concert Hall to the cheers of the audience his intention to open a new theatre. (99) The magistrates' surrender was an important milestone in English theatrical history. Stanley and Cowen now joined forces to create Newcastle's second theatre. Cowen, it appeared, had a burning interest in the theatre which led him into organising Newcastle's celebration of the Shakespeare ter-centenary in 1864. (100) He also mixed with people who had a working knowledge of the stage. W.E. Adams had been involved with travelling drama groups in the 1840s and often discussed the theatre with John Kane, the north east iron workers' leader and one of Cowen's associates in the Northern Reform Union. (101) From whatever sources, Joseph Cowen progressively accumulated "an apparently inexhaustible knowledge of the stage", (102) although he could still be easily diverted into "hot political discussion" in the middle of watching a play. (103) The Cowen generosity rescued "many a troubled entertainer from despondency" (104) and, in the 1860s, he described his theatrical acquaintinces as some of his "best and most intimate friends ... the most intelligent of men, and the most reliable and estimable of women."

But Cowen's eye was really on the stage as a "powerful" channel of communication which "if properly directed would only be second to the press, or platform in its power to instruct." (105) Between 1865 and 1868 the *Chronicle* carried numerous leaders on the value of drama, (106) possibly reflecting the fact that Cowen and Stanley were in the process of starting and managing a new theatre. Cowen largely raised the money and in September 1867 he and Stanley opened the Tyne Theatre and Opera House in Newcastle's Westgate Road. (107) Launched amid a countrywide wave of theatre-building, the Tyne Theatre was no ordinary provincial playhouse. The Tyne's natural lighting, general grandure and above all in a period of "poor" technical standards, its specially designed and intricate stage machinery placed the theatre in a class of its own. (108) Stanley also shared Cowen's perspective on the educative potential of drama - "an adjunct of the school" - but the two partners agreed that the enterprise should be a paying proposition. (109) Cowen, leaving nothing to chance, "practically managed" the Tyne Theatre for its first couple of years and accompanied Stanley in negotiations with London theatre companies. (110) The partners had early notable triumphs in promoting light dramas dealing with issues of class discrimination and within three years they had virtually bankrupted the Theatre Royal. (111)

The *Chronicle* in the 1860s casts fresh light on Joseph Cowen. His earlier links with European exiles had showed his imaginative skills, the revival of the mechanics' institutes and participation in his father's business revealed organising abilities, and Chartism, republicanism and the Northern Reform Union had marked him out as a Radical politician. Through the *Chronicle*, however, Joseph Cowen came to control something of his own for the first time and he resolutely intended to succeed. The paper was there primarily to promote the rights of the working classes and Radical principles but the foundations of its broad appeal rested in Cowen's awareness of working class communities as composed of human beings with talents, creativity, varieties of interests and suppressed potential. There would have been no need to push the *Chronicle* so far along the Radical road if making money and gaining a little political influence had been the only aims. It should be noted, also, that Cowen's appearance as a tough operator at the helm of the *Chronicle* was not at the expense of his own notion of "fairness". At the beginning of 1870, the proprietors of the beleagured Theatre Royal decided to get rid of Edward Davis. In an echo of the fate of the Chartist, John Brown, the proprietors seized Davis's possessions to meet some outstanding debts. This provoked a public outcry and a Testimonial, or fund, was raised enabling Davis to take the lease of a Sunderland theatre. The organisers of the Testimonial were Joseph Cowen and the *Newcastle Daily Chronicle*. (112)

CHAPTER SIX : AGITATIONS AND EMPIRE

The first play performed at the Tyne Theatre and Opera House in September 1867 was *Arrah-na-Pogue*. Written by Dion Bouciault, "the unchallenged king of melodrama" in the 1860s, the production's "strong card [was] the appeal to Irish patriotism: though the play was set in 1798, the old revolutionary tune, *The Wearin' o'the Green*, with revised verses by the author, had a Fenian ring." (1) As an opener the play had crowds flocking to the new theatre and was a roaring success for Cowen and George Stanley. No doubt part of the popularity rested with the Tyneside's enormous Irish population which had settled in the area from the 1830s onwards (figures of 20,000 Irish male adults resident in Northumberland and Durham by the 1860s have been claimed), propelled to the north east by poverty and colonial repression in Ireland. Although there were instances of racial antipathy, preventing Irish access to better paid industrial jobs, the immigrants fought back - for example, 120 Irish labourers went on strike at Mitchell's Low Walker shipyard in July 1869 over a foreman's offensive remarks - or they forged close links with other workers, notably in the revived miners' unions. (2)

Cowen's and Stanley's decision to stage *Arrah-na-Pogue* was daring, not least because of a Fenian scare as the Irish Republican Brotherhood, or Fenians, mounted an armed challenge to the British Empire between 1865-67 with attacks launched against the British government in Canada, Ireland and England. Riddled with internal division and informers, the Fenians could not match the strength of the world's most powerful state but they did re-establish the demand for Irish freedom. This was especially true in the north east of England where Fenianism was not short of sympathisers. "Tyneside was honeycombed with Fenians" spending "half the night in dark cellars, planning and organising and getting *the stuff* - which meant rifles, revolvers and ammunition - aboard harmless looking boats waiting at the quays." It was said "many a hunted Fenian, escaping from the English police, found welcome and safe-hiding in the home of a poor Tyneside worker" or in the houses of the more prosperous Irish who appeared "above suspicion." (3) A Fenian society held secret meetings in Burn's Tavern at Newcastle's Amen Corner until forcibly evicted by a new landlord in September 1865. Proclamations urging preparation for revolt were posted at Shotley Bridge Iron Works in February 1866, extra police, troops and volunteer rifle corps were deployed at Newcastle, Sunderland and Jarrow to forestall rumoured Fenian outbreaks in March, and the *Newcastle Daily Chronicle* reported that "American officers, who are suspected of possessing Fenian proclivities" were known to be on Tyneside. (4) In February 1867 an arms cache was discovered at an Irish shop in Newcastle and in October, as the Tyne Theatre enjoyed the triumph of *Arrah-na-Pogue*, special constables were enrolled and armed at Middlesbrough, revolvers were ordered for the Sunderland police and military security was tightened at North Shields, Newcastle, Berwick and Carlisle. There were tales of Fenians secretly drilling near South Shields. (5)

Joseph Cowen's interest in Fenianism was more tentative than the staging of Bouciault's play might suggest. He rejected what he saw as the "folly" of the Fenians' "wild and violent" tactics, and looked towards a constitutional rather than conspiratorial approach for solving Irish grievances. On the other hand, the *Chronicle* did not condemn Fenianism outright. The paper respected the movement's principles. It even printed letters stating that "physical force" was the only way to secure Ireland's freedom and pointedly asking why English Liberals were not willing to allow the Irish the same rights of revolt as those accorded to Poles and Italians. (6) The newspaper opposed Fenian "outrages", but insisted that the Fenians had "compelled the public to consider afresh the condition and disorders of Ireland ... Fenianism is nothing more than the sign and fruit of existing wrongs." (7) A series of articles on "the present condition of Ireland" appeared in the *Newcastle Daily Chronicle* from 10 December 1867. And Cowen, whose secretary at the *Chronicle*, William Heenan, was deeply involved in Newcastle's Irish politics, (8) took a more public position on Irish affairs from 1868. He chaired a large meeting in July 1869 in favour of Irish church disestablishment and in October gave strong support to a mass demonstration on Newcastle's Town Moor which called for the release of imprisoned Fenians. The mayor of Newcastle judiciously ordered the police to keep away from the meeting. (9)

Cowen's newspaper took a firm stand against attempts to manufacture fear of the Fenians by the authorities and particularly the police. The paper was scathing in October 1867 about the police reaction to rumours:

> "To sustain the excitement, the Police even seem to invent tales of horror of their own. Certainly they are willing to become victims of any wag who cares to haunt them. Two nights ago, in obedience to a stupid telegram he had received, the Chief Constable marched a body of his men down to the railway station, there to await the arrival of Kelly [the American Fenian Colonel who had escaped from police custody in Manchester] by the midnight train. The Police actually believed that the fugitive ... was about to unfurl in the streets of Newcastle the flag of the Irish Republic! ... the Police should take proper precautions. But should they endeavour to make themselves look ridiculous?"

The police, the *Chronicle* believed, were trying to concoct a Fenian panic purely as "a pretence to frighten us into an unpopular choice"; to establish an armed police force. (10) Cowen was attaching to the Fenian scare Tyneside's traditional suspicion of the police. Newcastle Radicals had fought the creation of a uniformed police force in 1829 and 1836 (11) and, quite apart from the Chartists' experience of the police, there had been further clashes. Violence by constables near Blaydon had prompted Cowen to lead a protest campaign in 1862 exposing "cruel and cowardly policemen." (12) Sidney Milnes Hawkes, in April 1862, described chief constables as running "a quasi-military dictatorship", (13) a view shared by the lower ranks of the Newcastle police the following November when they held public demonstrations and lobbied the town's watch committee over their chief constable's "tyranny" in matters of working conditions. (14) The *Chronicle* castigated police conduct during the Cramlington miners' evictions of 1865 and complained about police intimidation of a reporter. The following year saw the paper highlighting police brutality towards prisoners in the Newcastle cells. And in 1868, Joseph Cowen as a member of the Newcastle town council (he was elected unopposed in 1862), demanded the police stop "furtively stealing up back lanes to cut clothes ropes" to enforce a by-law. (15) When the police began to focus on Fenianism, the *Chronicle* raised the spectre of Peterloo and warned that "the emergency they predict is not likely to arise unless they provoke it." (16) Amid a countrywide Fenian panic in January 1868, as the Newcastle police wildly predicted an Irish rising, the *Chronicle* denied there was such "a terrible conspiracy" and accused the police of "crying wolf." (17)

The Fenians nevertheless exposed a boundary to Joseph Cowen's radicalism by advocating the constitutional separation of Ireland and challenging English Radicals to declare their position. The Chartists had met a similar challenge without great difficulty. In April 1848, the Newcastle Chartists passed a resolution typical of the movement's general stance demanding repeal of the Union with Ireland. (18) But there were sensitive areas threatening unity between Irish nationalists and English Radicals on Tyneside. The intimate mixture of Irish politics and Catholicism could have conservative outcomes. One problem erupted as early as January 1843 when an Irish crowd broke up a Newcastle meeting addressed by Robert Owen, "the well-known Socialist", (19) and another in June 1866 when a 300-strong Irish group paraded around Newcastle's Town Moor during Race Week. Waving shillelaghs, the Irish attacked anyone who gave the wrong answer to whether they were for "Garibaldi or the Pope?" The police and the courts treated the incident as Fenian in inspiration although this could have been a convenient excuse to fuel a scare. (20) If the conservative strand in Irish politics made Cowen cautious of the Fenians, there was also the British Empire to be taken into account. Cowen could denounce the Union with England as founded on bribery of the "basest" kind, but he was committed to preserving the integration of Ireland and England, albeit with the cement of social reforms. This quickly caused difficulties for Cowen with Irish audiences. He told a public meeting in support of Gladstone's Irish Land Bill in April 1870 that the English and the Irish were really one nation. As if this was not sailing close to the wind, Cowen went on to claim with a hint of Mazzini's influence that the unity of the two countries could be compared with the Garibaldi's unification of Italy. This analogy failed to impress many at the meeting who, in any event, regarded Gladstone's land reform as timid. (21) And there was certainly dissension from Cowen's conviction that the Land Bill might inaugurate "a reign of justice and consolidate the unity of the Empire." (22) At first sight, there is little more to be said about Joseph Cowen and Irish liberty. But this would be to miss an exceptional departure in Cowen's engagement with Ireland - one rooted in his advocacy that the Irish should raise their voices in England (23) - which was to emerge later.

Ireland was not the only international excitement animating the 1860s. Looking back, W.E. Adams believed that "no crisis in which we ourselves were not directly concerned ever excited, I think, the interest in England that the American War did. It entered into all our thoughts, seasoned all our conversation, formed the one topic of discussion at thousands of public meetings." (24) The American Civil War (1861-65) was a major preoccupation of Radicals and former Chartists like Adams and Joseph Cowen. They saw "there wasn't much to choose between Liberals and Tories" on the abolition of slavery, "the greatest question of the centuries", (25) and hurled themselves into an unequal confrontation with the generally pro-Confederate British government, commerce and newspapers. The pressure to assist the Confederates was immense. Radicals such as Charles Bradlaugh had been reticent about a rapid abolition of slavery in the United States. (26) Confederate views found prominence in important sectors of the labour press (27) and MPs, including in the north east the Sunderland Member, W.S. Lindsay, energetically advocated recognition of the slave owners' regime. (28) The pace of the issue also began to be forced on Tyneside by Liberal cabinet ministers. Earl Russell, the Foreign Secretary, attacked the United States government in a speech at Newcastle town hall in October 1861. Twelve months later, Joseph Cowen, sitting in the audience at a Newcastle banquet, heard the Chancellor of the Exchequer, Gladstone, describe the Confederacy as "a nation" separate from the United States. Gladstone's remarks, greeted with "loud and prolonged" applause and made just prior to Lincoln's Emancipation Proclamation, sickened and alarmed Radical opinion. (29)

The shock of Gladstone's Newcastle speech probably helped convince Cowen to boost his own moderately active campaigning for the Federal cause. Before the outbreak of the war his *Chronicle* had been cautious about the efficacy of military action against the slave owners but once the slavers started the war the newspaper immediately took the Federal side. (30) Cowen had kept himself informed about the American anti-slavery movement for many years. He collected newspaper cuttings of William Lloyd Garrison's visit to Tyneside in 1846, subscribed to Garrison's journal, *The Liberator*, and acquired further knowledge through William Wells Brown and Jessie White Mario (who had risked lynching in the United States by lecturing on abolition in front of an audience of slave-owners). (31) That Cowen does not seem to have paid a lot of attention to the war through 1861-62 may have been due to the Italian and

Polish struggles as well as pressures generated by the *Chronicle*. But a further reason explaining Cowen's relatively slight early involvement was the absence of the abolition of slavery from Federal war aims. The *Chronicle* was consistently critical of Lincoln "for not taking a bolder course in the War, and hoisting the banner of Emancipation." (32) Much coverage was consequently given to a pro-emancipation speaking tour of Tyneside in April 1862 by James Watkins "a fugitive slave" from Maryland. Watkins addressed meetings at Newcastle, Blaydon, Wallsend and North Shields. He also wrote a long letter to the *Newcastle Daily Chronicle* in October rebutting Lincoln's suggestion that black Americans might be persuaded to emigrate to specially purchased "colonies" in Central America and Africa. The idea incensed abolitionists and Watkins, writing "as a citizen of America, born a slave" angrily rejected the "diabolical emigration scheme." The *Chronicle* agreed and described the plan as "impractical" and "chimerical". (33)

On 1 January 1863 the situation changed dramatically. Lincoln finally signed the Emancipation Proclamation, sounding the death-knell of slavery. Cowen quickly organised a huge meeting in Newcastle's Nelson Street Music Hall to welcome Emancipation. From the chair, he admonished Lincoln for not moving against slavery earlier nor "from a higher motive than military expediency." After several speakers had addressed the meeting, Cowen put forward a resolution which was adopted by acclaim:

> "That the revolt of the Southern States of America against the Federal Government having avowedly originated in the determination not only to maintain but to extend slavery, and having been followed by the organising of a Confederacy based upon the denial of human rights to the negro race, this meeting indignantly repels the assumption that the English people sympathise with a rebellion that violates every principle of political justice, or with institutions framed in defiance of the moral sense of mankind."

The Newcastle meeting was one of the earliest to be called in provincial and Scottish towns and cities prior to the great St. James's Hall meeting at London in March which is usually taken as the starting point of the campaign to prevent British intervention in the American War. (34) Cowen's Newcastle resolution had a special status because it directly refuted Gladstone's use of a Tyneside platform to promote the standing of the slavers. Cowen now poured more energy into helping the Federal cause, and his *Chronicle* distinguished itself as one of the tiny minority of English newspapers to take an anti-Confederate stand. Cowen also became a vice-president of the Emancipation Society which he and other Radicals, including John Bright, Peter Taylor and W.E. Adams, formed to counter the slave states' propaganda. Adams wrote the Society's most powerful pamphlet, *The Slaveholders' War: an argument for the North and the Negro* published in 1863. The pamphlet was even translated in Gujarati and was circulating in India (35) as Adams lectured on the American War to "working men" at North Shields in the autumn of 1864 after accepting Cowen's invitation to edit the *Newcastle Weekly Chronicle*. (36)

The alliance between Joseph Cowen and W.E. Adams - which it is worth recalling extended back through the Emancipation Society, the Friends of Poland, the outer edges of the Orsini Plot and into republicanism - produced a stunning coup in the bid to stem Confederate influence. In the summer of 1863 the British Association for the Advancement of Science held its annual congress in Newcastle. One section of the congress was allocated to learned papers on "Ethnology" and among the contributors were two well-known Confederate apologists, Dr. James Hunt and C. Carter Blake. Their purpose was to justify the racist philosophy of slavery and Hunt read a paper claiming that black people were not really human beings. Cowen and Adams together with Holyoake had thoroughly prepared for the occasion. Holyoake, acting on Cowen's instructions, wrote in "private" to Professor Phillips of Oxford seeking early notification of the arrangements for congress sessions. Phillips was a little curious at the clandestine nature of the enquiry and had to be reassured that whilst Holyoake was not writing on behalf of "any Committee of the British Association in Newcastle" and information was being sought "purposely outside of Newcastle", the request could be considered as being "in furtherance of the [Association"s] objectives, as will in due course appear." (37) What happened "in due course" was the appearence of William Craft, a famous escaped slave, who took an active part in the "Ethnology" section of the congress. Craft's prime purpose was to stalk Hunt and Carter Blake, challenging them at crucial moments. The Tyneside anti-slavery societies ensured that Craft always had supporters in the audience, and Cowen and Adams used the *Chronicle* to publicise Craft as the star debater. By these means Craft was able to deal with several procedural obstacles to speaking placed in his way by congress organisers.

Every time Hunt spoke, Craft was there to derail him with a mixture of skillful debating and humour. At one stage Hunt tried to extricate himself from a tight corner by stating that Craft had a white ancestor and could not be seen as black or solely of African descent. Craft deftly countered by calmly observing that he had been "black enough for slavery." As William Craft cut a dash through the congress to the accompaniment of "cheers" and "loud and prolonged applause", the *Chronicle* provided a public commentary:

> "These gentlemen [Hunt and Carter Blake], it seems, have a "mission", and that is to run the negro to death, and fix him in his "proper place". Well, these gentlemen ... attempt[ed] to prove that if you were to cross the white with the black, you would breed the whole human race off the face of the earth. But Mr. Blake, let the cat out, by blurting out that the negro was better used in the Southern States of America than in the North ... Mr. William Craft ... got up to reply to him ... and the gentleman from the South ... seemed rather astonished."

And, finally, the spurious "scientific" concepts of "Ethnology" were turned against their exponents:

> "Mr. Carter Blake attempted to rescue his friend, and was well and deservedly hissed. Mr. Blake's is a very miserable type of Anglo-Saxon head. Somewhat narrow, and loping away from a large apex at the back part, showing that he has a thundering self-esteem. He is long-jawed, has a very conceited manner, and while speaking has the knack of striking an attitude after the manner of Napoleon at St. Helena which makes the ladies laugh. Dr. Hunt was not happy in his reply, and evidently felt his defeat, and I advise him the next time he comes with his "insulting" airs not to try it on in Newcastle, where a Negro is treated as a friend and a brother." (38)

The congress ended in a points victory for the Emancipation Society.

"A Man and a Brother" was the traditional rallying cry of the British anti-slavery movement active on Tyneside since the late-eighteenth century. This was one of the seams tapped by Cowen and Adams in relation to the American War. The Tyneside movement was on the whole the province of Nonconformist churches and the Quakers who had often invited William Craft and other former slaves to speak in Newcastle. During the American War these efforts increased considerably and visiting black Americans became a familiar sight on the Tyne. The Radicals, contrastingly, had a different emphasis in their approach to the abolition of slavery. Whereas the Nonconformists tended towards paternalistic "missionary" work to protect the "poor negro", the Radicals pursued a political concept of equality inspired by the American and French Revolutions. This notion was fundamental to Joseph Cowen's outlook on the world and could be applied to black and white alike. A segment of Radicalism also saw the slave-system as a threat to free labour everywhere. For this reason Adams aimed much of his *Slaveholders' War* to exposing Confederate claims that slavery abolished the conflict between labour and capital. Seen in these terms, the slave-system potentially threatened white as well as black workers and consequently raised the possibility of a united multi-racial opposition. Radicals such as Sidney Milnes Hawkes were equally at ease with both sources of inspiration and, in his case, opportunities to stress the common interests of black and white workers were taken up through the *Chronicle*. During the 1866 seafarers' strike, for instance, Hawkes commented on the sailors' demonstrations at South Shields that: "Whatever may be the feeling of the people of America or elsewhere against colour, it is not participated in by our tars, who walk arm in arm with the coloured men." The *Chronicle* as the voice of Cowen and the Radicals attacked racial prejudice forcefully between 1865-68. An editorial in January 1865 deplored "prejudice against colour" and was "severely censorious against those who exhibit it."

This consciousness of race which was not apparent prior to the 1860s may have been reinforced partly by Tyneside's direct contact with black people. The 1860s conveyed a constant procession of black music hall performers, sailors, religious ministers, politicians and even cricketers through Newcastle and North and South Shields. According to one account, the presence of black singers helped persuade Joseph Cowen to build the Tyne Theatre. There was also evidence of black people settling permanently in the area as labourers, restauranteurs, entertainers and, in several well-reported cases, existing as beggars or trinket-makers. But it was the American War that heightened the awareness of racial inequality. (39)

"A Man and a Brother", unfortunately, remained largely a slogan. There were plenty of people who denied that black and white were equal. Some years after the end of the war, Joseph Cowen still felt it important to open a speech at a mammoth meeting of Northumberland miners with an impassioned defence of the time spent on solidarity with "negroes suffering from the lash in the United States" during the mid-1860s. He may well have been directing his remarks at the prominent miners' leader, Thomas Glassey, whose own oratory always seemed to include derogatory and racially abusive references to the fact that black Americans could vote but Northumberland miners were denied the franchise. Glassey later emigrated to Australia and, as a Queensland Senator at the opening of the twentieth century, was an architect of the "White Australia" policy. (40) But even the *Chronicle*'s calls for racial equality were circumscribed by other considerations. Blind spots abounded. Legal abolition of slavery in the British Empire made little difference to the lives of Her Majesty's black Caribbean subjects because the law was not properly enforced. Furthermore, black opposition to colonialism was discouraged by both the Radicals and the anti-slavery lobby. Just occasionally, the *Newcastle Daily Chronicle* might vaguely sympathise with the Maori or Ashanti resistence to the spread of colonial rule. Yet there were limits to this exercise in "fraternity" which exposed another roughly drawn boundary to Joseph Cowen's own Radicalism.

A few months after the end of the American War there was a reported black uprising in Jamaica. The English press swiftly decided the defeat of the Confederacy had ignited a world-wide move by the black race to eliminate whites and this was beginning in the West Indies. A frenzy was whipped-up. Cowen's *Chronicle* reacted by cautioning its readers to wait until firm news had been received from Jamaica before jumping to conclusions. When hard news did arrive it presented a very different kind of horror story. The white planter regime on the island had ruthlessly dealt with complaints about social grievances by executing a black political leader, killing 493 black men, women and children and flogging some 600 others with wire-cord "cats". This was the infamous Jamaica Outrage of November 1865. The atrocity raised a public outcry all over Britain. Local mayors convened protest meetings - North Shields, Newcastle, South Shields and Darlington all held meetings in December - and a national deputation of 300 civic dignitaries, mainly mayors of

towns and cities, went to Downing Street to demand the suspension
of the governor of Jamaica. At Newcastle's meeting the mayor
invited Joseph Cowen out of the audience to make an impromptu
speech. Cowen vehemently denounced the Jamaican governor for
murder, demanded an inquiry and was immediately included in the
deputation to call on the Prime Minister. So far there was little
difference between Cowen's advocacy of equal treatment for black
Americans and his concern for black Jamaicans. Two months later,
a difference emerged. An editorial in the *Newcastle Daily Chronicle*,
pressing for retribution on those accountable for the massacre,
defined the unmistakeably imperial context in which justice should
be administered:

> "We have a right to see that our coloured countrymen are not
> wronged. But it is not so much out of regard for the rights of the
> negro as out of regard for the honour of England that we are
> disposed to demand the strictest justice. We owe it to England
> even more than we owe it to the outraged black man that the
> crimes committed under English authority should be adequately
> and justly punished." (41)

The Empire made the difference. Cowen and his newspapers were
prepared to criticise the neglect, scandals and the ill-treatment of
black peoples accompanying British rule in the West Indies, India,
Australia and New Zealand. (42) But the *Chronicle* also welcomed
the formation of the Colonial Society in March 1869 as a way of
disseminating the supposedly positive English virtues of the Empire.
These virtues embraced the notion that all the inhabitants of the
Empire - British (including the Irish), Indian, African - were
brothers. India, especially, was seen as "content" with British
government and administered through the strength of English ideas.
Slightly over a week later, in a step characteristic of the paper when
it could not quite make up its mind, a further editorial questioned
whether India really was bound to Britain by contentment or by
force. A lingering element of doubt was revealed, possibly related to
Cowen's youthful belief that colonial expansion was both wasteful
and anti-democratic, (43) possibly stemming from Cowen's mixing
of ideals of universal equality with English nationalism. It was an
uncertainty about the Empire, combining a fundamental commitment to the idea of Empire with an occasional uncomfortable
awareness of the harsher realities of imperial rule.

In the meantime, there were other preoccupations. Reviewing the record of a tumultuous few years, Joseph Cowen declared that the abolition of slavery in the United States had been the greatest event of 1864-65. (44) He could have added that a major event in his life during 1864 had been a visit to England by Garibaldi. The Italian "liberator" was still regarded as a super-hero by working class opinion in Britain. Thousands turned out to greet him *en route* from Southampton in April 1864 and half-a-million people mobbed his arrival in the capital. Behind the scenes his stay was the object of intense intrigue. Among Italian nationalists there was a desire to use the visit as an opportunity to reconcile differences between Mazzini and Garibaldi but this had to be broached with care. It was a measure of the trust enjoyed by Cowen that he was selected to act as a "go-between". Mazzini asked Cowen to be "the first to see" Garibaldi in England: "it would be important for somebody of ours - like you - [to] see him without delay ... I would send you a letter of mine to be delivered to Garibaldi." Cowen agreed and with Mazzini's plea "try to succeed" ringing in his ears he forced his way through the crowds on a steamer taking Garibaldi from Southampton to the Isle of Wight. Garibaldi was delighted to meet Cowen again, embracing and "kissing him several times." (45) Cowen's mission was conceived by anxious Mazzinians afraid that Garibaldi was becoming too influenced by London "society" and the aristocracy. Mazzini told Cowen he thought Garibaldi was "badly surrounded and weak." (46) The element of truth in the Mazzinian assessment of Garibaldi's visit was borne out by the Prime Minister, Palmerston, who reassured Queen Victoria that Garibaldi had been "taken up by the aristocracy" precisely to prevent him being "left in the hands of agitators." (47) Cowen preferred to avoid becoming embroiled in disputes between European nationalists and seems to have done only what was originally asked, delivering Mazzini's letter to Garibaldi. Returning to Newcastle, Cowen busied himself preparing a reception for Garibaldi who intended making a country-wide tour. A welcoming committee was formed with Cowen in the chair and Adams as secretary, (48) and the *Newcastle Daily Chronicle* announced that Garibaldi would "stay at Blaydon with Mr. Cowen during his visit to Tyneside." (49)

Mysteriously, Garibaldi's visit to England was abruptly terminated and the planned national tour cancelled. Exactly why Garibaldi decided to leave England so unexpectedly remains a matter of

controversy. On 20 April Cowen received a telegram "from Garibaldi
or those accompanying him" apparently stating that the General was
ill. (50) Garibaldi's rumoured ill-health was one explanation for his
departure though it was widely disbelieved at the time. The
Newcastle Daily Chronicle even claimed the Queen's personal
physician had invented the excuse of illness at the request of the
British government. (51) There were, it appears, other telegrams
sent to Cowen by Mazzini and the London Working Men's
[Garibaldi] Reception Committee asking Cowen urgently to come
to London and persuade Garibaldi to continue the tour. Cowen did
go to London and met Garibaldi at 11.30 pm on 19 April. (52)
Accounts of the ensuing conversation have left the impression that
Garibaldi was being forced out of the country by the government.
The *Newcastle Daily Chronicle* roared that Garibaldi was being
"expelled" purely to appease Louis Napoleon and the paper
demanded the cabinet's immediate resignation. (53) Jane Cowen was
sure Garibaldi had told her father that Gladstone had "prevailed"
upon him to leave England out of fear of enthusiastic provincial
"demonstrations." (54) A fear of renewed working class unrest,
inspired now by Garibaldi's presence, was very evident. *The Times*
described Garibaldi's London reception as dominated by the working
classes "from first to last." (55) J.M. McFarlane of the *Glasgow
Herald* told Cowen "there would have been trouble" had Garibaldi
visited Glasgow because the local working men's council planned a
demonstration "or general shouting exhibition of the advanced
Radical type." Similarly, the Roman Catholic Cardinal Manning
warned that Garibaldi's speeches would stimulate "the seditious and
Socialist revolution which at the present moment threatens every
government, absolute or constitutional, throughout Europe." (56)

The authorities' nervousness erupted when working class activists
held a rally in early May on London's Primrose Hill to protest
against Garibaldi's "expulsion". The police broke up the meeting
though not before one of the speakers, William Shaen, had accused
Gladstone of wanting Garibaldi out of the country. Gladstone
denied the allegation at a meeting with the Working Men's
Reception Committee on 10 May but appeared to hedge on the
reasons for Garibaldi's departure. Shaen nevertheless stood by his
accusation and the *Newcastle Daily Chronicle* reported that his
information had come from Joseph Cowen and had been
double-checked for the exact content of Cowen's conversation with

Garibaldi. To add to the confusion, Cowen denied that he and Shaen had ever spoken a word on "the Garibaldi business" but did not contradict the generally held belief that the government had arm-twisted the Italian leader to leave. (57) The following year, Cowen had a statue of Garibaldi erected at Summerhill, near Blaydon, as a permanent reminder of Tyneside's links with the General.

Garibaldi's 1864 visit was poised as a catalyst for working class unrest. As it happened, the situation was contained by the simple expedients of hustling Garibaldi out of the country and leaving the police to tidy up any loose ends at Primrose Hill. But dealing with Garibaldi as an individual was easier than sweeping aside the growing restiveness over a lack of political rights in Britain. Joseph Cowen found himself in the midst of a diffuse development encouraged by freedom struggles in America, the Caribbean, Ireland, Poland and Italy. These "internationalist" dimensions of the 1860s found a strong receptiveness among the working classes, and especially Radicals and old Chartists. The Polish Insurrection of 1863-64 aroused interest in England and Cowen had been involved in this episode. British intervention in the American War had been prevented and Cowen had played a dynamic part in this "immense impetus" (58) given to the demand for democratic government. Garibaldi's visit highlighted working class impatience for reform (59) and, again, Cowen was at the centre of the action. The Jamaica Outrage of 1865 may have indicated the limitations of Radicalism but Cowen adeptly publicised an alarming implication: "If agitation is to be punished as treason in Jamaica, how long will agitation be permitted in England!" (60) Fenianism, too, was drawing Cowen into new relationships with the large Irish population of Northumberland and Durham. And the north east itself was serving as a crucible, absorbing and shaping the facets of a democratic political culture. Stimulated by economic and population growth a virtual new working class society was coming together - its media fashioned by Cowenite Radicals; its cultural tastes encouraged and influenced by Cowenite campaigns, newspapers and theatre; its trade unions and everyday concerns befriended by Cowenism.

CHAPTER SEVEN : QUEEN VICTORIA DRAWS THE BLINDS

Queen Victoria had her own ways of signifying disapproval. For "some years" during the 1870s she reputedly had a disdain for Newcastle upon Tyne, ordering "the blinds of her railway carriage" to be "drawn down whenever she passed through Newcastle on her way to and from Scotland." The cause of royal disfavour was the town's supposed "sympathy...to Republican principles." (1) Numbers of Newcastle's "leading men" felt the Queen's displeasure acutely and once profferred a Loyal Address accompanied by a less than reverent description of the republican Sir Charles Dilke as "scum". (2) Dilke had only recently spoken in Newcastle on the virtues of a republic. But the difficulty faced by the monarchy did not rest with the principal citizens of the town. It flowed from attitudes struck by militant workers of the sort who physically took over a public meeting held by the Sunderland MP, John Candlish, in April 1871 and ended the evening with a rousing "3 cheers for a Republic." (3) Republican sympathies among the lower orders was a worrying development for those classes which had ruled England for so long. It was particularly disturbing when republican sentiments were combined with appeals to working men to realise "the extent of the power placed in their hands" under the Second Reform Act. This appeal was made at the very meeting in Newcastle which had prompted the town council's Loyal Address, and came from the lips of the man accused by the Tories of being the genius behind the Newcastle Republican Club - Joseph Cowen. (4) As if this were not terror enough, the republicans wanted votes for women. (5)

The journey from the passing of the Second Reform Act in 1867 to the republican upsurge of 1871-72 was an important phase in the growth of Joseph Cowen's Radicalism. Cowen played a central role in marshalling the north east for the reform campaign sweeping the country in 1866-67. This movement had its roots in the political awareness stimulated by international incidents - the Polish insurrection, the American War, the Jamaica Outrage and Garibaldi's 1864 visit - and in the strength of trade unionism and co-operative societies. In addition, Liberal gains at the 1865 general election, which saw Cowen's father elected as an MP for Newcastle, together with intense manoeuvring for position by the Conservative and Liberal leaderships, suggested the possibility of renewed parliamentary support for enlarging the suffrage. Reform organisations such as the Reform League, emerging out of the anger caused by Garibaldi's expulsion from Britain, reflected a powerful alliance of middle class Radicals and trade union leaders. Joseph Cowen became a vice-president of the Reform League in 1866, attracted by the League's commitment to manhood suffrage, but choose to concentrate his efforts and "a great deal of his own money" on a separate Northern Reform League. (6) On the surface, the Northern League was a revival of the Northern Reform Union. Indeed the objects and rules of the League, including manhood suffrage, were those of the Union except for a few minor alterations made in Cowen's handwriting. (7) The chief difference was that the trade unions took a major interest in the League. Cowen acted as president but the secretary and treasurer were workers and at least a third of the one hundred members of the League's governing council were miners. The Northern Reform League differed from other regional reform organisations. It was dominated by working class representatives and definitely not part of the middle class "attempt to keep control" of a working class agitation which characterised much of the Liberal relationship with the reform movement. (8)

Much of the initiative in arranging a host of public meetings and demonstrations climaxing towards the end of 1866 and the beginning of 1867 was taken by the miners' unions in Northumberland and Durham. These public demonstrations were crucial to the carrying of the Reform Bill and the Newcastle meetings conveyed the vital impression that demands for reform were not limited simply to the highly organised London working classes. The contemporary labour newspaper, *The Beehive*, regarded "the political demonstrations ... of 1866 and 1867" held in Newcastle as "among the most memorable events in the public history of that epoch." (9) Cowen addressed an open-air NRL demonstration at Newcastle's Sandhill on 10 December 1866, urging the 4000-strong audience to adopt "revolutionary sentiments" in their struggle. Underlining the inspiration provided by the American War all the speakers at the Sandhill rally referred to the United States as a model of democracy. Similar large meetings addressed by Cowen were held at Gateshead on the following day and in Newcastle on 12 December. (10) The clamour rose to a crescendo with the planning of a massive demonstration for January 1867. Delegates from over fifty unions and factories met on 19 December and agreed to arrange a reform demonstration to be held on an ordinary working day. In other words, they planned a political strike. This meeting reconvened on 8 January at the *Chronicle* offices with Cowen in the chair when it was decided to use the newspaper offices as the organising centre. The date of the demonstration was set for Monday 28 January and the *Chronicle* printed numerous advertisements from trade unions directing their members to assembly points. (11) Hopes were more than fulfilled. Cowen wrote ebulliently to George Howell, secretary of the Reform League, informing him that the procession through the town had been supported by "25,000 men" and the subsequent meeting on Newcastle's Town Moor, attracting 40-50,000 people to hear speakers at six platforms, "was the greatest of its kind ever held in the North of England" (although there had been bigger demonstrations). (12) Reform agitation continued at an intense level throughout Tyneside, Wearside and Durham in the spring of 1867, complementing the movement elsewhere in the country. Cowen was "unwell" and "confined to the house" in February, preventing his attendance at a London demonstration, but was keenly active again by the summer. (13)

The 1867 Reform Act was a great disappointment. Cowen and the Reform Leagues had hoped for manhood suffrage as a right but the Act conceded only a male householder franchise largely restricted to towns and cities. This cautious measure was not intended to herald an age of democracy. Instead, it reflected the intentions of the principal Conservative and Liberal leaders (chiefly the Tories under Disraeli's guidance) to enhance their own parties' standing. Achieving any reform at all was, undoubtedly, a victory for popular agitation and Cowen was prepared to accept the more limited extension of the vote as a temporary "compromise". (14) In common with most Radicals, he thought that the winning of reform would open the way for further changes fairly quickly. In this connection, he supported the old Chartist Ernest Jones's unsuccessful bid to represent Manchester as a working class MP and he organised public meetings for Jones on Tyneside to consider the impact of the Reform Act. (15) Cowen also publicised and chaired a Newcastle meeting in favour of votes for women in March 1869. (16) But there was to be no more reform for several years and the newly-enfranchised segment of the working classes, fragmented along

Liberal-Tory lines, made little obvious impression. There was an extra unforseen and disillusioning problem. Most miners, particularly in Northumberland and Durham, remained excluded from the franchise because they were not recognised as householders under their tenancies. It looked as though the battles of 1866-67 had been all in vain.

The election of Gladstone's Liberal government in 1868 did momentarily encourage optimism about further social and political reforms but was another false dawn. The enlarged franchise had not produced working class representation in the new House of Commons and Radical influence on government policy was barely evident. Before long there was widespread disenchantment and the government came under outspoken attack from its own supporters in the country. The trade unions were angered by the Liberals' Criminal Law Amendment Act, 1871, which criminalised many trade union activities including picketing. Several Radical MPs voted for the Act and others, including Cowen's father, were according to the Trades Union Congress "conspicuous by their absence." The passage of the 1871 Act caused a "massive" rupture in the trade union "alliance with middle-class radicalism." Cowen's *Chronicle* maintained a deafening silence over the Act, merely reporting trade union protest meetings. Possibly this lack of comment indicated deference within the Cowen family although Joseph Cowen, jnr, did criticise the Act's "questionable clauses" at a Northumberland miners' demonstration in July 1871. (17) The *Chronicle* was by no means so retiring towards Gladstone's repression of Ireland, accusing him of associating with "reaction" and, when his government suppressed a public meeting in Dublin, equated his approach with "the dark days of Peterloo." In a sideswipe at the Irish Peace Preservation Act, 1870, that imposed press censorship on Ireland, the *Chronicle* joined the *Pall Mall Gazette* in publishing a nationalist pamphlet (*The Farmers' Catechism*) banned in Dublin. The move flagrantly breached the law to the delight of the Tyneside Irish who sent copies of the *Chronicle* home to Ireland. (18)

For Cowen, one of the most absorbing controversies was education. The introduction of household suffrage helped to nudge the Victorian establishment in the direction of substantial educational reform if only to try to shape the outlook of the new voters (though there were, of course, many religious and economic sources of pressure for extending access to education). Accordingly, Gladstone's education minister, W.E. Forster, embarked on an Education Bill designed to create an elementary schools system. From 1869-71 educational reform also enlisted Cowen's "most devoted advocacy." (19) He had been aware for years that adult education was of limited effectiveness. Cowen argued "the cause of the only partial success of the mechanics' institutions was the want of elementary education" and schools were needed to acquaint children with the basic skills of learning. (20) At the same time he warned that other national economies were challenging British industrial dominance and a programme of technical education was "urgent" to match competition. (21) Cowen therefore employed the *Chronicle* in raising funds for the establishment of a College of Science at Newcastle in 1871 as a branch of Durham University. (22) Yet the Cowen philosophy of education went beyond a bare utilitarian case for wider educational opportunities. A deep commitment to education as a tool for social emancipation was still burning. Speaking about the new school boards in December 1870, Cowen "took it that the education of the people and their mental, social and moral improvement were the chief objects they should seek to obtain. They must pay either for the schoolmaster or the policeman; and he would pay rather for the former than the latter." (23) Echoing Mazzini, Cowen told the Durham miners' Big Meeting in June 1873 that education was a political question:

> "Your liberty, your rights, your emancipation from every injustice
> in your social position, the task each of you is bound to fulfill on
> earth; all these depend upon the degree of education that you
> are able to obtain." (24)

Cowen originally opposed state schooling but in November 1869 he changed his mind because the Reform Act had potentially taken government out of the hands of a "class or caste" and "the people now were masters." He advanced the case for a national, secular and compulsory schools system, locally directed and free for the poor. (25) Cowen was one of many speakers contributing to a two-day conference on educational reform held in Newcastle on 24-25 November 1869 which led to the formation of a Newcastle branch of the National Education League (Cowen became a national vice-president of the NEL). Through the League he renewed contacts with allies in the trade union leaderships and worked with up-and-coming Radicals including Birmingham's Joseph

Chamberlain. In December, Cowen organised and chaired a League "public breakfast" for General Carey, a former chairman of the US Congress education committee. Cowen was impressed by the American "democratic" public education system . It was an emphasis, as Sidney Milnes Hawkes observed, that led "the country gentry" to "taunt us poor Radicals with wanting to Americanise our institutions." (26) Forster's Education Bill, on the other hand, was a half-hearted measure. It represented a surrender to religious vested interests by building the state system around existing church schools instead of replacing them, and it gave religious pressure groups considerable influence within the state framework. The Education League campaigned furiously to amend the Bill and Cowen even tried, unsuccessfully, to persuade his fellow Newcastle town councillors to petition Parliament against Forster's proposals in April 1870. (27) Thereafter he had to alter tactics. He denounced the 1870 Education Act as essentially Tory (28) and full of contradictions typical of a measure "conceived by a Whig", but was prepared to seek to implement the Act's few positive features. (29)

A democratic element in the 1870 Act was the local election of school boards charged with building and running schools. Cowen continually pressed for the formation of a school board for Newcastle after the Act was passed and, following a delay of some months, elections took place in January 1871. A list of "unsectarian" candidates (including Cowen) was nominated to contest the election on a platform of building non-denominational schools open to all, accepting some scripture teaching in the curriculum and insisting on compulsory school attendance to ensure the right of children to an education. The campaign was hard-fought because, as Cowen told an election meeting, the Act's concessions to religious groups "simply propagated sectarian feelings." Cowen and four "unsectarian" candidates were elected to the new board although Cowen came eleventh in the poll for fifteen seats. Denominational candidates emerged as the strongest force on the board and at once plunged its meetings into "confusion", acrimony, indecisiveness, "intrigues and squabbles" over religious doctrine. (30)

Unable to make headway with his imaginative approach to education, Cowen resigned from the board in disgust in 1874. Cowen passionately rejected authoritarian methods to instil knowledge into children "by three feet of cane, a birch-end, or a strap of leather."

Schooling, he suggested, ought to be about "teaching children how to think for themselves" rather than "what to think." (31) Arguing that a school syllabus should avoid classics and cover modern languages and subjects relevant to contemporary life, (32) Cowen believed that education was something "in which the people themselves, and not the parsons, should have the main direction." (33) As always, he carefully avoided a completely secularist stance, although it was "in vain that anyone tried to obtain from him any definite or distinct statement of a formal religious creed." (34) He took a firm stand against prejudice, sharply telling a clerical opponent of educational reform who claimed English workmen were inherently superior to foreigners that "it is not in the power of patriotism to make an ignorant people free and happy." (35) On the Newcastle school board he accused the sectarians of discriminating against Jews in their proposed use of the Bible in schools. (36) Cowen's humanistic vision of education for equality was especially evident in 1871 when he acknowledged that he was:

> "a great many things: he professed to be a maker of fire-bricks; he professed to be a printer of newspapers; for a long time, also, he had professed to be a Radical politician - or, if they liked it better, a Democrat (cheers)." (37)

And as a democrat he wanted:

> "The children of the various sections of the People [to] be brought together while in the elementary schools. A mutual respect would spring up; and, as a consequence, they would find, in another generation, the social feeling of the community would be altogether different." (38)

The disappointments of both the 1867 reform and the Liberal government were the more keenly felt when compared with the sometimes thrilling and almost non-stop episodes of Radicalism and revolution through which Cowen had lived since the launching of the Northern Reform Union. But if little appeared to be happening in the party or electoral arenas, a strong labour agitation for a nine hours working day was building up on Tyneside in the early months of 1871. The "9-hours Strike" that lasted for twenty weeks from 25 May 1871 is generally regarded as "one of the most significant industrial disputes of nineteenth-century Britain ... a major confrontation of national importance." (39) It flowed from years of trade union efforts to reduce the length of the basic working week in the engineering trades from fifty-nine hours to fifty-four. The decision of trade union (and non-union) workers on Tyneside to take industrial action, and the fierce determination of the employers to resist, linked with Tyneside's pre-eminence in engineering, meant the result of the strike would influence conditions in much of British industry. Ample accounts of the strike have been produced,(40) but it is important to note that the Nine Hours League - a workshop-based delegate organisation conducting the strike - was "a genuine working-class leadership" backed by an absolute desire to win on the part of the engineering workers. (41) The League's leaders were also well-versed in strategy (keeping sections of their members at work so as to sustain a levy for strike funds), they received substantial help from other trades (the Northumberland and Durham miners gave regular contributions), and were concerned to see "their case should stand well with the people", stamping them "as apt politicians." (42)

The character of the Nine Hours League has been recalled to set the context of Joseph Cowen's association with the strike. Cowen's name was already "a household word in Northumberland and Durham" among the miners, (43) a reputation achieved through consistent efforts on their behalf and respect for the autonomy of their unions. He applied the same principles in relation to the Nine Hours League whose strike Cowen backed "first to last." (44) From an early stage in the dispute Cowen instructed the *Newcastle Daily Chronicle*'s editorial staff to "keep a sharp look-out for news from the engineers. Tell Burnett [the League's president] we will print all he wants printed in the way of news." (45) Burnett in turn made sure there were proper facilities for the *Chronicle*'s journalists at strike meetings, and Cowen provided free copies of the newspaper for circulation in other engineering centres. (46) It was hardly surprising to find an engineers' mass meeting on Newcastle's Town Moor in June 1871 ending with cheers for the *Newcastle Daily Chronicle*. The labour press commented that "working men on strike never had so powerful a friend in any journal in England" as in the *Newcastle Chronicle*. (47)

The participation of non-union as well as union members in the strike placed an exceptional burden on the League's funds during the summer of 1871. There was talk of lowering the level of strike pay and fears that this could weaken the workers' solidarity. Cowen at once offered to help, writing to the League that he would "see that there is no deficiency" (48) in the strike funds. An admirer later claimed Cowen gave £80 a week to the strike funds for part of the dispute. (49) Cowen went on to help defeat the employers' attempt to break the strike when they hired strikebreakers from Europe. Cowen learned of the employers' plan and rapidly informed Burnett, urging him to ask the International Working Men's Association in London to send an agent to Belgium to counter the employers. The IWMA did send a representative who was eventually expelled by the Belgium government. Towards the end of August, hundreds of German, French and Belgium workers started to arrive on Tyneside but Cowen and the League made the incomers aware of the exact reasons why they had been offered jobs and a free passage to Tyneside. This produced a startling effect as a proportion of the German workers joined the strike. There followed an exodus of foreign workmen from Newcastle, eased by Cowen's payment of a large part of their return fares (he certainly paid £80 towards the cost of shipping three hundred workers home to Hamburg). (50)

The failure of the strike breaking gambit left the engineeering employers with no more cards to play. Competition from companies unaffected by the dispute was gnawing away at Tyneside firms and the League's position appeared stronger than ever. In September Cowen was able to arrange arbitration and on 6 October, together with the Newcastle town clerk, Ralph Park Philipson (a butt of the *Chronicle*'s crusade for theatrical freedom a decade earlier), facilitated an agreement to end the strike - on the League's terms. (51) The nine-hours day was won. When news of the final victory was announced at a huge trade union demonstration on 9 October in London's Trafalgar Square, Cowen was included in the votes of thanks. George Odger, secretary of the London Trades Council, who chaired the demonstration, praised Cowen fulsomely - "long may he live to do more good (Cheers)" - and the general secretary of the House Decorators' Society eulogised:

> "Mr. Joseph Cowen, jun - (hear, hear, and cheers) - who had used his paper, the **Newcastle Chronicle**, as a barrier between the oppressor and the oppressed - who had stood between the working-men and their tyrannical employers - who had declared for the right against wrong, for truth against falsehood (Cheers)." (52)

On Tyneside Cowen was now seen as "the most canny man in canny Newcastle", (53) at least by his friends among the industrial workers. The engineering employers held a very different opinion. Embittered by their defeat, the employers' association prepared a prosecution for conspiracy against leaders of the Nine Hours League. Cowen discovered this plan through his own sources and told Burnett:

> "the remarkable thing is that my name is included in the list, while yours is not. The idea is that you are left out so that you may be subpoenoed as the chief witness." (54)

For some undisclosed reason the charge was not pressed, yet its contemplation exposed the divide between Cowen and other members of his own social and economic class. He had defiantly challenged the industrial barons of Tyneside and in close connection with a working class movement. The 1871 strike was consequently a watershed for Cowen's emergent political identity.

1871 was a year of drama. One group of Tyneside workers after another showed the spirit of the Nine Hours League as militancy gripped joiners, riveters, carters, pipe-makers, and slaters. By the end of August the unrest had led to the controversial deployment of the Newcastle police in the protection of factories and strikebreakers. The police force, for its part, was preoccupied with internal grievances concerning low pay and petty discipline. Cowen, whose long-term disdain for the police had been compounded by the policing of the Cramlington evictions and the rough handling of the Primrose Hill protest against Garibaldi's expulsion, seized the chance to weaken the Newcastle force. Firstly, he encouraged public hostility to the conduct of the police during the engineering strike. The *Newcastle Daily Chronicle* of 1 September 1871 publicised the case of two off-duty police officers who had gone looking for strikers, used their truncheons on two men "and tore off a woman's clothes" in the street. The officers were gaoled and the chief constable admitted it was not the only case of its kind. (55) Three days later the *Chronicle*'s "Elfin" column gave details of a previous incident of police violence against a woman. (56) On 6 September the mayor reported to a town council meeting that he had asked for police reinforcements from Northumberland and Durham "owing to the disturbed state of the town." Cowen protested against police protection for "a special section of the community" - the engineering employers - at the expense of protecting "the people generally" from crime. (57) Throughout September the *Chronicle* hammered the police for overlooking the violence of strikebreakers and being more interested in public order incidents than in detecting crime. (58) At the end of the month public meetings were held criticising the policing of the nine-hours strike and condemning the chief constable's preference for "obnoxious military regulations" over "civil rights and civil liberties." (59)

The mention of "obnoxious military regulations" was at the centre of Cowen's assault. He realised that a great many policemen were unhappy about petty regulations and service conditions. Their concern was made public on 6 September when a "memorial" signed by 101 out of the force's 160 officers, and complaining of "injustice" at the hands of the chief constable, was presented to the town council. Cowen, the *Chronicle* and successive public meetings highlighted the police grievances, quite probably to inflame the chief constable's difficulties and depress police self-esteem. The chief constable had ordered his officers not "to talk to anybody in the street." So, Cowen took the opportunity to ask directions from a policeman and received the anticipated answer from a constable that to talk to the public would "be an infringement of his duty, and would imperil his situation." The story ridiculed the police but had a more serious point as another constable "had been ordered off his beat" for speaking to two women worried about a lost deaf and dumb boy. (60) Publicity was also given to the record of the police for "drunkeness" and "idling their time in public houses." (61) A *Chronicle* editorial noted police training was poor and it was no wonder if a man

> "who up to yesterday had consorted principally with horses, kine and pigs, and who today is the representative of law and authority in the busy haunts of city life, occasionally misconceives the true nature of his new functions." (62)

These attacks, plus the unwillingness of the chief constable and the watch committee to consider police grievances (a secret decision "leaked" by the *Newcastle Daily Chronicle* on 14 October), had an effect. Over half of the force threatened to resign, and on 11 November the vast majority of Newcastle's policemen collectively handed in their uniforms and left the town. A week later Cowen went to a large public meeting convened to demand police reform. He was "loudly called from the body of the room", cheered on to the platform and crowned his victory with a call for a full investigation into local policing. (63)

The ferment of 1871 was not confined to Tyneside and Britain. An earth-shaking upheaval took place in France. The hated tyrant Louis Napoleon at last fell from power in the aftermath of the Franco-Prussian War. A new French Republic was proclaimed, and warmly welcomed at Radical meetings in England. Cowen had been the main speaker at a Newcastle public meeting on 6 September 1870 when he again denounced Louis Napoleon as "the miserable conspirator." (64) But on 18 March 1871 the working population of Paris rose in revolt against the new French leaders whom they suspected were anti-Republican. This became the Paris Commune which sent a shock tremor across Europe. The Communards shot several generals and were branded as murderers in the English press. Cowen's newspapers echoed the revulsion at the executions but also pleaded "let us endeavour to understand the situation." At this stage, the *Newcastle Daily Chronicle* believed the Commune should give the French government a chance to prove itself. (65) Within a few days the thrust of the *Chronicle*'s editorial policy had veered towards open sympathy with the Commune as an expression of municipal autonomy against a centralising state. (66) By late April the newspaper decided that "whatever errors or excesses" the Communards may have committed, "they are martyrs of a just idea ... their dream will be realised." (67) The *Newcastle Weekly Chronicle* was even stronger, asserting that contrary to English press opinion there was "no reign of terror in Paris" and "in spite of all its follies and faults" the Commune "represented a great principle" of democracy. (68) Cowen's press offered:

> "no apology for any act of Paris outraging national honour or individual morality ... it is impossible to maintain that the programme of the Commune is not perfectly compatible with both ...nothing less invigorating than faith in an idea, could sustain the Commune." (69)

According to the *Chronicle*, the ideas of the Commune were "yet destined to revolutionise France" even if the French government was now drowning the uprising in blood. (70) With the crushing of the Commune, those who could escape from the carnage of Paris sought asylum in other countries including Britain. When French diplomats pressed for the return of the refugees, the *Chronicle* called upon the

British government not to "surrender" the exiles "merely because they were engaged in the late Parisian insurrection" but to "distinguish between political offences and crimes." (71) Cowen, it was believed, assisted several of the Communard refugees financially. (72)

The *Chronicle*'s sympathy for the Commune had at least a coterminous relationship with the nine-hours strike, but there were other linkages between the Parisian events and the Tyne. In July 1871 the Liberals' new Criminal Law Amendment Act was used against workers picketing in Gateshead. One young picket named Joseph Ward, who had been heard to shout Communard slogans, was arrested and sentenced to fourteen days imprisonment by the magistrates because, in the words of the mayor of Gateshead, Ward had committed "a very dastardly outrage." The mayor told Ward he

> "hoped the case would prove a warning to him, that he would become wiser, and that he would leave all these Communist notions alone. To imagine that persons in this country could shout for the Commune and obstruct their neighbours with impunity, was to imagine something much too preposterous to be tolerated." (73)

The International Working Men's Association, which also supported the Commune, was linked with the nine-hours strike courtesy of Joseph Cowen. Just before Ward's sentence the IWMA had formed a branch at Sunderland led by "Citizen William Holmes and Citizen John Lennon" and a further branch opened at Middlesbrough in October 1871. (74) And James Dellow, a Tory, recalling his "first attempt at canvassing" at about this time in the Mill Lane district of Newcastle's predominently working class west end, claimed he and a companion were forced to abandon their efforts due to hostility towards the "toady Tories":

> "This place was a notorious haunt of intolerant Radicals. I'm not sure that Republicanism and Communism were not largely represented in that locality." (75)

The reference to "Communism" implied the Paris Commune and Dellow's mention of "Republicanism" acknowledged another wild child of 1871.

Sidney Milnes Hawkes, during the course of an "Elfin" column in the *Newcastle Daily Chronicle* of 20 February 1871, casually announced that a Republican Club was to be formed in Newcastle. The same evening a crowded meeting at the Nelson Street Lecture Room listened to Charles Bradlaugh counterpose republican principles to the expensive parasitism of the Royal House of Hanover headed, in Britain, by Queen Victoria. (76) Holyoake then appeared at the co-operative hall in Bedlington, Northumberland, invited by the local miners to speak on republicanism, defined as egalitarian democracy encompassing votes for women and the end of class distinctions. (77) The new movement's journal, The Republican, was circulating at Blyth at the end of February 1871, (78) and on 1 March a Republican Club with one hundred members was founded at Newcastle. (79) Two days later the *Newcastle Daily Chronicle* reprinted a lengthy article on republicanism by Mazzini. (80) Republican clubs spread like a bushfire with groups forming at Bedlington, Jarrow and Sunderland. *The Republican* declared its support for the Paris Commune and in May reiterated a demand for the rights of women, and in June the *Chronicle* expressed a broad sympathy for the movement. The connection with labour was underlined when George Odger, on Tyneside to assist the nine-hours strike, told the revamped Newcastle and Gateshead Republican Club that republicanism was a higher stage of political development than Radicalism. Here, then, were the foundations for the "strong" republican organisation active in the Northumberland and Durham coalfields throughout the early 1870s. (81)

It was a fairly amorphous array of people who came together as republicans. Holyoake, Bradlaugh and Odger opposed the Commune but other elements in the movement took a different view. There were middle class Radicals - Joseph Chamberlain, for example - who saw republicanism as an administrative modernising tendency; Joseph Cowen looked to the revival as a means of advancing popular democracy; and there were "Social Republicans" who sensed a vehicle for social reforms and land nationalisation. Demarcation lines between these factions could be blurred but the general thrust was supplied by the expense of the monarchy, the rise of republicanism in Europe (and Queen Victoria's connections with "despotic" royal families) together with Radical and working class disenchantment with Liberalism. (82) Joseph Cowen stoked the flames in November 1871. The Newcastle Republican Club invited

Sir Charles Dilke, MP, a leading critic of the costs of the monarchy, to address a meeting on "Representation and Royalty." The intention was to link the republican campaign with calls for a wider franchise, and Newcastle's Nelson Street Lecture Room was "fully occupied" by a "very crowded and enthusiastic" audience anticipating Dilke's speech. The organiser of the Newcastle Club, Bayfield, proposed Cowen to chair the meeting. Among those on the platform was John Burnett of the Nine Hours League. Cowen soon warmed up the atmosphere, describing the 1867 Reform Act as "neither a perfect nor a final measure (Hear, hear)" and calling for the "old Chartist plan - (applause)" of equal electoral districts and the election of working class MPs who would not be seduced by the attractions of Court and "society". (83) The hapless Dilke was carried away by Cowen's introduction, and attacked the iniquities of the Civil List to an extent he later thought "possibly unwise." (84) *The Times* made an issue of the speech and Queen Victoria was furious, informing Gladstone:

> "At present, and now for many days these Revolutionary Theories are allowed to produce what effect they may in the minds of the working classes. Gross misstatements and fabrications injurious to the credit of the Queen and injurious to the Monarchy remain unnoticed and uncontradicted"

by the government. (85) Gladstone, conscious that Chamberlain had greeted Dilke's speech as a sign that a British Republic "will come in our generation", was wary of tackling Dilke and Cowen directly. He advised the Queen that a government denunciation "would have tended to exasperate and harden such persons as composed the Newcastle meeting" (86) and a more tactful way had to be found to extinguish the agitation: "for it could never be satisfactory that there should exist even a fraction of the nation republican in its views." (87) There were, however, other problems.

Following Newcastle, Dilke's presence elsewhere sparked riots and Gladstone became entangled with a further difficulty concerning the Cowens. Holyoake, acting as secretary to Cowen's father, had been angling since 1869 for the award of a knighthood to Cowen, snr. Some sensitive footwork had been necessary to ensure that Cowen, jun, would not "prevent" the knighthood out of hostility to the honours system, especially as it looked as though the father was unwilling to accept the award without his son's consent. As it happened, there was no objection within the Cowen family. (88) Neither Cowen, snr, nor Holyoake, nor Gladstone knew in advance that the mischievous younger Cowen was on the point of unleashing the Dilke meeting upon an unsuspecting country. This alignment of the outrageous Newcastle incident and the granting of a knighthood to Cowen's father clearly caused Gladstone concern. The government's Lord Privy Seal, Halifax, appears to have conveyed to Gladstone a volume of "society" and parliamentary criticism of the award, causing the Prime Minister to reply defensively:

> "It is true as you suppose that the Cowen knighthood virtually preceeded the Dilke speech. But what you say upon the subject is beyond my comprehension. I have heard but cannot vouch for it that the son is an ultra-politician [an extreme Radical] & perhaps the critics think the distinction immaterial." (89)

The main reaction to the Newcastle meeting came in January 1872 when the Prince of Wales's recovery from a serious illness was made the object of a "loyalty fever" generated by the press and town councils. Newcastle's councillors promoted a Loyal Address to the Throne with the mayor pointedly referring to "all the noise that has been made in the town of late" and, in relation to Dilke, "the scum that has appeared." (90) The mayor had previously told an Anglican soiree he "felt proud" to condemn "those revolutionary, socialistic and communistic sentiments which had so recently been scattered in Newcastle." Naturally, the soiree closed with a rousing *God Save the Queen!* (91) The *Newcastle Daily Chronicle* was disparaging about the mayor and new republican clubs were formed at Windy Nook, Felling and Blackhill. By this time a Northern Republican League had been organised to campaign for "equality as between man and man, not forgetting the conferring of those rights on women also." (92) Over the summer the Newcastle Republican Club held open-air meetings at the town's traditional "speakers' corner", the Sandhill, where a favourite target of republican venom was the House of Lords. (93) As the authority of the mayor was being flouted, the police were called. The chief constable, intending to halt the republicans by preventing all open-air meetings, ordered a police "swoop" on the Sandhill. It ended in ignominy when the temperance society (with whom Cowen was closely associated) dared the officers to arrest their speakers. The police retreated amid a familiar editorial barrage from Cowen's *Chronicle* in defence of free speech. (94)

CHAPTER EIGHT : "THE MILITANT DEMOCRACY"

It is questionable whether Joseph Cowen would have appreciated his treatment by historians. Theodore Rothstein, in an otherwise brilliant analysis of the elements of Chartism and labourism, consigned Cowen to the margins as merely a "bourgeois radical and republican." (1) F.E. Gillespie in her *Labour and Politics in England 1850-67* went a step further and included Cowen - "the miners' champion of Tyneside" - in a list of assorted Radicals who sought to attach the working classes to middle class leadership and causes through adhesion to Liberalism. (2) A.R. Schoyen's biography of Julian Harney regarded Cowen purely as a personification of "middle class Radicalism." (3) Similarly, John Vincent's account of the formation of the Liberal Party focussed on Cowen as a provincial press magnate - running "the leading daily paper in the north east" - effectively engaged in Liberalism's historic mission to help the "poor and powerless...accept a most inequitable distribution of wealth and authority." (4) A related perspective informed Maurice Cowling's equating of Cowen with John Bright and sundry provincial Radicals in mobilising working class agitation as a controlled adjunct to Radical pretensions within the Liberal Party. (5) The same point was refined into an accusation by T. Tholfsen who argued "Cowen's idealism often did no more than put a gloss on existing patterns of class relations" by advancing social improvement restricted within an unaltered structure of capitalism, and that Cowen "did not differ from the middle class as a whole. "(6) Meanwhile, W. Hamish Fraser's survey of trade unions and mid-Victorian society positioned Cowen as one of a number of middle class leaders mainly concerned to enrol working class "support in pro-Italy and pro-Poland agitations" and assisting the growth of trade unionism's cautious "respectability" in order to "incorporate the working class into the body politic." (7) The broadly agreed verdict of modern historians is that Cowen served the purposes of Liberalism in ways relatively indistinguishable from other Radicals and contributed to the diversion of the working class into a Liberal hegemony. The origins of this judgement are readily intelligible but the conclusion is somewhat misplaced.

Joseph Cowen's speeches and journalism were phrased in the

conventional language of mid-nineteenth century Radicalism. There are ample references to self-help, responsible social reform, encouragement of social harmony and standard terms of respectfulness towards public figures. Integrated into this orthodox phraseology of Liberalism were observations about the realities of the market economy and the usual emphasis on English "greatness" and "fairness" as essential criteria in reaching decisions. Within this unexceptional linguistic framework dwelt statements conveying apparently more "extreme" advice. There was another side to Cowenism which emerges through a detailed reconstruction of his long-term connection with popular movements. When Cowen's own aims and context are unravelled, *and when attention is paid to what he actually did,* it becomes possible to begin to identify the real Joseph Cowen.

That there was something different about Cowen was clear to his contemporaries. The *Co-operative News* said of him in 1873:

> "Belonging by birth and position to the middle classes, [Cowen] has, for more than thirty years to our knowledge, familiarised himself with all the aspirations of working men, and has been ready to assist, by his personal influence and by pecuniary means, in every effort to improve their physical and moral condition." (8)

"Every effort" meant the efforts of the working classes themselves under their own control and direction, recalling Cowen's declaration over twenty years previously "that if they [the people] are to be elevated, mentally, morally, physically and socially, they must accomplish the task themselves." (9) Cowen's exceptional identification with the working classes, confirmed vividly during the nine hours strike but extending across almost thirty years, was a pronounced feature of his public identity in the early 1870s. Speaking to a trade union gathering in 1873 he still exhibited an unrepentant disdain for the middle classes (the "respectable classes") for whom "he had a most complete aversion." (10) Cowen continued to believe the middle classes were selfish and opposed to democracy, and he was not averse to ridiculing the

> "very common practice for a man to be an earnest Radical when he is at the bottom of the ladder, but when he gets up in the world, procures a good shop and is able to live in an excellent house, he very often quits the Methodist meeting in order to

attend the Church, and gradually emerges into a comfortable
Whig. Let us not follow in such a course." (11)

The strength of Cowen's choice of class allies set him apart from
other Radicals. It also brought the stinging criticism that he pursued
a "burlesqued" Radicalism distinct from the "advanced Liberalism"
of men like Joseph Chamberlain. (12) In a similar vein, Cowen was
seen as identifying with the "destruction and subversion" typical of
republicanism in contrast to Radicalism. (13)

A Cowen distinctiveness was obvious during the years 1871-73.
The point has been explored already through Cowen's involvement
with the nine hours strike, his destabilisation of the Newcastle police
and his response to the Commune and republicanism. At the height
of the engineers' strike, however, Cowen spoke to 30,000 people at
the Northumberland miners' July "picnic" near Blyth. What he said
remains a key to interpreting the meaning of "Cowenism". His
arrival at the demonstration "called forth a burst of cheering" and he
started speaking with a justification of the support given to the
anti-slavery campaign in the United States in 1861-65. He next
turned to review improvements in housing, food quality and prices,
railway links between pit villages and towns, and safety in the mines.
The speech also welcomed the expansion of education. But there
were shortcomings and inadequacies in this "progress". Cowen
especially criticised the depopulation of rural areas and the
concentration of land ownership in the hands of the wealthy. These
were familiar facets of Radicalism which Cowen decorated in the
terminology of the age, saying that "driving people from the land"
would undermine democracy and stability and create landless
labourers "less concerned about the interests of their country, and
[whose] patriotic feelings were necessarily weakened." There was
then a sharp twist in the argument.

Cowen observed that the fate of the agricultural labourers
reflected a deeper problem, namely "the masses of the people had
not participated fully and fairly in the increase" in national wealth.
The purpose of reform now was to extend the country's wealth to
those left out in the cold. It was as much a challenge to the existing
organisations of labour, which appealed to the better paid or "labour
aristocracy", as it was to Liberalism. Having described the situation
facing Radicals and the working classes, Cowen moved to outline a

programme for the future. This consisted of three inter-connected themes grounded in material reality rather than in political abstractions or general aspirations. Two social movements - trade unionism and co-operation - formed the basis of two themes. Trade unions could "protect" their members' rights and gain the "best possible market prices" for their labour. The growth of trade union organisation was to be encouraged although there had to be a recognition that the economic system restricted trade unionism. Co-operatives, on the other hand, provided methods for enhancing the power of the working classes by enabling them to collectively "buy goods and carry on a business at a profit." This was abundantly true in retail distribution but Cowen was anxious to suggest the "broader aspect of the movement was its application to manufactures; and the principle as applied to manufactures or to mining was as sound as when applied to distribution." For all their advantages, though, trade unions and co-operatives were only "remedial measures" and could not be a panacea for every social ill. The third paramount theme had to be the struggle for "political freedom." Cowen warned that despite the 1867 Reform Act many people "were not so alive to their political interests." He advocated agitational work to ensure "the working class would more fully appreciate their position." The aim was for working class constituencies to elect their own MPs able to represent "the feelings and principles and the prejudices, if they would, of their class", and abandon representation by "mere wealthy tradesmen and successful manufacturers." (14) Superficially, Cowen's Blyth speech could be read as typical mainstream Radicalism. But in linking the speech with the events of 1871 it is possible to detect a manifesto for working class economic and political ascendancy. This interpretation of Cowen's purpose is strengthened when developments in 1872-73 are taken into account.

An opportunity to grasp the question of those "masses" excluded from the increase in national wealth arose graphically in the early months of 1872. A widespread "revolt" by agricultural labourers protesting against archaic working conditions and low rates of pay swept through one county after another. By February, the agitation had reached Northumberland and the *Chronicle* began to report meetings of farm labourers in the villages. The meetings listed a reduction in the length of the working day, either a shortening in the number of months covered by "bonded" labour contracts or the total abolition of the "bond", and the creation of an agricultural labourers' union as their principal claims. At some meetings there were discussions about "possibly joining with the miners' union", reflecting the mobility of workers between coal mining and farm labour in Northumberland. (15) Cowen placed the resources of the *Chronicle* behind the labourers. Highly detailed reports of meetings at Earsdon, Kenton, Heddon, Mitford, Longhorsley, Horton, Prudhoe, Ponteland, Whalton, High Usworth and other villages appeared in the newspaper between February and the founding of the Northumberland Agricultural Labourers' Union at the end of June. Special care was taken to preserve the anonymity of speakers at the labourers' meetings and the method of reporting almost certainly encouraged the agitation. On two occasions the *Newcastle Daily Chronicle* carried leading articles fully supportive of the labourers. Additionally, the paper reported on demonstrations and victories over hours and pay at the Newcastle, Morpeth and Long Benton "hiring fairs" (a degrading system which the *Chronicle* condemned as barbaric). (16) The organisation of the Northumberland union happened rapidly due to the determination of the labourers, financial help from the Northumberland Miners' Association, and the presence of a sympathetic newspaper able to distribute news about the movement's growth. And a year later it was Joseph Cowen who chaired a public meeting in Newcastle addressed by Joseph Arch, the national leader of the agricultural labourers. (17) There were many "friends" eager to push Arch onwards. Radicalism and Liberalism tended to be overjoyed at the prospect of rural unrest since it was a challenge to the Tories in their traditional countryside heartlands. Cowen, arguably, went a step further by using the *Chronicle* as an unofficial organiser on behalf of the labourers.

Assisting oppressed farm labourers was a fairly safe way of implementing the Blyth Manifesto. Among other considerations, the labourers' movement was mainly a male preserve within an overwhelmingly male culture. Even so, the *Chronicle* did gently chide the movement in March for not giving a higher priority to improving the conditions of women on the land:

> "Greater freedom [from the "bond"] and better pay should be demanded for the women ... the rate of pay accorded to women, compared with all other workpeople in the north, is miserable"

- and the women, by their own efforts, won wage rises at the Newcastle "hiring fair" in April. (18) Cowen's commitment to women's rights was more evident in the early 1870s. As Radicals including John Bright withdrew their support from the enfranchisement of women after 1867, (19) Cowen turned towards a republicanism that stressed women's freedom; or, in Holyoake's words at a miners' meeting in Bedlington in February 1871: "A republic implies equality, and cannot be based on masculine votes. It would never do for republicans to declare in favour of an old aristocracy of sex." Republicans, said Holyoake, wanted "a Parliament elected by the entire people - of adult men and women." (20) Two months afterwards, Cowen's *Newcastle Daily Chronicle* called for the right of all women to vote at parliamentary elections. (21)

Cowen's principles faced an unexpected test over the summer of 1872. There was a sharp rise in meat prices and the cost of milk, bread and potatoes. Throughout County Durham, a suspicion grew that the butchers, whose travelling vans served the mining villages, had deliberately increased their prices to exploit advances gained in miners' wages. The discontent exploded at a remarkable meeting held in an enclosed field at Murton Colliery on Wednesday 12 June 1872. At least 300 women from the village gathered together, elected the local miners' union official or checkweighman, Martin Thompson, to chair the meeting "but with this one exception the whole business of the meeting was conducted by the ladies." The women then decided to fix the prices they were prepared to pay for meat, milk and potatoes. This was, in effect, a strike or boycott and was conducted in the language of trade unionism. After Murton the women's agitation tore through the villages. Two hundred Seaham Colliery women met the next day and "tin panning" was used to identify and shame "strikebreakers". One thousand women met at North Seaham Colliery on the following Monday and "meetings in support of the new movement had also been held by the women of the bottle works, chemical works, and iron works at Seaham Harbour." The village bellman had been sent around the streets on the previous Saturday night to announce the prices set by the women, and the Monday meeting denounced the *Seaham Weekly News* that had "ridiculed the movement." A miners' union delegate, Mr. Kellet, took the chair explaining he had been invited to do so ("You should have sent the wife") but tactfully withdrew in favour of Mary Errington "who had come to the field nursing a child, which was imbibing milk from its feeding bottle." A "women's union" was at once formed with Mary Errington as president, warning:

> "And we'll have to frighten the men that oppose us. I wish I had been a man. (Great cheers and laughter) We are ordered to be quiet, to keep silence in the church ... we are not going to be frightened, but you must excuse me if I am going too far. ("No, no" and cries of "Go on") You will make all right; if not, we'll have a bonny lot of men offering to speak. Petticoat government's been a long time in starting, but we will exert our rights, and prove faithful to our cause." (22)

There were further demonstrations at Ryhope (chaired by a woman), Thornley and at Murton. The Murton meeting again attracted 300 women and Martin Thompson was allowed into the chair (all other men being "ordered to keep outside" the field) but a woman conducted the debate. Levels of prices were fixed and it was agreed to buy Martin Thomson a white hat and neck tie both for his services and so the Murton miners would agree to march behind him to the Durham Big Meeting. On 18 June the butchers met at Newcastle to decide how to break the strike. Their discussion was frantic with reports that the butchers had been "cruelly treated" by "the mob" in several places, "tin panned" out of other villages and at Murton "had escaped from the fury of the women at the risk of their lives." The tradesmen resolved to boycott villages where the strike was in force, although this only admitted the impossibility of getting anywhere near the villages except on the women's terms. Undeterred by the butchers' blustering, the women forged ahead. Three hundred met at Ryhope carrying tricolour flags of pink, white and calico adorned with rosettes and were joined by women from Silksworth. Meetings mushroomed at Shotten, Houghton-le-Spring, Philadelphia and West Rainton. Two hundred women from Hebburn Colliery marched to Jarrow and held street meetings about "this determined strike of the women-people." Strikebreakers' effigies were burnt at Ryhope and everywhere meals were revolving around bacon or herrings in preference to butchers' meat. At Okenshaw Colliery on 20 June a meeting of 300 women, chaired by a woman, demanded the village policeman should be prohibited from buying meat. The tricolour flags reappeared at a meeting of 500 women at Sunniside on 21 June, and at Wheatley Hill the "men were ordered off the ground, with the exception of two or three" to assist the female organisers. The *Chronicle* reported on 24 June that "meetings are still being held all over the pit districts" and included:

> "a very imposing demonstration ... at New Seaham Colliery on Saturday, in which a magnificent banner, specially manufactured for the agitation, played a prominent part. These meetings are got up by the promoters of the movement apparently to strengthen each others hand [in] ... a general strike against the butchers' prices." (23)

Encouraged by the power of the the "women's union" the washerwomen and female farmhands at Ryhope started their own trade union and soon afterwards the women farmworkers at Seaham struck for an increase in wages and "an allowance of beer." At Blaydon a tricolour banner, decorated with a red-herring to denote independence from the butchers, led the procession to a meeting, which gave three cheers for the "women's union" and firm support for the local secretary whose husband had called her "stupid" because she could not write. A further meeting held in the pouring rain half-way between Hebburn and Jarrow forced a male speaker to "shut up" and replaced him with a woman. Simultaneously the butchers founded an association to defend themselves "as a body of Englishmen" against the "ruffianism, blackguardism and deceit" as well as the "tyranny" of the women. The following day "a whole hillside crowded with women and children" at Blackhill, near Consett, decided to picket the Durham shops and ordered the men to keep away from their demonstrations ("their retreat was not a little precipitated by a shower of stones"). A female strikebreaker at Colliery Dykes was "seized and tarred" and at Wardley a committee was appointed "to go round next Sunday and examine pots to see what was cooking." By 8 July the movement was spreading into Gateshead and the Walker district of Newcastle, although in both places hundreds of women had to cope with abuse and disruption by men and boys. At Gateshead the women were eventually able to meet in the town hall by invitation of the town's chief constable, John Elliot, who as a former Chartist was just about the only policeman ever to be a friend of Joseph Cowen. Five hundred women met at Wallsend on 12 July and there were reports of meetings at Bedlington ("they wished for one man to take the Chair, and no one but ladies to be admitted"). The agitation seems to have continued through August and into September, extending from Durham, Tyneside and Northumberland to the Cumberland coast, south Lancashire and London. It is impossible to assess the exact impact on prices but some victories were won in the north east and the turmoil seems to have attracted greater competition in the form of Australian meat promoters. (24) From the middle of August, the "women's union" in County Durham vanished from the public scene as suddenly as it had arisen.

For its brief life span the women's agitation was a new star in the heavens. There had been no comparable movement initiated by working class women since the female Chartist societies of 1839 and a similar price-setting movement in Durham in 1845. (25) As with the agricultural labourers, the women demonstrated how those most excluded from power and wealth were prepared to challenge their traditional subordination. It was a challenge which in theory fitted the framework of Joseph Cowen's Blyth Manifesto. In practice Cowen went a considerable distance to support the women's struggle but encountered one or two problems on the way. Cowen was unwell and out of action for much of the women's strike, perhaps explaining an absence of direct comment, (26) but his press conveyed his outlook. Indeed, the detailed accounts of the women's union owe everything to the *Chronicle*. Repeating the type of coverage given to the agricultural labourers, Cowen's army of journalists was despatched to report in depth on large numbers of the women's meetings. At the beginning of the strike a *Chronicle* report included a remark about the drinking habits of women at Seaham, bringing condemnation from the women. (27) From then onwards the *Chronicle* related women's meetings in a sympathetic manner quite at variance with usual male attitudes. The women, as noted, were very selective about which men if any should be allowed near their meetings, so the *Chronicle*'s informative reports produced by male journalists imply their acceptability to the women. There is evidence of the *Chronicle* acting as an organiser on behalf of the women in much the same way seen during the agricultural labourers' movement. Women read the *Chronicle*'s reports out loud at meetings in at least Seaham, Wheatley Hill and Jarrow, (28) to reinforce the self-confidence of the union's members. An outstanding editorial on "the Women's Agitation", published in the *Newcastle Daily Chronicle* of 24 June, insisted "necessity has taught" the women "to argue, to calculate, to protest, and to organise, as well as to declaim and appeal with an eloquence" not used by men. The women had put "the price of meat ... in the domain of politics" and were acquiring a "political training" for the time when they would have the right to vote. But, the *Chronicle* stated, if the men are enfranchised first they should act "in obedience to the counsels of their wives."

The relationship between Cowen's newspapers and the women's union was not entirely comfortable. Some difficulties centred on the Blaydon co-operative society which Cowen had helped to start in 1858 and had since grown into the flagship of the north east co-operative movement. The Blaydon co-operative store aimed to provide cheap food for its working class members at prices they could afford. Unlike private retailers the co-op was managed through a committee elected by the membership and had no obvious interest in exploiting its customers. The weakness in this theory rested on the fact that the co-operative society's prices were also dependent on the general state of the market. Co-operative meat was not necessarily cheaper and consequently the women's union did not always distinguish between private butchers and the co-operatives. The point was driven home in the latter part of June when the Blaydon co-operative society's butchery carts were also boycotted by women at two nearby pit villages. This incident represented, too, a dichotomy between an established working class movement administered by men, selling food at price levels broadly geared to paying a dividend to the members, and a fresh movement organised by women excluded from co-operative committees (and, often, from membership altogether until the 1880s and 1890s). (29) The *Newcastle Daily Chronicle* could not comprehend the subtlety of the affair and argued that the co-operative society's butchers were not the principal villains. The fundamental cause of the problem, the newspaper believed, was located in "unwise and unjust laws ... made in the interests of the wealthy and privilged classes." The women's union should direct its attention to land reform and the abolition of the game laws so as to open up more land for agricultural production. (30) Whilst the women may well have broadly agreed with the *Chronicle*, they were not greatly impressed by the advice and continued with their strike. The women's union, as it happened, also formed co-operatives at Ryhope - where several women were elected to a committee to "form a Co-operative Butchery Union as soon as possible" - Murton, Thornley, New Seaham, Wheatley Hill, Dipton and Hebburn. Most of these "co-operatives" were simple temporary associations set up to buy a sheep or cow for slaughter. In a few cases, as at West Cornforth, the strike provided the basis for a more permanently constituted co-operative society. (31) On the whole the surfacing of co-operative ideas within the food agitation supplied a further meeting stage between Cowen and the women's movement.

Cowen's Blyth Manifesto mentioned co-operative societies as a source of working class economic power. This was a sphere of tremendous attraction to Cowen and he threw his energies into the co-operative movement with characteristic enthusiasm, spending substantial amounts of time on the development of co-operatives. The decade after 1860 was a period of spectacular growth for the movement in the north east with no less than seventy-one local societies formed, (32) making Newcastle and its surroundings "one of the main centres of Co-operative activity" in the country. (33) The origins of the movement in this area - i.e. societies founded on the model of the Rochdale Pioneers of 1844 - were intimately linked with "the work of individuals such as Joseph Cowen." (34) Cowen floated the notion of launching a co-operative society by reading "lessons from G.J. Holyoake's famous little book *Self-Help*" during concerts at the Blaydon and Stella mechanics' institute in 1858. (35) The Blaydon co-operative society was started at the end of 1858 on the Rochdale "principles" of one member-one vote, payment of a dividend related to the value of a member's purchases, a low and fixed rate of interest on share-capital to eliminate speculation, the allocation of two-and-a-half-percent of profits to an education fund and avoidance of both credit trading and adulterated food. Blaydon was the first of the modern co-operative societies in the north east and "was for at least a decade after its formation a centre of co-operative propaganda and effort." Cowen's part in "the Blaydon store was all important, for the magnetism of his personality and his continued interest in the store ensured the success of Co-operation on Tyneside." (36)

Cowen's motives for encouraging co-operation stemmed from a recognition of working class interest in "social reform as embodied in co-operative societies", (37) and a belief that the democracy of the co-operatives could be "the preparation for participation of the working classes in the running of government." (38) These were highly political motives which Cowen advanced at co-operative meetings, arguing against a narrow preoccupation with shopkeeping. Co-operators, he insisted, must not be "indifferent to all other considerations" and should see themselves as part of a wider movement for social and political reform. (39) The preface to the Blaydon society's rules sermonised: "Never forget that the safe way for the working man to raise himself is to raise his class." (40) Such ideas disturbed hostile local newspapers which labelled Cowen's encouragement of co-operatives as an attempt "to establish the worn out theories of revolutionary France," (41) and Northumberland landowners tried to prevent the erection of co-operative stores in mining districts. (42) After Blaydon, co-operatives spread fairly quickly as groups of workers at pits, shipyards, engine works and factories formed their own societies, creating a lively and thriving network of enthusiasts. A "striking feature" of the movement in the north east was that "it was the seizure of an opportunity created by the growth of industry and population" to create a new economic organisation through an alliance between "prominent Radicals and the working classes." (43) Cowen, especially, "visited all, or nearly all, of the large co-operative stores in the country" over the first half of the 1860s to study their experience and apply their successes. (44) He concluded that the north eastern societies should establish a "central co-operative agency" as their own wholesaler and business adviser, and first proposed the agency as early as October 1861. (45) In 1862 he tried again and this time moves were made to form a Northern Union of Co-operative Stores at Newcastle (the pioneering stores of Lancashire "were still only meditating the establishment" of a wholesale agency). (46) Cowen and the management committee of the Blaydon society "initiated the Northern Co-operative Union" which survived for two years (47) until the "ideas and spirit" of the north eastern co-operatives proved an inadequate substitute for "the necessary volume of purchases" and the union faded away. (48)

This excursion into the *minutiae* of co-operative history indicates not only Cowen's deep involvement with the movement but also the core of his ambitions. Cowen wanted the co-ops to grow into a powerful force and after 1862 "much of the unity and direction of co-operative effort" in Northumberland and Durham flowed from Cowen and like-minded Radicals. (49) He embarked on extensive "missionary" work to form new societies. At Walker, Cowen asked a public meeting of iron-workers to consider "the adoption of co-operative principles both as to distribution and production" integrated into an economic policy encompassing land reform and lower taxation. The result was the founding of the Walker co-operative society in 1870 to undermine an employer's "tommy shop". (50) The pages of the *Chronicle* were used to disseminate information and propaganda about the movement, including a four-page special supplement in the *Newcastle Weekly Chronicle* in June 1871 detailing the balance sheets of the Northumberland and Durham societies and carrying articles on co-operation by leading co-operators and Radicals including Holyoake, John Stuart Mill, Lloyd Jones and Millicent Fawcett. (51) By the early 1870s "the energetic work of Joseph Cowen and his fellow Radicals" had led to the opening of "well over a hundred co-operative stores in the North East." (52) The ultimate vision was more far-reaching. Cowen urged the movement to reach beyond "the buying and selling or the mere paying of dividends." For him "it was the national and social aspect ... that was a source of attraction" and if co-operatives were to engage with education and industrial production they would "revolutionise the institutions of the country." (53) The Jarrow and Sunderland societies developed their own libraries and the Sunderland co-operators, who formed an education committee in 1863, proudly retained a letter from Mazzini congratulating them on their library. The Wallsend society, too, had a library and "for a short while an elementary school (1872-75) run by the society." (54) Such societies were a minority, however, but many others did open newspaper reading rooms attached to their shops.

Cowen found considerable interest in extending the co-operative movement into industrial production. Holyoake was a passionate advocate of producer co-operation by the late 1860s and many other co-operators and middle class exponents of co-operation saw the industrial rather than the retail sphere as of primary importance. At the same time there were plenty of active co-operators content to stay with shopkeeping. A prolonged debate took place over the direction to be taken but in the north east the argument was carried in favour of entering production by Cowen, Dr. J.H. Rutherford, an educator and Radical and their supporters. In 1866, Cowen proposed that trade union funds might be invested in co-operative factories and banks. (55) He went on pressing the case for producer co-operatives through the movement's evolving structures, particularly, in 1872, the creation of the national Co-operative Union's regional committees (in which Cowen played an active part), and the opening of a Newcastle branch of the Co-operative Wholesale Society for which he had argued twelve months earlier. (56) The seeds soon grew into plants. A co-operative cabinet makers' society and a tailoring co-operative opened on Tyneside in 1867 and 1871 respectively, and a co-operative corn mill began at Bedlington in 1868. (57)

The producer co-operatives received their most powerful boost under the impact of the nine hours strike which "led to the formation of the greatest Co-operative manufacturing establishment ... attempted in England." (58) This "most ambitious of all the Co-operative speculations" (59) was the Ouseburn Engineering Works at Newcastle. The Ouseburn experiment, largely inspired by Rutherford, was meant to demonstrate that co-operative principles applied to engineering could guarantee decent employment practices including profit-sharing as well as quality products (principally, marine engines). With the keen assistance of Cowen and the *Chronicle*, together with financial help from the north east's retail co-operatives, the Ouseburn Works got under way in July 1871. It took advantage of the weakness of the private engineering firms caught in the nine hours strike and the goodwill of the Nine Hours League. The workforce rapidly increased from 300 to 800 people and membership of the co-operative was open to individual workers and the retail societies. Cowen kept in touch with Rutherford and the Ouseburn Works but was unable to participate directly in the co-operative, explaining to the workers that he "had been much pressed to join the undertaking but he was in a position of having already as much to do as he could attend to." (60)

The Ouseburn was just the start. Rutherford and Cowen had wide-ranging plans to construct a co-operative economy. An "Industrial Land and Building Society" was proposed by Rutherford to erect "model dwellings" next to the Ousesburn Works as the nucleus of a co-operative community. (61) And at the "inaugural soiree" of the Works in November 1871 (attended by Cowen and Charles Dilke the day after Dilke's republican speech) Cowen looked forward to the appearance of "co-operative farms, collieries and other undertakings" which would "be instrumental" in achieving "a more equitable distribution of wealth." (62) Co-operative schemes flowed thick and fast. A co-operative engineering factory was planned at Sunderland in November 1871, a co-operative printing society at Newcastle in February 1872, a co-operative bank (the Industrial Bank) was opened in Newcastle with backing from the retail societies and the Northumberland miners in May 1872, and a national co-operative mining society was formed on Tyneside at the end of the year. Co-operative shipbuilding societies were active at Jarrow and Walker and launched ships at Blyth in 1873, the same year as the founding of a co-operative dairy society at North Seaton, a brushmakers' society at Newcastle and a gas and lighting society at Newbiggin. (63) Producer societies were founded in various parts of the country during the early 1870s but the interest on Tyneside was pronounced: "The point of view ... captivating co-operators" in the north east was the "theory of Co-operation ... held by Joseph Cowen and his fellow radicals." The theory considered co-operative societies "a shadow of a good thing" unless they were constructing "a sound industrial socialism" based upon profit-sharing encompassing workers in addition to share-owning members. (64)

From July 1871 the contours of Cowen's Blyth Manifesto took practical shape in the sophisticated projection of a co-operative economy, the nine hours strike, the unionism of the agricultural labourers and the women's agitation. Integral to these substantial movements of working class opinion was the organising role of the *Chronicle*, consolidating the confident assertiveness that broke the Newcastle police, upheld the ideals of the Paris Commune and conveyed republicanism from public meetings to street corners to mining villages. Joseph Cowen was at the centre of it all. It was not that he was simply more deeply involved than most Radicals; he had a perspective capable of connecting the distinctive movements and pointing towards a vision of popular empowerment expressed graphically in the democratic "festival" of 12 April 1873.

Saturday 12 April 1873 saw Newcastle upon Tyne hosting two significant assemblies. The first was the annual co-operative congress or "parliament" of the British co-operative movement, attracting the attention of newspapers and politicians throughout the country. It was a conference representing almost half-a-million people, in a movement barely detectable a decade earlier, and now conducting an annual trade of around £18 millions and with over £5 millions in capital at its disposal. The 1873 congress was also one of unusual importance to co-operators. A national advisory, propagandist and representative organisation, the Co-operative Union, had been recently created and a national newspaper, the *Co-operative News*, had just been launched as the voice of all shades of co-operative opinion. These were crucial topics for delegates attending a congress which could now justly claim to be "national" in scope. Additionally, the conference met to debate the movement's attitude towards producer co-operatives and co-operative banks. Presiding over the congress was Joseph Cowen. To be invited to act as congress president was a mark of the esteem in which an individual was held by co-operators. Cowen spared no effort to impress. The *Newcastle Weekly Chronicle* produced a supplement containing verbatim reports of the congress speeches, sessions and associated meetings. A thirty-two page special edition of the *Co-operative News* reporting the congress was in fact a reprint from the *Chronicle*, (65) and something like 100,000 copies of the *Weekly Chronicle* supplement were printed. All the arrangements were on the grand scale, illustrating:

> "Cowen's value as a stage-manager - abundant publicity, sumptious meals, a [Co-operative Union] Central Board meeting in a pleasure steamer on the Tyne, and to cap it all a 42-gun salute for the Board's 42 members ... undoubtedly the movement was put in the public eye." (66)

Cowen's presidential address juggled three elements. There was a review of the strength of the movement, noting the retail societies in Northumberland and Durham had over 40,000 members, held £200,000 in share capital and enjoyed an annual trade approaching £1½ millions. A second element touched on the advantages of co-operation to co-operators and the community, embracing everything from healthy food to economic stability. But the third strand in Cowen's speech laid out the centrepiece of his philosophy:

> "What we wish is this - not that labour is to dominate over capital, but we do say that the man who represents labour should be treated upon perfect equality with the man who represents capital (Hear, hear), and further and better still, we hope to see the day when the working men will be their own employers. (Cheers) We hope, gentlemen, to see a better state of things. At the present time, our commercial pursuits are carried on upon two principles - unlimited competition and unrestricted rivalry. The only struggle with a man of wealth is how to make more of it. We mean to preach a higher and better doctrine. (Hear, hear) We wish the be-all and end-all of this existence not to be more money and greater material prosperity; we want to make men citizens, we want to preach the doctrine of brotherhood and fellowship - (hear, hear) - we wish to preach to you a new gospel, and I believe the time will arrive when the competition in which we are now engaged will be set aside, and men will live together

not as mere rivals in trade, but in a community of common
interests, labouring for the advantage of themselves and each
other, and every man's advancement will be promoted by
contributing to the welfare and comfort of his neighbours.
(Cheers) These are the benefits and advantages which we expect
will spring from the dissemination of the principles of
Co-operation, and from the establishment of co-operative
societies throughout the country. (Hear, hear)"

Cowen believed that co-operatives would "bring about a more even
and equitable distribution of wealth" without risking "that system of
doleful patronage to which the working men have been treated in
the past" as a consequence of government interventions in
economics. Cowen concluded "we are now coming to a new era"
heralded by producer co-operatives. It was a short but energising
speech brought to a close by Cowen's urgent need to leave the
congress for an appointment in the streets of Newcastle. (67)

Cowen had begun his congress address by flouting the
co-operative convention of "no politics", saying:

"In Lancashire, he believed, there were "Conservative working
men", but this was a commodity they did not possess on
Tyneside." (68)

Outside the congress hall delegates would have found ample
evidence sustaining Cowen's claim. The streets were thronged with
80,000 trade unionists assembling in a huge procession for the right
of manhoood suffrage. Some 500 extra carriages had been hired by
the North Eastern Railway Company to provide special trains to
Newcastle from Northumberland and Durham. Work had stopped
in factories and pits, and streets had been specially decorated. And
then the great march lumbered into motion behind numerous bands
- the Tyne Dock Garibaldi Band, the Seaham Bottleworks Brass
Band and many more - and symbols of the various trades (models of
steam hammers, ships and engines). Prominently displayed were
"upwards of 150" banners of the different unions. The Ouseburn
Engineering Works and Co-operative Smiths carried their own
banners as well as Garibaldi's sea flag and a bullet-holed battle flag
once used by Mazzini (both loaned for the procession by Holyoake).
The miners' banners included three - Edmondsley, Pegswood and
Waterhouses - containing Joseph Cowen's portrait. Cowen was at
the head of the gigantic column. As the trade unionists slowly

wound their way through the town, walking four-deep and taking over two hours to pass, the only discordant voices were those of a few shopkeepers calling for Cowen to be hanged. Eventually the marchers reached the Town Moor where a vast crowd of 200,000 people grouped around six platforms of speakers (Cowen chaired the No. 1 platform), registered demands for the further extension of the franchise to all working men and especially those, like the Northumberland and Durham miners, left out of the 1867 reform. Naturally, the *Newcastle Weekly Chronicle* published a special supplement. (69)

The manhood suffrage demonstration had been planned for months. An impetus for a reform campaign was provided by the Northumberland-based Miners' Franchise Association, founded early in 1872, and a similar Durham County Franchise Association, whose president underlined a connection with Cowen at a miners' meeting in January 1873 by praising the *Chronicle* as "the only friendly newspaper to which they could look for help." (70) In February 1873 Cowen chaired a joint meeting of the two associations at which the Town Moor demonstration was mooted. A fortnight later he conducted a manhood suffrage public meeting in Newcastle addressed by Thomas Burt and over the following weeks there were further meetings and rallies throughout the coalfields. At one stage queries were raised about the clash of dates with the co-operative congress but it was decided to keep to the original plan for 12 April. (71) After the immense Newcastle demonstration the agitation for manhood suffrage was intensified. Cowen urged the trade unions to become involved in politics when he chaired the principal platform at the Durham miners' Big Meeting in June 1873. (72) Towards the end of the same month he presided at a Newcastle meeting which revived the Northern Reform League "as the outcome of the Manhood Suffrage Demonstration of 12th April." Cowen was elected president of the NRL and Thomas Burt and Dr. Rutherford became vice-presidents. The League then embarked on a campaign for manhood suffrage as a right, triennial parliaments, payment of MPs and equal electoral districts. (73) Numerous meetings of the League were held across the north east in the summer and autumn of 1873 with Cowen taking a leading part, reminding audiences that all major reforms had required "compulsion by popular pressure." (74) And "popular pressure" clearly proved effective for the Northumberland miners, whose applications to be admitted to the franchise were accompanied by an organised boycott of the Morpeth shopkeepers and talk of occupying the town. A right to vote was quickly conceded.

Saturday 12 April 1873 was, in Cowen's words to the co-operative congress, the day when "the militant democracy" was displayed in all its glory. (76) The quest for political freedom paraded the streets and, at the same time, an economic system to supplant capitalism was debated in the conference hall. A spectacular display of working class opinion, strength and optimism flourished in Newcastle on that Saturday, and it was Cowen who conducted the orchestra of political and economic movements. His Blyth Manifesto set out a route and his mixture of Chartism and Mazzinism, a blend of revolutionary and reformist principles and tactics finely tuned to the conditions of the early 1870s, supplied the motivation to encompass a form of plebeian democracy. When Cowen was invited to chair a triumphant meeting of Northumberland miners, held at Morpeth in October 1873 to nominate Thomas Burt as the miners' candidate for the next parliamentary election, the prospects for the "militant democracy" looked bright. This rising tide was also taking Joseph Cowen to new prominence. Although ill from "overwork" (77) his "political influence" was considered as powerful or even exceeding "that which Chamberlain was beginning to wield in the Birmingham district." (78) Cowen was now seen as "one of the most popular men in the North of England" (79) - even the formidable Durham coalowner Lord Londonderry "dreaded" him (80) - and his "national reputation" was reaching new heights (81) as "one of the most powerful Radicals in England." (82) The *Daily Telegraph* (then a Liberal newspaper) described Cowen at the beginning of 1874 "one of the few English Reds." Cowen, the *Telegraph* warned, was "a most estimable man, with the courage of his convictions in an eminent degree" and a person to be watched: "He has nothing but good intentions, a warm heart, and a conviction that the best thing for England would be the rule of Tyneside Radicalism." In a word, he was "dangerous". (83)

CHAPTER NINE : THROWING A BRICK AT MR. GLADSTONE.

Joseph Cowen was riding the floodtide of the "militant democracy." When asked by a less resolute Radical how he came to be so popular with the working classes, Cowen replied:

> "Well, this is the explanation. While you have been sitting at home in the cold nights with your feet comfortable in the rug before your drawing room fire, I have been for twenty years travelling about, in sunshine or storm, to every Tyneside place or distant colliery village, talking to the pitmen, assisting in establishing their humble institutions, and giving them what information was in my power; and it now comes to pass that they happen to remember it, and be grateful for it." (1)

An 1873 commentary on Tyneside "celebrities" described Cowen as "a powerful, well-informed writer as well as an effective public speaker" ("notwithstanding his local accent") and anticipated "he will yet both seek and secure a seat in Parliament." (2) If Joseph Cowen seriously entertained parliamentary ambitions he had not yet appeared eager to pursue them. Holyoake unsuccessfully pressed Cowen in 1860 to contest the next election at Newcastle, (3) and Cowen was also "repeatedly solicited" to stand elsewhere. (4) Even when Cowen, snr, looked likely to retire from Parliament, Cowen, jnr, seemed more interested in "sounding out" other Radicals to fill the vacancy than in pushing himself forward, although it has been suggested these "soundings" carried an ulterior motive of gradually dislodging Newcastle's second MP (the Whig, Thomas Headlam) and smoothing a path for the younger Cowen at a later date. (5) The issue was unexpectedly brought to a head in December 1873 when Cowen's father died. The sudden death caught Cowen, jnr, unprepared for a by-election. In order to forestall the Tories, and probably the Whigs or "moderate" Liberals as well, Cowen and Holyoake secretly persuaded the government to call the by-election quickly. Cowen "expected to be pressed to stand" but told Holyoake he would "do so only if no other man likely to be elected came forward." (6) In fact, his "candidacy was carefully planned" (7) and, before attending his candidate adoption meeting, Cowen already had his election literature printed and inserted into envelopes addressed to each voter. (8) Cowen's campaign properly began on Christmas Eve 1873 when, in the absence of any Liberal organisation, a Radical public meetmg adopted Cowen as a candidate on Dr. Rutherford's nomination.

Liberal "moderates" were furious that the Radicals had stolen a march on them. As Cowen spent Christmas Day planning his campaign, the "moderates" were organising their own meeting for New Year's Eve to choose a different candidate. Their meeting, however, ended in confusion when Cowen's supporters challenged allegations that Cowen was unacceptable to Liberals because of his past political affiliations, and several Tories intervened producing chaos. (9) Cowen's election techniques aroused further sharp controversy. His election literature included a form for electors to complete and return to his agent, Spence Watson, indicating an intention to vote for Cowen. The form was defended on the shaky grounds that it would not be possible to personally canvass every voter but was attacked in the local and national press as breaching the spirit of the secret ballot. (10) Cowen's election platform, too, made few concessions to the Liberal "moderates". The stock Liberalism of free trade and disestablishment of the Church of England were included. So was the neo-Chartist programme of the Northern Reform League (triennial parliaments, universal suffrage - defined by Cowen's promise to "most unhesitatingly support any proposal for granting the suffrage to women" (11) - redistribution of seats, payment of MPs). And the Radical shopping list of abolition of the death penalty, the game laws, the Contagious Diseases Act and, significantly, the Liberals' own Criminal Law Amendment Act also featured. At first Cowen seems to have been equivocal about committing himself to Irish Home Rule. But, with the qualification that it should not "disorganise or break-up the empire", (12) he took Home Rule on board and symbolically "added green to his white election emblem." (13)

Orthodox Liberalism came out strongly against Cowen's "uncompromising" Radicalism, insisting: "Such wild Republicans as Mr. Cowen" were not wanted in the House of Commons. (14) The Tories also concentrated their fire on Cowen's "extremism", circulating a cutting little broadside:

> "I"m a rank and Red Republican, And a Freethinker also;
> For neither Queen nor Creed, you see, Will satisfy young Joe." (15)

These themes were repeated in the *Newcastle Journal* which saw

Cowen as a "professional revolutionist and a radical of the most extreme hue", warning that a vote for him would be "an insult to the Queen." (16) Cowen was particularly attacked for his republican past and vagueness about his religious identity. But the Tories had problems with their own candidate, Charles Hamond, and his "personal creed of independent Toryism" (he had supported the nine hours strike). Hamond was a vocal town councillor, "tall, florid, dandified, corsetted, bewigged and the possessor of a dyed moustache" and exceptionally determined. Just as Cowen rode over the "moderate" Liberals so Hamond dragooned the reluctant Newcastle Conservative Association into accepting him as their candidate. (17)

Cowen's election strategy was heavily grounded in public meetings and lavishly financed (Spence Watson spent £10,000 of Cowen's money on the campaign without telling Cowen at the time). (18) Since his support came mainly from the working class suburbs of Elswick and Byker, Cowen wanted the election held on a Saturday to maximise the workers' votes. The town council, sympathetic to Hamond, decided to hold the polling on a Wednesday, taking advice from the under-sheriff who happened to be the legal adviser to the local publicans' association - a body fiercely opposed to the temperance Cowen. Polling was set from 8.00 am - 4.00 pm, coinciding with factory working hours and illustrating that every possible obstacle was placed in the way of Cowen. Yet labour demonstrated its strength. Factories were forced to close down at noon to allow workers to vote and, remarkably for a hard drinking town, there was a boycott of the numerous public houses where the brewers were hoping to "lubricate" Hamond's election prospects. The "moderate" Liberals voted against Cowen as did the shopkeepers with the exception of 500 "perenially radical" tailors. (19) The Radical workers won the day. Cowen was easily elected on 14 January 1874 with a majority of 1,003 votes over Hamond. The Tory vote of 6,353 had substantially risen from its 1868 total of 2,727, but Cowen had also increased the Radical vote from his father's 7,057 to 7,356. No sooner had Cowen emerged victoriously from the by-election than Gladstone dissolved Parliament. Cowen did not even have time to take his seat in the Commons before being thrust back into a second round of electioneering. A contemporary cartoon portrayed Cowen finding the door of Parliament slammed shut in his face by a worried Gladstone. There was a widespread suspicion that

"Mr. Cowen's return ... alarmed Mr. Gladstone into the hasty dissolution of 1874. Mr. Cowen's was an ominous name in those days." It was said of Gladstone: "Somebody threw a Blaydon brick at him ... a Blaydon brick being known over a great part of the world as something of Cowen manufacture." (20)

Gladstone called a general election for several reasons. He was confronted with cabinet splits and disturbed by the rise in the Tory vote at Newcastle coming as it did at the end of a string of Liberal by-election losses. Holding an election seemed to be a way out of the immediate predicaments facing an unpopular and divided government, but the decision posed a new problem in Newcastle because of the town's status as a two-member constituency. Essentially, the Radicals and the Whigs, bitterly divided but inhabiting the same party, had to find a means of running Headlam and Cowen in tandem. Their difficulty was compounded by the contrast between Cowen's meticulous attention to Tyneside politics and Headlam's reputation as an indolent MP who "rarely visited Newcastle." Within both the Radical and "moderate" camps there were groups keen to oust Headlam. Cowen appears to have made efforts to prevent a damaging civil war among Liberals at the very start of the by-election and visited Headlam in London to discuss a joint campaign. As a result a public meeting did adopt Cowen and Headlam as the Liberal candidates. Unity was fragile. Before long the Liberal campaign had divided into two election organisations, one Radical and the other Whig. (21) Headlam's poor performance in the course of the election finally snapped the patience of the Radicals who also suspected him of conniving with the Tories to ensure his re-election in partnership with Charles Hamond. This antagonism between the Radicals and the Whigs became highly public towards the end of the campaign when Cowen's *Chronicle* printed a facsimile of a ballot paper marked only in Cowen's favour. (22)

The end for Headlam was confirmed at midnight on the eve of poll when Cowen, Rutherford and Radical election organisers, but not Cowen's agent Spence Watson, met secretly in Cowen's private office at the *Chronicle* and decided to instruct Radical ward election agents to urge their canvassed supporters to vote only for Cowen. (23) The election result finally finished Whig influence in Newcastle. Cowen's vote soared to 8,464, Headlam came bottom of the poll with 5,807 votes and Charles Hamond held his by-election support and was elected with 6,479 votes. Blistering recriminations followed. Headlam, in a letter to *The Times*, accused Cowen of engineering his defeat by duplicity, and Cowen was apparently denied a right of reply by the newspaper. (24) The *Chronicle*, on the other hand, blamed the "Whiggish section of the Liberal Party" for disunity and claimed "weak-kneed Whigs" had voted for the Tories. (25) Had Headlam been a Radical, the Cowenites argued, then the Tories would not have won a seat in Newcastle and the town would have emulated Northumberland and Durham, returning Liberal candidates sympathetic to Radicalism. (26) The Radicals drawing on the "militant democracy" had indeed scored a distinctive success in the north east including the election of Thomas Burt at Morpeth as one of the first "labour" MPs. By dismal contrast, Liberals in other parts of the country had been overwhelmed by the Tories and Disraeli was about to become Prime Minister.

The two elections represented a huge endorsement for Cowenite Radicalism, though the jubilation was abruptly cut short. The "strain of the elections" on Cowen's health was devastating and "drove him from politics for a year." (27) He was unable to take his seat in Parliament until two-thirds of the way through the 1874 session and was seriously affected by ill-health for two years. (28) Holyoake wrote to the Liberal chief whip, Arthur Peel, that Cowen had suffered from the effects of overwork prior to the elections and by "severe disablement" afterwards. Peel may have learned more about the cause of Cowen's illness verbally from Holyoake and evidently considered the matter as requiring "discretion." (29) The nature of Cowen's problems is unclear. A few clues were provided in the autumn of 1874 when Cowen admitted the events of the past months were "in a sort of haze" and he had been ordered by his doctors to "avoid all excitement." (30) He spent months in convalescence on the south coast and in the south of France, (31) and confided to Joseph Chamberlain that he had overworked, experienced painful sciatica and, because he had refused to rest, had suffered "tortures ... since January 1874" inducing the "entire prostration of mind and body" and would rather have died. (32) From time to time in 1875 he was "in tolerably fair health" but Parliament's "long sittings and late hours" were "exhausting". (33) The impact of this major breakdown in Cowen's health should not be discounted. After the 1874 elections his personality altered and became more prone to emotion. Holyoake saw Cowen as moving from being placid but purposeful to becoming resentful and implacable. (34) It should be borne in mind, however, that Holyoake's assessment may have been coloured by political disagreements with Cowen as the later 1870s unfolded. Whatever the exact details of the illness, Cowen was effectively removed from active politics between February 1874 and the spring of 1876 and this absence had serious consequences.

While Cowen was incapacitated a number of changes took place. In Newcastle, Spence Watson established a Liberal Association. The proposal was welcomed by W.E. Adams in the *Newcastle Weekly Chronicle* as a means of avoiding future Liberal defeats and was also encouraged by James Annand as editor of the *Newcastle Daily Chronicle*. (35) Associations already existed at Rochdale and Birmingham and Spence Watson seems to have taken up the idea after a conversation with John Bright at whose "instigation, I held meetings in the different Wards of Newcastle." (36) Ward committees and a Newcastle-wide general committee were formed and, in March 1874, a Newcastle Liberal Club or Association was founded. (37) Crucially, the general committee of the Newcastle Liberal Association acquired the right to select the official Liberal candidates for parliamentary elections. This was the birth of an infamous "caucus" which, as a new departure, threatened the freedom of those diverse groupings vying for power in the loose milieu of Liberalism.

From the start the Newcastle caucus was firmly controlled by the middle classes, its principal members being "shipowners, solicitors, merchants, manufacturers and an accountant." A "money qualification" for membership was maintained to deter "working class extremists" from joining. (38) The caucus members were precisely the sort of people whom Cowen regarded as "well-to-do, conventional, non-political ... satisfied with their material success, and ... indifferent to the condition of their less favoured and less fortunate fellow-countrymen." (39) The men who oiled the Newcastle Liberal Association were drawn from the same social elite then running local government which Cowen believed to be corrupt. (40) Cowen tended to oppose the "municipal socialism" of Joseph Chamberlain out of concern about the integrity of local authorities. In Newcastle's case Cowen's scepticism was well-founded against a background both of sustained council resistance to providing a free public library and revelations of fraud and maladministration throughout the 1870s and 1880s. (41) On occasion, Cowen teased the town council, observing "generally when he proposed anything in the Council he stood alone." Referring to the council's taste for glittering social functions, Cowen once delighted a public meeting by pointedly stating "he had never attended a municipal or other dinner in any way connected with his duties as a town councillor." (42) If Cowen's long-term opposition to the watch committee's policing policies are taken into account, it can be seen that the creation of the middle-class dominated caucus produced an additional arena for conflict between the Radical MP and the local social hierarchy.

Had Cowen been active immediately following the 1874 elections then conceivably the story might have been different: "Had he been involved, the Association might have taken a different form, if only in financial dependence on [his] wealth." (43) The interregnum in Cowen's political activism caused by illness is pregnant with "might-have-beens". Shortly after the 1874 general election it seemed Liberalism might disintegrate. The labour newspaper, *The Beehive*, pronounced the Liberal Party "dead" at the end of the year and called on Radicals to form a new party. (44) To some extent, W.E. Adams concurred, writing in the *Newcastle Weekly Chronicle* that Liberal leaders were "insipid politicians" and the prospects for Radicalism within the Liberal party were "anything but encouraging." Cowen, too, in a letter from his sick-bed to the Northumberland miners in June 1875 saw the Liberals as "divided - they have no common bond of union, and there is little spirit or energy in their proceedings." (45) Could a new politics have emerged linking labour and co-operative organisations, embracing republican and Radical principles, and spearheaded by the "militant democracy" of the north east? Had Cowen been fit enough to act as a catalyst, employing his newspapers to develop a fresh political alignment, might there have been the earlier appearance of a type of "labour party"? And could the Northern Reform League, still active in the coalfields during 1874-75, have served as the vehicle for the new party? The questions are highly speculative and the answers depend a great deal on the presence of one individual. But Cowen was a person of substantial influence and status and had the resources to promote a new departure. He also had the political vision to transcend the immediate and narrow considerations pulling other Radicals back into Liberalism. As it happened, Cowen was unable to continue at what could have been a turning point. The field was consequently clear for Robert Spence Watson, among others, to strengthen the Liberal "machine" and reduce the Northern Reform League to a mere propaganda adjunct of the caucus. (46)

Further changes drained the infant "militant democracy" of its vitality and independence. An economic recession from 1874 replaced the boom of the early 1870s. This "great depression" affected the various sectors of the economy with degrees of severity, but those hardest hit by pressures to lower wages and shed labour included agricultural labourers and the Northumberland and Durham miners. By 1877 Thomas Burt could tell Holyoake he was totally absorbed in trying "to keep our union afloat" against the slump, (47) and a few months later the *Chronicle* was appealing for donations to aid Burt's union in opposition to an employers' lock-out. (48) The producer co-operatives formed between 1871-73 were decimated in 1874-75. Even the pride of producer co-operation on Tyneside, the Ouseburn Engineering Works, collapsed. Rutherford's poor management of the concern had not helped, raising another speculative "might-have been":

> "With Joseph Cowen instead of Dr. Rutherford at the helm, any co-operative ventures into the field of production might well have stood a chance of success. Experience and confidence would have been allied to ambition, instead of which ambition was dashed on the rocks of business incompetence." (49)

Again, whether Cowen's participation in the Ouseburn Works would have made a difference remains an untested theory. Cowen's final part in the saga was to assist Rutherford financially, repeating a familiar role he had played already in relation to Holyoake, W.J. Linton and many other people when they were down on their luck. (50)

From the mid-1870s the economic foundations of the "militant democracy" were weakened in a winnowing process which enhanced cautious and less radical tendencies. The co-operative movement retained an interest in co-operative production but the experience of the 'seventies disposed co-operators to concentrate on their retail societies whose stronger financial base withstood the icy blasts of recession. Co-operators limited their aims to maintaining dividends and in the north east kept away from grandiose schemes for many years. The same trend could be found among trade unionists who achieved their own settlement with capitalist society through a closer relationship with the Liberal Party. Thomas Burt, MP, for example, discovered he did not really have a "strong prejudice against the Whigs" after all, and in Cowen's absence also led the Northern Reform League into an alliance with the supposedly anti-Whig Gladstone in January 1875; opportunism was in vogue. (51) A pattern of compromise was set in the second half of the 1870s shaping north eastern labour political attitudes for much of the rest of the century. One implication was that the eventual capture:

> "by the mining unions of several parliamentary divisions, meant
> in practice not the election of any very subversive figures, but
> the despatch to Westminster of reforming figures of society's
> established order." (52)

While Cowen was confined by ill-health, his "militant democracy" was dying.

During the period of "might-have-beens" Cowen did manage a few commitments at Westminster. He made his first House of Commons speech on 25 February 1875 in a debate on the Friendly Societies Bill, arguing that the working classes suffered great discrimination due to the inequitable distribution of power and wealth and required friendly societies, co-operatives and trade unions as counter-balancing collective organisations. The following July he helped the Amalgamated Society of Engineers to lobby the government for repeal of the Criminal Law Amendment Act. (53) But in March 1876 Cowen finally made his presence felt. Disraeli produced a Royal Titles Bill conferring the title of Empress of India upon Queen Victoria. The Bill was a gesture towards popularising both empire and monarchy yet ran into a storm of criticism. An opportunity was offered for the disorientated Liberal opposition to unite in an onslaught on the government.

And at the end of a debate characterised by the usual parliamentary formalities Joseph Cowen intervened, creating an atmosphere approaching melodrama. Breaking the convention barring further contributions after those of the Prime Minister and the Leader of the Opposition, Cowen made a short but emotive speech striking at the irrelevance of the Bill, the "superstition" of monarchy and warning that imperial titles were often associated with despotism. He insisted there was no support for the title among Indians who "despised" their English rulers and on whom the Bill was an "imposition". (54) The speech made Cowen's reputation as one of "the highest rank of parliamentary orators." (55) It was widely seen as "one of the most unqualified triumphs which parliament has ever witnessed", (56) and copies were circulated in conjunction with the numerous protest meetings. Spence Watson, chairing a meeting in Newcastle, congratulated Cowen on his "true English oratory" and for ending "those six months of silence, when he was looked upon as a man who had been misestimated by his native town." (57) Cowen's speech nevertheless had a broader significance since it was considered:

> "to be the great success of that session, indicating that a new Radical star was rising rapidly, and encouraging hope among some Radicals that he might assume their leadership...it appeared possible that the energy and organising power which the diverse forces of Radicalism so badly needed might be supplied by Joseph Cowen." (58)

Contempories thought it "certain" Cowen would become "not merely the most popular but the most powerful Radical in the House of Commons", (59) and "the lead is practically in the hands of Mr. Cowen." (60) For Cowen the speech represented a welcome personal achievement: "My old confidence has nearly returned. I am not now so nervous as I was." (61)

The uproar surrounding the Royal Titles Bill pinpointed Cowen as the coming leader of Radicalism. But it was more difficult to build on these expectations in Parliament than in the meeting rooms of Tyneside. At Westminster, Cowen was the outsider. His "rough northern accent" was seen as a "personal disadvantage" even though he "clung to it as one of the most precious of his possessions." (62) Disraeli listened to Cowen's speech and claimed he "did not understand the tongue in which the speech was delivered." (63) Other MPs "thought Cowen was speaking in Latin." (64) To this problem of communication, part real and part probably invented by Westminster condescension, Cowen made no allowances. A "genuine Tynesider", Cowen exhibited a pride in the language and culture of the north east, projected it incessantly through the pages of the *Chronicle* and carried it flamboyantly to London. (65) He also held a deep suspicion of metropolitan politics. Cowen had been irritated by the London Radicals' failure to match the aims and single-mindedness of the Northern Reform Union in 1859, and angrily rejected the London-based Reform League's description of the Northern Reform League as its "North Eastern Department (Newcastle)" in 1867. (66) The *Chronicle's* fight with W.H. Smith in 1864 had underscored Cowen's fierce northern independence, defending "the rights and liberties of the Newcastle press" against the London monopolist. In the same year Cowen had written privately to Holyoake saying he was "heartily sick" of metropolitan intrigues over Garibaldi's expulsion and "had grounds of complaint against some of our London friends." (67) Added to this "distance" between Cowen and London politics was the complication of William Ewart Gladstone.

Gladstone censured Cowen's Royal Titles Bill speech as "smelling of the lamp." (68) The two men did not like each other and, on Cowen's eventual arrival at the House, Gladstone had snubbed him. According to some commentators, the slight was an "accident" and "unintentional". (69) Cowen took the incident badly, telling his daughter "Gladstone had always been very cruel to him." (70) The prickly reaction (possibly exaggerated by the effects of illness) was taken by some to be "the beginning of an estrangement with the Liberals" (71) and indicative of Cowen's "vanity, jealousy, disappointment" (72) or "hatred". (73) Convenient though these personal explanations may have been to Cowen's Liberal critics there was a political cause at the root of the hostility between Cowen and Gladstone. Cowen had been doubtful about Gladstone since at least 1859. Gladstone had not been a strong supporter of extending the suffrage and Cowen had needed reassuring about Gladstone's intentions in proposing a visit to Newcastle. (74) When Gladstone did go to Tyneside in October 1862 it was Cowen who organised an elaborate public reception (75) - only to see Gladstone abuse the occasion by lauding the Confederate slave-states. Then there was Gladstone's mysterious interference in Garibaldi's 1864 visit, and it was Gladstone again who led the disappointing Liberal government of 1868-74. Despite all this, Gladstone enjoyed enormous prestige among Liberals, so Cowen was not above trading on the great man's name in order to confuse "moderate" Liberals and therefore "praised Gladstone." By identifying with Gladstone, Cowen could claim the support of the whole Liberal Party "but he frequently advocated that which Gladstone would not or could not give." (76) The frenzy unleashed by Dilke's republican speech at Newcastle in 1871 unquestionably made Gladstone take notice of Cowen. This meant that when Cowen appeared at Westminster "he found that he was not acceptable to the Front Bench Olympians" not just because of what had happened to the luckless Headlam but due to:

> "a feeling that he might prove more dangerous if the party took him to its bosom than if he were left on the extreme wing. A friend of Anarchists and Fenians, a republican to boot, however brilliant and influential in his own district might be a very uncomfortable fellow-passenger on the voyage back to office."
> (77)

Gladstone - and John Bright who "rudely and grossly insulted" Cowen (78) - were prepared in advance to keep the Tyneside "Red" at arms-length.

The possibility that Cowen might lead a new Radical grouping depended on the presence of a handful of MPs whom, it was thought, shared a common outlook. Press reports in April 1876 envisaged "a distinct Radical Party - an extreme Left" being formed with Cowen as leader. (79) This small, select band included Cowen, Joseph Chamberlain, Sir Charles Dilke, Thomas Burt and, outside Parliament, the journalist John Morley. (80) Known as the "New Party" the little group held meetings and discussions but found differences tended to outweigh areas of agreement. Cohesion was doomed due to the "inability of Chamberlain and Cowen to agree on anything." (81) This was hardly surprising. Chamberlain was "the first "professional" politician" (82) in the sense that he looked to a combination of programmes, party organisation, plotting and a political career. His alter ego was John Morley, a man beset by personal ambition shrouded in intellectual high-mindedness. Periodically, Morley cherished hopes of becoming an MP for Newcastle (and other places) and once excitedly boasted to Chamberlain how his prospects had brightened by gaining the confidence of Robert Spence Watson's wife through "the spirituality of my conversations." (83) Chamberlain and Morley were a thoroughly detestable duo full of "contempt" for other Radicals who might "threaten their own speedy advancement." They were mainly interested in "concentrating the representation of Radicalism, at the highest levels of the government, in their own hands." (84) And neither of them regarded the working class as central to social reform and democracy. Chamberlain acknowledged the need for "a more generous recognition of the claims of the masses" but, at heart, he was more interested in Nonconformism and the personal exercise of power. (85) Morley had opposed franchise reform out of a fear of the "destruction the sleeping giant of the working class electorate might wreak", and believed in rule by an educated elite (or, put another way, rule by Chamberlain and Morley) to compensate for "the indigenous intellectual laziness of the majority." (86)

This was anathema to Joseph Cowen whose politics were grounded in popular movements, a keen commitment to working class education and the proletarian "militant democracy". Whereas Chamberlain and Morley envisaged political development as a process directed and controlled from "the top", Cowen came from a Radical tradition in which "the people" gained reforms and liberties by action from "below". Cowen also still owed a lot to the revolutionary ideals of Mazzini and it was probably this influence rather than vanity or an inability to work with others that "made him stand somewhat alone in Parliament." (87) Racked by these quite fundamental divergences, the "New Party" rapidly fell apart. Cowen left and Chamberlain excluded Burt whose interest was slight anyway. (88) The gulf between Cowenite popular Radicalism and "machine" politics widened as Chamberlain turned to constructing a National Liberal Federation in 1877 with the aim of extending caucus power even more widely. Deliberately, Chamberlain cultivated the support of Gladstone and Spence Watson for the Federation but "ignored" Cowen. (89)

Cowen found Parliament a bleak environment. In spite of poor health he actively participated in parliamentary business, voting in 232 divisions out of 240 in the 1876 session and 242 out of 314 in 1877, (90) although he "rarely took part in the give-and-take of Committee work" at this time. (91) He felt the slow pace of parliamentarianism and the general atmosphere was frustrating and unproductive. A comment he made in 1883 could apply with equal force to his impressions in 1876-79:

> "A member of a municipal board sees the consequences of his work ... If the literary man writes a book, or the artist paints a picture, or the journalist produces matter for a newspaper, he

has the results before him ... But if a man labours in Parliament
... he would see little result from this work. It is this sense of
sterility and incompetence that chafes against eager and earnest
men." (92)

By 1878 Cowen decribed being an MP as "a perfectly useless
occupation" and one he would like to "quit". "It was" he wrote, "the
worst thing I ever did to come to the House of Commons." (93) A
few months later he noted that he had "lost" much of his "old
political fervour." (94)

Cowen's view was no doubt informed by the depressive aspects of
ill-health and in the context of a Tory Parliament and the changes
affecting Liberalism and Radicalism it was easy to slip into gloom.
A more balanced analysis of Cowen's record after the Royal Titles
speech, on the other hand, reveals interesting features. Cowen was
not so "isolated" as has often been suggested. (95) He remained very
close to Thomas Burt and the two MPs went together to the
Commons daily "as if it were their business office, and remained
until the close." (96) Burt, as one of the first "labour" Members, was
another outsider on the Westminster scene and shared Cowen's
pronounced north east cultural identity. A further set of outsiders
with whom Cowen developed a strong relationship was the Irish
Home Rule Party. He established a warm connection with the Irish
MPs through fulfilling his 1874 election pledge to press for the
release of Fenian prisoners. This was a major issue on Tyneside and
one capable of attracting vast crowds to demonstrations (30,000
attended an amnesty rally on Newcastle's Town Moor in October
1872, for example). (97) Cowen was apparently on good terms with
the Fenians around Blaydon (98) and even in May 1874 he had
written in support of the amnesty campaign. (99) Cowen's next
substantial contribution to a parliamentary debate after the Royal
Titles row was on the question of the Fenian prisoners. O'Connor
Power, MP, proposed an amnesty for the Fenians on 1 August 1876
and Cowen became the first English MP to argue in favour of the
Irish motion. Cowen told the House "it was not sufficient that the
only protest ... should come from Irish representatives", and
compared the Fenians with the Polish insurrectionists of 1831. The
Poles, he pointed out, had "attempted to do for their country what
the Fenians attempted to do for Ireland" and whereas the British
government had rewarded the Poles with refugee funds the Irish had
received "persecution". This position was well in advance of Liberal

thinking, which usually suppressed any comparison between Irish and European nationalists, and signified a shift taking Cowen considerably nearer to the Irish cause. (100) The amnesty proposal was heavily defeated but in April 1877 Cowen joined Parnell, the emerging leader of the Irish party, in an attempt to win official recognition for "political prisoners" in British gaols. Cowen maintained that "repressive and arbitrary" martial law in Ireland meant "every man's liberty was at the mercy of an ignorant police constable" and political prisoners were the product of this oppression. He took the opportunity to expand the case against English double standards reminding Gladstone, whose strictures on Italian political prisons were well-known but who had refused to release all the Fenians when he was Prime Minister: "It was easy to see the defects of other people's characters and modes of procedure; but it was not quite so easy to discover the shortcomings of their own." (101) Gladstone was not convinced.

Two weeks later, Cowen and Parnell were again busy. Parnell moved a reduction in the government's allocation for the secret services on the grounds that ministers refused to disclose information about secret service activities in Ireland. Cowen supported Parnell's motion, arguing the money was

> "paid to spies and informers, who went among the people, misled the innocent, excited them to insurrection and then gave evidence against them."

He alleged that informers had been used to imprison the Fenians in much the same "way in which this money was spent during the Chartist movement." (102) Parnell and Cowen lost but Cowen did enjoy two victories in 1879. His "decisive support", coupled with an "eloquent and ingenious" speech, managed to secure the repeal of the Conventions Act which had prohibited the convening of any elected assembley in Ireland. (103) The second success was linked with Parnell's bid to abolish flogging in the British Army in June 1879. A "secret committee" to orchestrate the campaign against flogging was formed composed of Cowen, Alexander McDonald, the miners' MP, and the Irish Member, F.H. O'Donnell

> "inside the House, and certain workmen leaders, notably the London Trades Council, outside the House ... to study public opinion, and excite it; to prolong discussion and procrastinate decision, whip-up recruits and suggest hostilities ..."

Cowen used the *Chronicle* to expose the use of the "cat" against private soldiers - "workmen's brothers and workmen's sons" - in contrast to officers who were left untouched. At a crucial stage he threatened to pay for placards to be posted in the constituencies of MPs who voted to continue flogging (showing each MP "in a cartoon in the act of flogging a British soldier"). A public outcry was generated and a gleeful Cowen told the "secret committee": "We might go to any lengths now, that the workmen would throw the colonels into the Thames if the "cats" were not thrown there first." (104) The campaign was partially successful and marked the beginning of the end of flogging in the army and navy.

Cowen's "consistent sympathy for the demands of the Irish Home Rulers" (107) from 1876 hardly helped to resolve worsening tensions with the Liberals. It was obvious by 1877 that he was deeply alienated from Liberalism and not least from the "advanced Liberalism" projected by Chamberlain and, in the words of Cowen's journalist friend Weymss Reid, "the mere machine men, the intriguers and the wire-pullers" of the National Liberal Federation. (106) Cowen had "old-fashioned notions of the duties of an independent member." He believed MPs should be left to reach judgements according to their own principles and saw in the caucus a cliquish ambition to dictate to elected representatives. Having experienced the problems of holding to his own convictions in Parliament, he became concerned that the rise of the local caucus might be used by the Liberal Party's national leaders as a mechanism to cut him adrift from popular support existing beyond the party organisation. (107) Moreover, the behaviour of Spence Watson and the Newcastle Liberal Association was beginning to give practical shape to Cowen's fears. A "quarrel" between Cowen and the Newcastle caucus "began in earnest" in 1877. (108) Cowen was invited to preside over a meeting of the Newcastle Liberal Association in February 1877 and from the chair advised the organisation to restrict itself to political education. Spence Watson had other ideas and encouraged the meeting to build an electoral machine. (109) Relations between Cowen and the caucus cooled considerably after February especially as the MP's disaffection with Liberalism became more apparent. Speaking in the Commons on 14 June, Cowen carefully described himself "as an English Radical" rather than a Liberal. (110) In December he went to Manchester and delivered a stinging rebuke to caucus tendencies, concerned "more about the machinery than the purpose which the machinery is intended to subserve." (111) Back in Newcastle the caucus launched "a merciless opposition to Cowen" setting

> "itself up as a sort of Holy Inquisition with the mission of watching every word that fell ... The most unfriendly construction for him was invariably placed upon them before the electors." (112)

The caucus's choosen courtroom for a public trial of Cowen's disloyalty was the convoluted and absorbing Eastern Question of 1876-78. Gladstone initially helped to give the topic prominence in Britain when he sensed that the Turkish Ottoman Empire's brutal repression of its Christian subjects in south eastern Europe (the "Bulgarian Atrocities") contained the potential for raising a popular agitation. (113) With the benefit of hindsight it can be seen that the Bulgarian agitation was the start of Gladstone's attempt to regain the leadership of the Liberal Party, relinquished to the Whig, Lord Hartington, in 1875, and drive Disraeli (now Lord Beaconsfield) from office. Over the summer and autumn of 1876, Gladstone stomped the country fuelling moral indignation about the atrocities and pressing the reticent Tory government to intervene against Turkey. Matters were complicated in April 1877 when Russia declared war on Turkey and the ferment ignited by Gladstone was turned into a call to permit the Czar a free hand in destroying the Ottoman Empire. Beaconsfield judged differently and regarded Turkey as a buffer preventing any Russian designs on the Suez canal and ultimately India. The Tories concocted a frenzy of imperial "jingoism" (the word dates from this period) and in 1878 mobilised the army and navy to warn-off the Russians. The domestic implications of this Great Power diplomacy and its inherent danger of war between Britain and Russia were breathtaking. Gladstone and his supporters ranted furiously against secret diplomacy and the absence of moral scruples in Beaconsfield's foreign policy. This was a little odd. Gladstone's own record in government had not been unblemished. As Cowen reminded the Grand Old Man during a heated argument, Gladstone had not shown any outstanding moral dispositon in relation to American slavery. (114) And Cowen could have recalled his own condemnation of Gladstone's last Liberal government for trying to spread "commerce and propagate Christianity" at "the mouth of a cannon, or at the point of a bayonet" in the 1873-74 Ashanti War. (115) The Eastern Question blotted everyone's reputation. The Liberals failed to present a united front, with Hartington supporting the Tories' military preparations. Cowen was also caught in the confusion, lending extravagant support to Beaconsfield in speeches of anti-Czarist purple prose. (116) By appearing to "go over" to the Tories, Cowen supplied the pro-Gladstone Newcastle caucus with its opportunity.

Cowen was pursued remorselessly by Spence Watson and the caucus for his sympathy towards Beaconsfield's apparent protection of Turkey. But Cowen was by no means an admirer of the decaying Ottoman Empire. He held the opinion of numbers of old Radicals like W.J. Linton that "the Turkish regime was doomed." (117) Cowen's preference was for reform in Turkey - undertaken by radical Turks and not Czarist armies - and "the creation of three independent states, Latin, Greek and Schlav along the Danube and the Balkans." He told Spence Watson: "I don't see how helping Russia will do this." (118) Anti-Czarism was the prime reason for Cowen's attraction to Beaconsfield's strategy, and an element of "bitter personal hatred" for Gladstone alleged by Charles Dilke may also have been involved. (119) However, Cowen genuinely believed the "worn out barbarism" of the Ottomans was less dangerous than the Czar's "new and active forces of organised slavery." (120) He outlined his considered position in a poignant letter to the *Newcastle Daily Chronicle* in January 1878. In the letter Cowen stated the British government's policy was "fair and temperate" and he refused to join in the "cry of national bitterness against the Russian or Turk." He also found it strange that Liberals could support Russia and "forget Siberia and Poland, and the sorrows that cluster around those names ... Poland and Hungary revive for me sad memories that time cannot efface." (121) The caucus may have questioned Cowen's loyalty to the Liberalism of the moment but Cowen remained loyal to older causes now deserted by the Gladstonians. During the Eastern Question Cowen renewed contact with Polish exiles in Newcastle and looked at the crisis through the eyes of those who had fought Czarist despotism in eastern Europe for fifty years. (122) This was certainly not a rash of Russophobia for which Cowen has frequently been accused, (123) but he was always clear that the real enemy was Czarism as a system:

> "Bribery, bayonets, banishment are the triple pillars upon which their politico-military-ecclesiastical system stands ... an aggressive, military, ecclesiastical autocracy [bringing] dangers

to human freedom, peace and civil progress." (124)

Cowen's antagonism towards Gladstone, and possibly the effects of illness, combined in the crisis to stimulate Cowen's latent imperialism. He made outlandish statements in the heat of parliamentary debates on the Eastern Question - "I will trust my own countrymen, whatever their politics, before the statesmen of either Russia or Germany" - afterwards expressing regret for his choice of words. (125) The same Cowen whose *Chronicle* in 1872 described the British Empire in Asia as "a pile of betrayed and slaughtered nations" seething with justified rebellion, (126) supported the British invasion of Afghanistan in 1879. And he told a Newcastle audience in January 1880 that the Empire had a mission:

> "to carry to distant countries and succeeding ages the loftiest form of civilisation ... Power so vast was never wielded with so sincere a desire to use it beneficially. Every tribe we touch acknowledges our supremacy, and looks to us either in conscious fear of weakness, or with brightening hope of participating in our elevation." (127)

Under their skins most Liberals believed the same appalling nonsense. But in the closing years of the 1870s caucus expediency pretended to take a different position for party advantage and a drive for power.

"In 1874 he would give up Gibraltar, in 1880 he hugs Cyprus to his heart", claimed a biting anti-Cowen pamphlet published in 1880 and entitled: *Mr. Cowen - apostle or apostate?* Written by James Annand (or, possibly, W.T. Stead), the widely circulated attack drew John Bright's approval as an exposure of Cowen's "treason to his party." (128) Annand was important in the caucus's war with Cowen because he had been editor of the *Newcastle Daily Chronicle* until 1877. Cowen and Annand spent May of that year at loggerheads over the Eastern Question. While the editor's leading articles advocated intervention against Turkey, Cowen used the paper's "London Letter" column to convey his own position. Such a sharp division involving editor and proprietor could be resolved only in Cowen's favour. Following an illness, Annand took a strong hint from Cowen and resigned. W.E. Adams was left free to relate a Gladstonian line, albeit less effusive than Annand's, in the *Weekly*

Chronicle. (129) The caucus, meanwhile, tried to set up a rival paper, the *Echo*, on Tyneside in April 1879. This posed no threat to the *Chronicle* but a more serious challenge emerged in the form of the *Northern Echo* edited at Darlington by W.T. Stead. An accomplished journalist, Stead was also a eulogist of Russia and the more so from 1877 when he joined forces with a notorious Czarist agent in London, Madame Novikoff (in whom Gladstone also took a keen interest). Under Stead's direction the *Northern Echo* became the voice of Gladstonian Liberalism in the north east so far as the Eastern Question was concerned. It was Stead who helped promote a subtle piece of anti-semitism about Cowen (anti-Jewish prejudices were prevalent in Radical circles in this period), writing "people used often to ask me whether the Russophobist Joseph Cowen of the Newcastle *Chronicle* was not really a Cohen" engaged in "race-sympathy" for the Turks. (130) Relationships deteriorated on all sides. Thomas Burt joined Spence Watson and the caucus on the Eastern Question, and Holyoake considered Cowen's views on foreign policy "utterly disastrous." (131) At Westminster, Gladstone was now referring to Cowen as his "hon. Friend, the Member for Newcastle - if I may still call him so", and Cowen was so completely absorbed in rebutting Gladstone that on one occasion he crushed G.O. Trevelyan's top hat with a clenched fist and did not even notice. (132)

Cowen and the caucus stoked their differences to a crescendo in the autumn of 1879 as a general election loomed. The caucus adopted Ashton Dilke, younger brother of Sir Charles Dilke, as their candidate to challenge Charles Hamond. Dilke possessed some Radical credentials which made it less likely that Cowen would refuse to work with him (Cowen had already undermined Spence Watson's previous choice, the Whig and anti-Home Rule Albert Grey). (133) But the caucus had not consulted Cowen about their choice and expected him to accept a joint election committee or, put another way, caucus control over the election campaign and policy. Cowen was not so easily ensnared. Determined not to give way to the caucus he embarked on a theatrical show of strength. In September he brought Hartington, the party leader, to speak in Newcastle. As the first visit by a national leader of the Liberal Party since before 1874, Hartington represented a coup for Cowen even if the choice was slightly bizarre. Cowen was an ultra-Radical and Hartington a dyed-in-the-wool Whig. At least they both disliked the

Gladstonians, and the visit conferred a certain status on Cowen. It also had the added advantage of displaying the party leader who had vehemently opposed the formation of the National Liberal Federation and who agreed to a degree with Cowen's approval of Beaconsfield's 1878 mobilisation. On the minor deficit side, Hartington rejected the obstructive parliamentary tactics of Cowen's friends among the Irish MPs. (134) Cowen next organised a vast public rally at Newcastle's town hall for 8 November. He used this meeting to criticise the Liberals for lacking firm commitments to both social reform and Irish Home Rule and he called for popular agitation to force the Tories out of office. The evening ended with an overwhelming vote of confidence in Cowen's record as an MP. (135) Three days later Cowen chaired a Newcastle Irish public meeting addressed by Arthur Sullivan, MP, who praised Cowen's assistance to the Irish cause: "it would be a hopeful day for Ireland when Joseph Cowens were multiplied in the House of Commons." Cowen noted with irony that he and the Irish MPs disagreed "frequently" but he had discovered "Irishmen did not object to men who differed with them (Hear, hear and laughter)." (136)

Cowen made sure the caucus received his message face-to-face. On 3 December he spoke at a Liberal gathering in North Shields. Opening the proceedings the chairman described the local organisation of the caucus in affectionate detail. The rest of the evening was overshadowed by Cowen's swingeing onslaught on the evils of the caucus system. He hammered a familiar complaint that the caucus had elevated a dispute on one aspect of foreign policy into a great issue of party loyalty. There should be room for disagreement, Cowen argued, affirming he was "more concerned for Liberal principles than for the Liberal Party." Neatly outflanking "caucus democracy", Cowen declared that real democracy would be achieved only when shorter parliaments and payment of MPs were introduced and the right to vote granted to all working men. Finally, he called on the working classes to act on their own, ignore the Liberal Party and take "the management of their own business into their own hands (Cheers)." (137)

The Newcastle caucus and the National Liberal Federation were dumbfounded. At a stroke Cowen was setting a new agenda for Radicalism, rekindling something like the spirit of the "militant democracy". His popularity on Tyneside meant the Liberals still needed him more than he needed them. (138) By good fortune he also stumbled across an "indiscretion" committed by the Newcastle Liberal Association in January 1880. The caucus had quietly resolved to regard Cowen as "a colleague" of Ashton Dilke. When the *Chronicle* exposed this attempt to subordinate Joseph Cowen in his native town to an unknown outsider, Cowen's supporters had a field day. Cowen threatened to retire and a public meeting was hurriedly called to give the Liberals a chance of begging him to seek re-election on his own terms and pull Dilke into Parliament on the Cowenite coat-tails. Even Gladstone had to visit Newcastle to repair the damage done by caucus ineptitude. Cowen therefore entered the 1880 general election unhindered by the caucus. Against this excited background, Cowen and Ashton Dilke were to address a joint public meeting at Newcastle's town hall on 19 March. As Cowen tried to make his way to the platform the movement of the crowd numbering "thousands" crushed him and he fainted. There followed twenty-six days of drugged sleep and speculation as to whether Cowen would live or die. Already under renewed nervous strain before the accident, Cowen's new injuries immobilised him completely for the rest of the election, but he once more topped the poll well ahead of Dilke and the now defeated Hamond. (139)

CHAPTER TEN : "THE MINISTRY OF COERCION"

"There are to be witnessed in Ireland" Joseph Cowen told the House of Commons in August 1880, "scenes of wretchedness and squalor such as it would be difficult to match in any country in the West of Europe." He was speaking with authority, having visited Ireland "more than once during the last few months" to investigate "upon the spot some of the causes of the dire distress that afflicts the people." (1) Cowen's membership of the Royal Commission on Land Tenure in Ireland had enabled him to see the desperate conditions created by the agricultural depression of 1879. The experience had a mesmerising effect and Cowen dragged himself back to Dublin within three months of being injured in Newcastle. (2) By now Ireland was in the grip of the Land War or a mass resistance to evictions led by Michael Davitt's Land League using the "boycott". Britain was back in the grasp of Gladstone and a Liberal government. Cowen was at first optimistic, believing the Liberals meant "to deal" with Ireland "in a vigorous and radical manner" through remedial measures. (3) Instead, Gladstone quickly surrendered to pressures from landlords in Ireland and the English authorities at Dublin Castle and acted to suppress the Land League. A Coercion Bill, or fresh set of repressive laws to "pacify" Ireland, was proposed. Along with the Irish MPs, Cowen's reaction was swift and alarmed:

> "Another Coercion Bill! that meant the fifth or sixth occasion on which the constitution had been suspended in half-a-century. They had been discussing for hours together, [in Parliament] whether the Irish people could most mercifully be shot down by bullets or buckshot." (4)

Within months the fears of the anti-coercionist MPs (mainly the Irish, now headed by Parnell, and a handful of English Members) were confirmed. Having failed to convict Parnell and the leadership of the Land League for seditious conspiracy at Dublin, the British government introduced a Bill on 24 January 1881 conferring sweeping powers on the colonial officials to arrest anyone they "reasonably suspected." The usually bland anonymity of *Hansard* was broken by the furious debates on the Coercion Bill. *Hansard's* editors prefaced their account with an apology for possible inaccuracies: "the greatest excitement and confusion prevailed" throughout the proceedings (5) as an heroic, eloquent and utterly doomed rearguard action was mounted by the Irish MPs and their allies to prevent the erosion of liberty. The debate simply on the Address announcing the Bill lasted for eleven sittings as the Irish Members spoke in relays often without sleep to delay the passage of the new law. When the government had Michael Davitt arrested at the beginning of February, the Parnellites' protests in the Commons brought their suspension from the House for that sitting. Most Radical MPs with the "exception of Joseph Cowen" found themselves in a dilemma between supporting a Liberal government and adhering to their principles. (6) There was no difficulty for Cowen. He was completely "ashamed" of the Liberal Party, seeing the arrest of Davitt as an example of double-standards on the part of Gladstone who, Cowen believed, would have been one of the first to complain if a European despot had done something similar. (7) During the struggle against the Coercion Bill "Cowen assumed the leadership of the opposition in Parliament" in a "moral or spiritual" sense, (8) so far as the English anti-coercionists (Charles Bradlaugh, Henry Labouchere, Alexander McDonald, Peter Taylor, E.T. Gourley, Thomas Burt and T.C. Thompson) were concerned. Cowen's public criticism of the government together with Bradlaugh's and Labouchere's speeches were also of real use to the Irish in the United States because they "deepened the American feeling that Ireland was being foully used." (9)

By speaking in opposition on every stage of the Coercion Bill Cowen went further than any of his English colleagues and, in some respects, took a different stand. Other Radicals, including Thomas Burt, opposed the Irish Party's obstruction of parliamentary business and were willing to tolerate Davitt's arrest and the attempted suppression of the Land League. (10) Cowen, in contrast, stood by Davitt and defended obstruction (in fact, in the previous Parliament Cowen had connived with the Irish Home Ruler, Joe Biggar, to test the obstruction tactic: they halted the proceedings of the Commons in order to have a "stranger" - the Prince of Wales - removed from the public gallery). Cowen bitterly fought Gladstone's "cloteur" - a change in parliamentary rules to bring debates to an end and prevent further Irish opposition - arguing the Irish MPs had a right to obstruct since "they were fighting a battle which was to them one of life and death." (11) He was almost howled down by English MPs.

But Cowen refused to be intimidated even by the "scores of threatening letters" sent from anonymous supporters of coercion offering to burn down his house and damage his businesses. (12) He pressed on as "a terrible thorn in the side of the Ministry", (13) condemning the Coercion Bill as placing "the liberties of the Irish people at the caprice of a prejudiced and perplexed police, a muddled magistracy, and a bewildered Government." English rule in Ireland, he said, "had been little else than a dreary record of starvation and agitation, conspiracy and insurrection, followed by brutal repression and reprisals." The government was assuming "despotic powers" and would go down in history as "the Ministry of Coercion." (14)

Cowen's stand won warm approval outside Parliament. His defiance was cheered at a Land League demonstration in Leeds. (15) And "the event of the evening" at an Anti-Coercion Association rally in Chelsea was the reading of a letter from Joseph Cowen describing the imprisonment of Michael Davitt as "the meanest and most cowardly act" undertaken by "an English Government in modern times." (16) Still fighting on through February, Cowen denounced the cloteur as "the establishment of a Dictatorship" and accused the Irish police of "a reign of terror." The Coercion Bill was a "nauseous draught" swallowed by the "mass of middle class Liberals" whereas Cowen was seeking to "sustain the honoured traditions of English Radicalism." In an oblique reference to caucus attitudes he stated a reality which most Liberal MPs did not want to hear:

> "According to the ethics of latter-day Liberalism, Coercion, when submitted by Tories, was a hateful and horrible enactment; but when proposed by a Liberal Administration, it was a beneficent provision for the protection of life and property." (17)

Cowen worked in concert with the Irish Parliamentary Party. In the middle of February, the anti-coercionists exposed government interception of the Irish MPs' mail. Cowen raised the allegation in the Commons on 17 February and the following day made public the fact that Irish Members were being watched by the police: "Detectives hung about their residences, followed them to the House of Commons, and were, at that moment, to be seen in the Lobby." (18) Later in the month he challenged silent ministers to deny they "had opened private letters, and subjected the freely chosen Representatives of the people to ... surveillance." (19) Cowen sought to counter the government's activities by "arranging to receive letters for Irish members under cover to himself", causing Morley to notice on a visit to Blaydon that Cowen's "letter bag ... was crammed with conspiracy." (20) Cowen also used his friendship with Hartington, now displaced as Liberal leader by Gladstone, to obtain "hints" about the cabinet's intentions which he then passed on to the Irish. (21) So the battle continued, long after the Coercion Act had been approved and employed to gaol organisers of the Land League across the west of Ireland. "A Liberal Parliament" observed Cowen, speaking above Liberal attempts to shout him down, "had handed over the liberties of the Irish people" to an "arbitrary magistracy, a vindictive police, and to that vilest of all created things, a political spy." But despite erecting "as arbitrary a mode of rule in Ireland as that which existed in Russia" the Coercion Act had "failed deservedly" (22) because the Land League had replaced its imprisoned organisers with fresh volunteers.

Faced with popular resistance to the Coercion Act, the Gladstone government turned to reform as a means of ending the Land War. A Land Bill was proposed to help tenants buy their farms. The measure was inadequate and Cowen, taking his cue from the Land League, argued the government "conceded nothing to Ireland from a sense of justice - only from force ... If there had been no Land League there would have been no Land Bill." (23) The real author of the aims of the Land Bill, Cowen insisted to an outraged House of Commons, was not an MP but a "convict", Michael Davitt, and his Irish agitation. (24) Tolerance of Cowen in the Commons almost reached breaking point in May 1881 when he was threatened with suspension. (25) Over the summer he kept up the pressure for the release of political prisoners. He visited Parnell who was detained in Kilmainham Gaol (26) and invited Davitt and other Irish leaders to write articles for the *Chronicle*. (27) Irish commentators felt Cowen's sympathy was "extraordinary" and "adored" him for defending Parnell's obstructionism and aiding the prisoners. What made Cowen's intense opposition to coercion more remarkable was his triumph of will over ever present bad health. The work and travelling connected with the Land Tenure Commission "had told seriously on his nervous system" (28) and he was suffering from frequent headaches. (29) The after-effects of the accident at the 1880 general election had also left him with "cardiac weakness". (30) In addition, Cowen's eyesight was deteriorating partly due to his refusal to wear spectacles. (31) By the spring of 1880 Cowen had complained to Holyoake "my eyes are so bad that I cannot write to you myself." (32) An acquaintance noted Cowen was "very ill" and "afraid of losing" his sight. (33) The late-night parliamentary sittings on the Coercion Bill meant that Cowen often went home "wearied and worn out." (34)

Cowen found support in the vibrant Irish movement on Tyneside. With over 54,000 Irish people in Northumberland and Durham by 1881, the Irish nationalist organisations enjoyed a huge base for their operations. Centred on the Irish Literary Institute formed at Newcastle's Portland Arms public house in 1871, Irish political and cultural activities had developed apace since the days of the Fenian scares. Most prominent Home Rulers visited Tyneside and Newcastle also produced several of the movement's leaders. John Barry, the skilful organiser of the Irish vote in Britain and subsequently an MP for County Wexford, T.M. Healey ("My brother and I owed much to Newcastle-on-Tyne") and Henry Campbell who became Parnell's secretary, all forged their political commitment on the Tyne. (35) Cowen could therefore pursue his "reckless courage" in advocating "a cause ... regarded with aversion or as disloyal, impracticable, visionary and perilous" (36) knowing he was not entirely alone. The Irish were apparently convinced Cowen was genuine and not an opportunist. This point was made both by Parnell's biographer, R.B. O'Brien:

> "We had influence in Cowen's constituency, but it was not our influence that weighed with Cowen. He would have voted for Home Rule anyway. He was thoroughly Irish in feeling",

and in a more recent independent study of the Irish in the north east:

> "Cowen had no vested interests in Ireland or the Irish nor did he act out of any self-interest for the Irish vote; He responded to what he believed to be purely democratic principles." (37)

It was from a discussion at the Newcastle Irish Literary Institute in 1880 that a local branch of the Land League was formed leading very quickly to the creation of a Northern Confederation of Land League branches. (38) In the panoply of nationalist politics Cowen appears to have been especially supportive of the League and Davitt.

Whilst happy to collaborate with the parliamentarian Parnell - "I believe him to be a thoroughly honest man" and a "very decent fellow ... frank and straightforward ... I have a very high regard for him" (39) - Cowen's political sympathies tended more towards the Socialist, Michael Davitt, and the League. Cowen believed the League was engaged in "something very like a social revolution", (40) and its objective of transferring land ownership from "the landlord class" to the tenants fitted with a central strand in his Radicalism. He campaigned ardently for Davitt's release, once again upsetting Queen Victoria, (41) and intimated to the Russian Anarchist Peter Kropotkin, an offer to place his own conspiratorial skills at the disposal of the Irish. (42) Davitt had other problems, too. In 1884, he visited Newcastle partly to thank Cowen "for all he did for me while I was in prison." At a public meeting in the town hall, Davitt was almost set upon by forty or fifty Fenians (apparently opposed to his downgrading of the armed struggle) and as they rushed the platform he "took out a revolver ... of the brightly polished or plated description" and "held it close to his side for about a couple of minutes" until the stewards restored order! (43)

The Land League evoked widespread enthusiasm in the north east, possibly explaining why Newcastle was chosen for the first conference of the National Land League of Great Britain on 29 August 1881. Joseph Cowen was a principal sponsor of this "Irish Convention". He directed the *Chronicle* to give the conference the treatment reserved for all significant national conferences held on Tyneside. A special free supplement to the *Newcastle Weekly Chronicle* was printed featuring a report of the Convention and the text of the Land Act. The Newcastle meeting adopted a constitution for the Land League in Britain and delegates from the League's branches elected Cowen to the executive committee along with a range of Irish leaders. But it was at a public meeting held at the close of the delegate assembly when Cowen - "the most conspicuous English supporter of the League" according to Davitt's biographer - came into his own. He was accorded equal prominence with the Irish MPs and was introduced as "one who had endeared himself to every Irish heart ... that real and grand Radical, Joseph Cowen." The audience went wild with "great cheering and waving of handkerchiefs" as Cowen rose to scorn yet again the imprisonment of Davitt. Cowen reiterated that Ireland could not rely on the Liberal government's sense of justice, only on "agitation" to force issues to the fore. The prison treatment of the Fenians had been the "most barbarous and inhuman" inflicted on political prisoners anywhere in western Europe and, Cowen declared: "If the Government cannot rule Ireland without coercion they are unfit to govern at all." In the vote of thanks to the speakers at the close of the meeting it was noted that "no other English Member in the House of Commons" could be "measured beside" Cowen and his contribution to the Irish cause. (44)

Gladstone's cabinet changed tactics. A secret agreement was concluded between Joseph Chamberlain and Parnell at Kilmainham Gaol in May 1882. It was agreed that the British government would release political prisoners and provide some financial assistance towards alleviating rent arrears among tenant farmers and that, in return, Parnell would assist the government's legislative programme and the Land League would call a halt to "agrarian crime" (revolt). Davitt was highly critical of the deal but the radicals in the national movement were momentarily powerless to constrain Parnell and his conservative nationalists. In any event, the "Kilmainham Compact" of 2 May looked like a substantial concession from the Liberals because the government's Irish ministers resigned in disgust. Any sense of "triumph", however, was extremely short-lived. Gladstone's new Irish minsters, Lord Frederick Cavendish and his under-secretary, Burke, were assassinated with amputating knives in Dublin's Pheonix Park on 6 May by disaffected terrorists. The murders destroyed Parnell's agreement and unleashed a torrent of anti-Irish fury in England. An immediate consequence was a further Coercion Bill. To remain firm to the Irish cause in the aftermath of the Pheonix Park murders was, in many respects, a supreme test of Cowen's commitment. Almost everybody else, Burt included, moved behind the 1882 Coercion Bill. Only Cowen (the sole English MP to speak against the Bill on its introduction into the Commons) (45) and the Durham MP, Thompson, stood out among the English Radicals. The new measure gave Dublin Castle unrestrained authority to abolish trial by jury, censor the press, ban public meetings and extend police surveillance and powers of arrest. Cowen fought the Bill clause by clause throughout June and July using all the "stirring oratory" at his disposal. (46) He and Thompson tried vainly to redirect attention to the deeper problems producing violence in Ireland and cautioned:

> "there had been murders as detestable and as dastardly, if not as
> daring, that had excited small comment and provoked little
> protest. Painful though these assassinations were, they did not
> constitute the most disturbing element of the situation." (47)

Cowen's opposition was brusquely dismissed by the government
- "We have become used to it" said one minister (48) - as was his
attempted censure of a government motion to suspend sixteen Irish
MPs in July to crush obstructionism. (49) At Newcastle, James
Annand reappeared with a critical pamphlet entitled *A Plain Letter
to Mr. Cowen* attacking Cowen's pro-Irish views: "On the morrow of
the assassination of Lord Frederick Cavendish you apologised for
the assassins." (50) Undaunted, Cowen kept on - "We are fighting
the Coercion Bill against heavy odds, and with little encouragement"
(51) - confiding to Kropotkin:

> "There are only five and twenty or thirty of us ... We have
> constantly to be on the watch to keep the opposition going. I do
> not talk much, as the Irishmen are loquacious enough
> themselves; but I have to do their work, which is just as
> onerous." (52)

Inside Parliament the atmosphere was full of hatred. Parnell was
shunned by John Bright, Chamberlain and all the other prominent
Radical leaders except Cowen. (53) Gladstone, Cowen suspected,
probably understood the need for reform but was imprisoned by the
frenzied "condition of Parliament and the temper of the country."
(54) This brought Cowen to conclude "the Grand Old Man has
made a grand mess of things" (55) and, in June, he wrote to the
Newry branch of the Land League saying "the English Liberals" had
"turned their backs on the principles they professed." (56)

Cowen had really broken with the Liberal Party. Shortly before
the 1880 general election he declined to be "a conventional adherent
of the fashionable Liberalism of the hour" concerned with "the
transfer of the offices of State from one set of men to another."
Instead he again proclaimed himself "a life-long Radical by
conviction, sympathy, training and taste." (57) Following re-election,
Cowen formally withdrew from the Newcastle Liberal Association in
September 1880 taking a third of the membership with him. (58)
The departure was not difficult because he considered the Liberals
a party "he had never been much in sympathy for - it just happened
there were certain points on which they were agreed." (59) And

Ireland, where Cowen was "five years ahead" of the Liberals, (60) confirmed his opinion that there were fewer points of agreement as time went on. Although he was prepared in 1881 to co-operate with the Liberals on a programme of radical reform (61) he rejected the persistent Liberal demands to acquiesce with the government's Irish policy, telling the Junior Liberal Club:

> "I do not wish you or your friends to have any doubts as to my intentions. I mean to oppose the Coercion Bill on every occasion and at every point by all the resources in my power." (62)

Relationships were not improved when Cowen wrote in the Parnellites' *Freeman's Journal* in November 1881 that the Liberals had committed "many mean and arbitrary acts ... in the enforcement of their hated coercion edicts." (63) Not long afterwards, Ashton Dilke who had voted for coercion tried to hold a public meeting in Newcastle and was barracked by Irish nationalists and Cowenites apparently to give him an experience of coercion. The names of Parnell and Cowen were chanted by the audience for fifty minutes until Dilke and the cream of the Liberal caucus abandoned the meeting. The *Chronicle* regretted Dilke had been denied a hearing but went to considerable lengths in excusing what had happened. (64)

Joseph Cowen was also cultivating other friendships. He spent time with Eleanor Marx in 1880, probably discussing Ireland, (65) and was on good terms with her father. In February 1881, Karl Marx and Cowen exchanged letters with Cowen enquiring after Marx's health and offering to call "one Sunday morning" when the "present troubles in Parliament have somewhat subsided." (66) This was a time of adventurous schemes. Marx had been attempting to bring trade union leaders into closer contact with Radical politicians (67) and Cowen was again actively exploring independent working class politics. In January 1881 *The Radical* had started a campaign to create "a new Radical Party" and Cowen's name was put forward as a likely leader because he was less "shaky" than other Radicals. (68) A meeting of delegates from the London Radical Clubs then met in Soho, on 2 March 1881, and, envisaging the formation of "a powerful Democratic Party", they sent a deputation to Cowen, (69) who was considered "the obvious leader." (70) Cowen was involved in preparations for a founding conference on 5 March. He arranged a venue at London's Westminster Palace Hotel and offered to provide "facilities" for Marx to attend the meeting. Resolutions were endorsed to form "a new and independent working class party" or "labour party" to be known as the Democratic Federation, and a committee including Cowen was appointed to draft a political programme. Cowen, from the conference chair, "strongly condemned" the Liberal caucus system which had made "the present House of Commons the most slavish ever known." (71) Engels was greatly excited:

> "a proletarian-radical party is now forming under the leadership of Joseph Cowen, an old Chartist, half, if not a whole Communist, and a very fine fellow ... Ireland is bringing all this about, Ireland is the driving force." (72)

One of the first provincial branches of the Democratic Federation was formed at Newcastle against the background of a hectic Land League agitation in the Durham coalfield. And when the Land League Convention met in Newcastle, on 29 August 1881, H.M. Hyndman, a key figure in the formation of the Democratic Federation, was among those elected to the League's executive. (73)

Hyndman and Cowen shared some opinions - the Eastern Question for example - and their affinity carried over into the initial programme of the Democratic Federation. The Federation adopted the old demand for shorter parliaments. This had been the very first issue Cowen had raised following his re-election in 1880, arguing in the Commons that "cliques and caucuses" could be eliminated by stimulating the "political intelligence" of the people through "making elections frequent." (74) Yet Cowen withdrew from the Federation soon after the founding conference, prompting speculation about disagreements with Hyndman. Both men liked to have their own way and if Cowen could be "implacable", Hyndman was renowned for being "dictatorial". (75) Cowen may have "disliked the kind of personal leaderhip and discipline" Hyndman "imposed on the Federation", (76) and there were sharp differences between Cowen's Radicalism and Hyndman's Marxism. Cowen's attack on the caucus system at the Federation's founding meeting was counterposed by Hyndman's call for "a centre of organisation" to direct working class politics. (77) Hyndman's perspective prevailed, pushing the Federation to seek (overambitiously) "to rival Joseph Chamberlain's National Liberal Federation." (78) Cowen would not countenance powerful, permanent organisation especially if the organisation's aims did not match his own beliefs. A further problem therefore emerged in the shape of Cowen's distance from Marxism. Cowen was integrating phrases with a "Marxian ring" into his speeches, notably his criticisms of the reduction of employer-employee relations to a "cash nexus". (79) But Cowenite Radicalism was deeply attached to the concept of private property ownership and this was a key to understanding Cowen's interest in the Land League (which declined to endorse Davitt's advocacy of land nationalisation). As the Democratic Federation moved towards a Socialism embracing land and other nationalisation in May 1882, Cowen grew more alienated. Finally, Cowen's individualism (80) distanced him from the rigid "tablets of stone" interpretation of Marxism preferred by Hyndman, to Engels's continuing despair.

Cowen seems to have been more impressed by the Anarchists he was meeting in 1881. During May, Cowen participated in the defence of Johann Most, editor of the Anarchist newspaper *Freiheit*. Most had been arrested by the London police for publishing a justification of tyrannicide against the Czar. Cowen demanded to know whether Most's detention had been at the instigation of "any foreign government" and if his contact lists had been passed to the Austrian police and used to detain Socialists in Vienna? The British government remained tight-lipped. (81) Cowen's interest in the Anarchists intensified over the summer of 1881. Noticing Kropotkin's connection with an Anarchist conference in July, Cowen invited the Russian exile to write for the *Newcastle Daily Chronicle* on life under the Czar. Kropotkin, finding the English press largely echoed "the opinions of Madame Novikoff - that is of ... the Russian State Police - was most happy" to accept Cowen's offer. (82) The two men became friends, and Cowen wrote in 1882: "I like him [Kropotkin] very much. He seems a good fellow. He wants to be able to put his case before an English audience and I promised to secure him one at Newcastle." (83) Using his influence with the Durham miners, Cowen got Kropotkin on to a speakers' platform at the miners' Big Meeting in July 1882 where the Anarchist talked at length on Czarist oppression and, in an aside at coercion in Ireland, noted "that in the English dominions people are also imprisoned without being judged." (84) Two days later, in a blaze of *Chronicle* publicity, Kropotkin appeared at the traditional stamping ground of Tyneside Radicalism, Newcastle's Nelson Street Lecture Room, to expose the evils of the Czar. Greeted with "rounds of applause" he

lost no time in stressing the significance of his link with Cowen and
Newcastle:

> "It is in Newcastle that a Russian revolutionary writer has, for
> the first time, found the means of disclosing in an English daily
> paper, the true state of Russia; and it is, again, in Newcastle that
> I have found for the first time the honour of addressing a large
> English audience, to relate, in plain words, the true state of
> Russia." (85)

Cowen was unable to attend the Nelson Street meeting due to the
parliamentary fight over the new Coercion Bill. But he did write a
public letter of apology to Kropotkin accusing the British
government of "legislating against opinion" even though "the
experiences of your country could have shown them the folly and
fatuity of such a course." Cowen told Kropotkin: "You will find no
feeling anywhere in England against the Russian people. Why should
there be? Our enemy and yours is despotism." (86) Cowen kept in
close touch with Kropotkin, introducing him to Hyndman, (87) and
pressing for his release from a French prison in 1883 ("with little
hope of success"). (88) Languishing in Lyon gaol, Kropotkin "with
some surprise ... received in his cell an English friend who had come
with a message from another Englishman (probably Cowen) offering
to go bail for him." (89) Kropotkin was also sent copies of the
Newcastle Weekly Chronicle by Cowen. (90) In later years Cowen had
Kropotkin included as a speaker for the popular Sunday evening
lectures delivered at the Tyne Theatre and Opera House (William
Morris, Oscar Wilde and Sergey Stepniak also lectured at the
theatre). (91) And in 1895-97 the *Chronicle* assisted several of
Kropotkin's Anarchist comrades who established the briefly famous
Clousden Hill land colony on Tyneside. (92) But Russia was the
principal meeting point between Cowen and Kropotkin. Cowen was
not an Anarchist and in arguments over communist theories neither
Kropotkin nor Cowen convinced the other of their beliefs. (93) Even
so, there was a mutual sympathy for co-operatives and voluntary
associations, combined with an antipathy towards the state, implying
an affinity between Cowen's Radicalism and Kropotkin's Anarchism.

It is tempting to contemplate another "might-have-been". Could
Joseph Cowen have used his status to mould the Democratic
Federation in the image of his own politics? What would have
happened if Cowen rather than Hyndman had guided this "labour

party"? Would Engels's vision of a "proletarian-radical" party have been realised with Cowen at the helm? Along with the anti-climax of the "militant democracy" of 1871-74, this is arguably one of the tantalizing missed turning points of British history. Possibly Cowen was too preoccupied with the coercion laws and restrained by poor health to conquer the consuming intrigues of a small organisation. On the other hand, Cowen was wedded to the preservation of private property, qualified by his advocacy of co-operatives, and this ultimately divided him from Marx, Hyndman and Kropotkin. However, the separation was not so exclusive as to prevent collaboration between Cowen and the Marxists and Anarchists, particularly over Ireland. Cowen chaired a Democratic Federation demonstration at London's Hyde Park on 11 June 1882. The rally - "one of the largest held for political purposes in London for a long time" - had been called to protest against the Coercion Bill introduced following the Pheonix Park murders. An estimated 80,000 people gathered at Hyde Park, ignoring heavy rain, and heard Cowen carefully explain that the protest had been organised by an English and not an Irish movement. He went on to say that until the Irish Question had been settled there could be little progress with social reform in Britain. (94) In Newcastle the local branch of the Federation received substantial publicity from the *Chronicle* and Cowen is believed to have made financial donations to the party's newspaper, *Justice*. (95)

Cowen's interest in the Socialists and Anarchists was linked with an alteration in his perception of class over the years 1881-84. He had always recognised the extreme stratification of the working classes by trade and craft and had persistently drawn attention to the needs of the poorest segments of working class communities. Underpinning Cowen's attitude was a strand of essentially Mazzinian idealism equating "the people" (the working classes) with a passion for democracy, equality and liberty. This facet of Cowenism was present in the 1881 anti-coercion struggle. Thomas Burt complained to Cowen that "all the working men with whom he had come into contact" in Northumberland and Durham "much blamed" him for voting against coercion. (96) Agreeing that opinions were divided, Cowen was more optimistic, refusing to "believe that the English workman" would desert the principles at stake "whatever the English middle classes may do." (97) Cowen retained his contempt for the middle classes whom he saw as "ignorant of politics" with "little

knowledge of the poor, and a poor conception of the future."
Gladstone, wrote Cowen, "fairly represents them." (98) In the
summer of 1881 Cowen paid for a delegation of "three workmen" to
go to Ireland and "enquire into the condition of the people." (99)
Their report was published in the *Chronicle* and one of the
delegates, John Bryson, a former president of the Northumberland
miners, returned as a convinced sympathiser of the Land League
much to Burt's annoyance. (100) But the situation in 1881 was not
straightforward. There was a popular agitation in the Durham
coalfield in favour of the Land League yet a growing undercurrent
of impatience with Irish issues was evident. By the mid-1880s this
undercurrent had become more apparent in the north east:

> "apathy, indifference or annoyance at Irish politics could often
> be found among the working classes, there was also a
> conservative element that openly repudiated Irish claims ...
> Related to these opinions was the racism that could be easily
> provoked when trade declined." (101)

This conservatism of powerful groupings within the working class
began to worry Cowen over the summer and autumn of 1882. In
August he wrote to W.H. Patterson of the Durham Miners'
Association that he was astonished "how workmen have acquiesced"
in the government's "coercion policy." At a trade union meeting in
September he chastised union leaders for their "conventional and
deferential" and "complacent" outlook. Trade union officials, Cowen
believed, "would be more effective if they had more political grit in
their composition, and if there was more robustness in their bearing
towards those now in authority." (102) The following February
Cowen came close to orchestrating "more robustness" by appearing
to encourage the Democratic Federation to nominate a "labour
candidate" for a Newcastle parliamentary by-election caused by
Ashton Dilke's retirement. Cowen's name was cheered at the
Federation's demonstrations in the town and the party's members
held clandestine planning sessions at the *Chronicle* offices (gaining
access through the private entrance). (103) The newspaper gave
ample coverage to the proposed "labour candidate", Elijah Copland,
a wood-carver and friend of Joseph Cowen. Alarmed, the Liberal
caucus acted speedily to undermine Copland's candidature. A display
of hostility from Liberal trade union officials was organised and the
financial deposit required from candidates was set at a punitive £250
at very short notice. These manoeuvres coupled with Irish

uncertainty about Copland's degree of support from organised labour forced the abandonment of the Federation's candidacy.

Cowen continued to stimulate "class" issues throughout 1883. At a teachers' conference in March, he called for free state education and free food and clothing to enable children to attend school. (104) In May he angrily attacked a police purge on betting in Newcastle. Sixty-nine men and women were arrested in public houses and marched through the streets in an incident which briefly became a national *cause celebre*, especially when sixty-two of the accused were discharged by the magistrates. Cowen contrasted the police raid on Newcastle's Derby Day with the Epsom Races where royalty, MPs and government ministers openly gambled and were "petted and protected by the police." (105) At the end of the year he told a public meeting he believed the "working men" possessed "a progressive spirit and broad sympathies": "They should be something more than a link in the chain of machine politicians. They should be propagandists of noble principles." These sentiments were qualified, however, with an open question. In "the unerring process of political and social revolution" the aristocracy had broken the power of the monarchy, and the middle classes had broken the power of the aristocracy. "The workmen", continued Cowen, "are in embryo. We cannot foretell their future." (106) An indication of what Cowen now feared the future might hold came a few weeks later in a reference to the co-operative movement. He felt that Robert Owen's albeit "dreamy" ideals had "not always been kept in view by recent co-operators" who had "shortcomings". (107) The economic success of the retail co-operatives had created an obsession with dividends drawing Cowen's comment that "no aristocrat stands up more stiffly for his vested interests than do the shrewd, cautious, careful shareholders in stores and building societies." (108)

Self-satisfaction, it seemed to Cowen, rather than hunger for social reform was a principal feature of the established working class movements of the mid-1880s. It was a situation he tried to analyse in a presidential address to the Northern Union of Mechanics' Institutes in September 1884. Recapping indicators of progress over wages, prices and conditions of life since 1854, Cowen concluded there had been significant improvements but the real picture was one of "gains and losses". Apart from tangible "gains" in incomes, the quality of food, some housing conditions, urban sanitation and the provision of libraries, art galleries, museums and parks, there were "losses" - "the atmosphere is impregnated with ... fumes, the streams are stained with refuse, and vegetation befilmed with soot." More ominously, Cowen saw the existence of

> "a hybrid class doomed to eat the bread of penury, drink the cup of misery. Precarious labour provides them with subsistence for the day, but the slightest interruption throws them destitute. A week of broken weather brings thousands to the brink of starvation ... Little share of our flaunting wealth has reached them ... society, ashamed and despairing, sweeps them, like refuse, into dismal receptacles, where, seething in their wretchedness, they constitute at once our weakness and our reproach. How to sweeten those receptacles and to help their forlorn occupants to help themselves is the problem of the hour. If society does not settle it, it will in time settle society." (109)

It is possible that Cowen would have liked to place himself at the head of a movement of the poorest and launch a new reform struggle addressing their conditions. But the route was blocked in two ways. Firstly, the very poor caught in the "dismal receptacles" of slum housing completely lacked political power. They were excluded from the household franchise of 1867. Secondly, the politics of reform outlined in Cowen's Blyth Manifesto of 1871 crucially depended on the active enthusiasm of organised labour in the co-operatives and trade unions to assist the "excluded masses." Cowen remained convinced of the efficacy of his 1871 perspective but in 1884 co-operators and trade unionists were less inclined, or, due to economic conditions, less able even if willing to look beyond the settled frontiers of their own particular organisations.

In any event, Cowen had little time to devote to the problem of the British poor in the early 1880s. Uproar over Ireland prevented attention to social reform. For Cowen, a further development threatened his very political survival: the revival of the Liberal caucus. Liberal Party managers had been infuriated by their upstaging in 1880 and "the more ardent partisans of Liberalism ... turned into embittered foes" of Cowen. (110) Cowen's anti-coercion stand ranged "the whole Liberal Party against him" (111) and "aroused evil passions" among the Newcastle Liberals. (112) Early in 1881 the Newcastle caucus passed a motion of censure on Cowen for his Irish policy in an atmosphere marked by "an anti-Irish feeling." (113) And the day after Ashton Dilke was shouted down at his abortive public meeting, the National Liberal Federation met in Newcastle "specifically to counter the *Chronicle*." (114) Behind the scenes Spence Watson was once more attempting to create a rival to the *Chronicle*. In a smooth piece of footwork Cowen published a special free supplement to his newspaper featuring the Liberal conference, (115) whilst keeping up a reciprocal stream of invective. He spoke against "the creation of an electoral oligarchy to control the constituencies", (116) "all the greasy apparatus of our caucuses", (117) and commented ruefully "there were no more intolerant persons in the world than illiberal Liberals." (118) The "war" ploughed on into 1882 with Cowen referring to "the malicious and slandering attacks" made against him in the Liberal press (chiefly the *Northern Echo*) as a way of rebutting Ashton Dilke's criticisms of the *Chronicle*. (119) Life was now highly vicious. Cowen's old ally of the early 1870s, Dr. Rutherford, was "purged" from a Liberal ward committee in January 1882 just as Cowen told an estimated 3000 people at a Newcastle meeting that the caucus wanted "three things":

> "They want, in the first place, that I should communicate with the people through them - that I use them as a funnel through which to speak to you. In the second place, I understand them to desire that I shall receive my orders from them on special subjects and on specific occasions. Their third demand, as far as I can make out, is that ... they shall share in the political directorate of the **Newcastle Chronicle**. I was not aware when I became a Member for this town, that I took the Liberal Party into partnership (loud laughter and cheering)." (120)

The caucus responded by deciding to select "a candidate to oppose Mr. Cowen at the next election" and circulating both an allegation from an anonymous MP that Cowen had lost the confidence of the House of Commons (121) and Annand's *Plain Letter* pamphlet. This gnawing hostility had a depressive effect on Cowen. In May 1882 he wrote to a friend despairing "of counteracting [the caucus] in any effectual way." (122) By June, the Liberals' behaviour over coercion in Parliament had reduced Cowen to "despondency" (123) and, in the following month, he felt it "impossible" to "accomplish anything in this country" without submitting to "regular party lines." (124) The caucus, meanwhile, was aware of Ashton Dilke's likely retirement and concluded that choosing "another eminent man ... might be the means of ousting Mr. Cowen." (125) Spence Watson alighted on John Morley, still striving for his own "swift advancement", as an ideal Liberal candidate. This was subtle because Cowen had suggested Morley as a potential candidate for Newcastle in 1877 and 1878, although Cowen's motives had more to do with teasing Morley's insatiable ambition by raising and then dashing his hopes. (126) Morley's adoption was accomplished in January 1883 at express speed to avoid alerting Cowen and to prevent the nomination of any other serious candidate. (127) The caucus was triumphant. They managed to sweep Morley into Parliament and, flushed with success, became "still more intolerant and intractable" towards Cowen. (128) The Liberal press announced that Cowen's "arrogant domination" of Newcastle's politics had been ended. (129) Morley conducted hostilities both openly - telling the House of Commons in 1883 that Cowen spoke for no one but himself (130) - and clandestinely, whispering to Irish MPs it was inadvisable for them to be seen talking to Cowen (131) and boasting to Spence Watson that he would "squash, pulverise and destroy" the enemy of the caucus. (132) Coming from someone who had once criticised Cowen for being "a conspirator to the ends of his fingers", (133) Morley revealed that he was less than the principled *prima donna* he liked to appear. But Cowen proved to be tougher and more resilient than Morley imagined. A year later Morley was bleating to Spence Watson that Cowen was surviving and even affable but "I hope I shall not be overtaken by him on a Dark night, with a Dagger; my chance would be small." (134)

With Morley doing his best against Cowen in London, the caucus kept up the pressure on Tyneside "by means of the old but always successful device, that if you only throw enough mud, some of it is sure to stick." Cowen was accused of being a "traitor...in league with the Tories" and subjected to Liberal "resolutions of censure, of indignation, of denunciation." (135) His newspapers' sports coverage was condemned as "immoral" in order to impress narrow-minded Nonconformists (136) and Liberal intellectuals claimed he had brought Radicalism into "discredit". (137) During 1884 the caucus and their trade union allies finally captured the political direction of the Northumberland and Durham miners' unions. Morley headed the lodge-by-lodge election of speakers to address the Northumberland miners' annual "picnic" and Cowen came bottom of the poll. It was Spence Watson and the Liberals who now organised the mass demonstrations for further franchise reform, and Cowen's support for extending the right to vote to women under the 1884 Franchise Bill was coldly brushed aside. (138) Morley summed up

Liberal attitudes by gladly confirming he was simply an "opportunist" and, in a surrender to male prejudice, refused to assist female enfranchisement. (139) It hardly helped Cowen when he allowed himself to be identified with the shipowners' lobby against tighter safety regulations on merchant ships in 1884, and then lost an arbitration case in which he represented Newcastle engineering workers in 1885.

Cowen collided head-on with the Liberals' dominance of miners' politics. He promoted Lloyd Jones as an "independent labour" candidate for Chester-le-Street at the expected 1885 general election only to discover that the leaders of the Durham Miners' Association had conceded the seat to James Joicey, a coal-owner, in return for a clear run for DMA candidates elsewhere. Apparently the Association offered Lloyd Jones another "safe" seat but "felt he was not free" to accept the offer. (140) Cowen deeply opposed deals with the Liberals' "wire-pullers" and continued with Lloyd Jones's candidacy, hoping to persuade the "working men generally" to "resolutely and earnestly" break away from the caucus. (141) The result was a fierce row between the DMA and the *Chronicle*. (142) Cowen may also have been insistent about opposing Joicey because the coal baron was financing a new Liberal newspaper. A *Newcastle Daily Leader*, edited by James Annand, was created by the caucus in the autumn of 1885 to compete with the *Chronicle*. (143) The challenge was easily deflected in newspaper terms. Cowen expanded both the daily and weekly *Chronicles* and launched a new *Evening Chronicle* with three afternoon editions in November 1885. (144) He also had the unshakeable support of the *Irish Tribune*, a lively national newspaper founded on Tyneside in December 1884 by the former Land Leaguer Charles Diamond as "the organ of Irish national thought" in England. (145) The *Tribune* enjoyed a considerable circulation in the north east, urged Irish support for Lloyd Jones at Chester-le-Street and described James Annand as "a mere nobody", Thomas Burt as "the so-called Radical" and "contemptible humbug" and Morley as "not worthy of trust." The *Chronicle*, in contrast, was "the able organ of an able man." (146) But where political influence was concerned the caucus claimed the greater power to move votes and the relative strengths of the two opposing camps were soon put to the test.

A year before the 1885 general election Cowen had decided to "fight" again though without much enthusiasm. (147) As he prepared for the contest he told Kropotkin it would not make "a great deal of difference which party wins." (148) The Irish were of the same opinion. The *Tribune* dismissed Morley for doing the Liberals' "hack work" (149) and was unimpressed by his sudden conversion to Home Rule as the election drew closer. Regarding Cowen's claim on the Irish vote as "paramount", (150) the *Tribune* voiced the broad sentiments of the Irish national movement on Tyneside and beyond. Cowen's speeches on the Irish Question were read aloud at meetings of the Irish National League, which had replaced the Land League, at Hunslet in Leeds in February 1885. The League's Newcastle No. 1 branch was registering Irish voters in June to secure the return of "the man who stood by us with an unswerving fidelity from the beginning" - or, in T.W. Moody's words, "the staunchest and most independent English supporter of home rule and the Land League" - and the South Shields INL was actually named the "Joseph Cowen Branch". (151) A League meeting at Newcastle in November cheered every mention of Cowen's name but loyally agreed to wait for Parnell's advice before deciding how to cast the Irish vote. An Irish MP nevertheless spoke "enthusiastically" in favour of Cowen "whose name was a household word" in Ireland. (152) Parnell's strategy was to vote against the Liberals, demonstrating the strength of the Irish vote in Britain and, hopefully, emerging from the election with the Irish MPs holding the balance in the new Parliament. Accordingly, Irish voters in Britain were asked to vote for the Tories with only a handful of exceptions, one of whom was Joseph Cowen - "the man who stood by Ireland in her darkest hour, the great Englishman, whose voice, pen and purse, have ever been at the service of our country." (153)

It was an strange coalition. Cowen and the Catholics were at odds over non-demoninational schooling and there were differences about the merits of the British Empire. The *Irish Tribune* resolved these problems by arguing that the "national question" was more pressing than the religious education issue which could always be settled in the future. (154) Cowen's reluctant acceptance of the British occupation of Egypt and the Sudan - seen by the Irish as "a disgraceful cut-throat mission" (155) - could be reconciled by accepting Cowen as "an English nationalist" whose views did not always coincide with those of Irish nationalists "on foreign affairs." (156) The differences with Cowen were taken as secondary to his long stand over Home Rule, his defence of obstructionism, his assistance to the political prisoners and his tenacious and exceptional opposition to coercion. For these reasons the *Tribune* urged its readers to "place Mr. Cowen at the top of the poll ... If he is not there it will be an Irish defeat." As for John Morley, he was simply a "fraud" and a "trimming opportunist" who should "not receive an Irish vote." (157)

Ironically, Cowen's promise of Irish support was a source of danger. Prejudice against the Irish had been rising in reaction to the Home Rule agitation and a number of bombings in London. "No Irish Need Apply" notices appeared at factory gates on Tyneside, (158) and Liberal canvassers told English voters that Cowen should "go to the Irish altogether." (159) A new and unscrupulous element was brought into electioneering. The Tories had always fought Cowen openly, portraying him as a menace to Crown, Church and Country, but the Liberals of the caucus were an altogether different and baser breed. They began the election by ousting Cowen's Radical ally, Eustace Smith, the MP for Tynemouth. This was achieved largely by exercising influence through Spence Watson's family connections with the local Liberal Association and exploiting Smith's acute embarrassment at the likely revelation that one of his married daughters was implicated in an affair with Sir Charles Dilke. The caucus ruthlessly used the pending scandal to have Smith replaced by a more pliable candidate. (160) Unfortunately for the caucus, so much effort was put into destroying Smith that the opportunity was lost to arrange for a second candidate to join Morley on the party ticket at Newcastle. The Liberals settled instead for trying to humiliate Cowen by pushing him into second place at the poll, probably hoping he would be beaten into third place by Charles Hamond, the perennial Tory candidate. Caucus canvassers informed Protestants that Cowen was a friend of the Catholics, and reminded Catholics he had helped Garibaldi against the Pope. Attempts were made to disrupt Cowen's public meetings and, as Morley toured industrial Elswick posing as the friend of the working man, the caucus suggested to the "trading classes" that Cowen was at the root of their troubles because of his sympathies for co-operatives, trade unions and the nine hours strike. (161) The Newcastle caucus presented Cowen's differences with them as a matter of principle affecting the rights of caucuses in general. They therefore appealed for "moral support and even more" to their counterparts in other towns. Canvassing teams were sent to Newcastle from elsewhere and Sunderland's distinctive contribution was to despatch:

> "a gang of energetic and roughish men who accentuated the tone of the electoral campaign in their own fashion ... Cowen was mobbed in the streets and had mud and stones thrown at him" (162)

and these "broke the windows" of his coach. (163)

Cowen's campaign was assisted informally by the Social-Democratic Federation. Elijah Copland had intended contesting the election as a labour candidate but, after debates at two public meetings, withdrew to avoid damaging Cowen's vote. (164) But Cowen's politics were a ramshackled bazaar. Home Rule for Ireland competed with adulation of the Empire and the need for social reforms at home. (165) Cowen choose not to canvass personally, sent each voter a copy of his election address - largely a recapitulation of his record - and organised his campaign around twelve public meetings. Against all the efforts of the caucus, he won. Cowen again topped the poll with 10,498 votes to Morley's 10,129 and the defeated Hamond's 9,500. Yet an analysis of the result showed Cowen had only 2,814 votes cast solely for him compared with John Morley's 7,105 and Hamond's 4,237. The "split" ballots revealed Cowen's dependence on votes from the Tories (hoping to keep Morley out) and from the Irish. With the strength of the caucus confirmed, Cowen was no longer his own man. At any future election he would depend on the power brokers of the new politics - either the Tories or a licence from Parnell. A return to the Liberal fold, hinted at by elements of the caucus as the Liberal Party fell apart over Home Rule after the election, (166) was unthinkable. Any reconciliation would be on the caucus's terms. In addition, Cowen was perversely obsessed with personal hatred of the caucus, accentuated by further strains on his health. He raged against the 7000 Liberal voters - "some of them accompanied their opposition by acts of personal violence" (167) - and condemned the "bilious party zealots" and their "vindictiveness and personal rancour" directed against his "opposition to coercion and support of Home Rule." (168)

Cowen believed "the bitterness of the Caucus's antagonism" was not "ordinary political opposition" but "personal enmity" and "there is no reconciliation possible." (169) He decided not to seek re-election as an MP at the general election called suddenly in 1886 when Chamberlain broke the Liberal Party into pieces in opposition to Home Rule. Cowen was finally destroyed by a bitter mixture of ruined health, party machines, antipathy towards the Irish and the incorporation of organised labour into the prevailing social order. As the early political scientist Ostrogorski observed, Joseph Cowen suffered "more than a personal defeat ... The old Radicalism was dead, quite dead." (170)

CHAPTER ELEVEN : EPILOGUE

There was something unique about Joseph Cowen. More than most Radicals of his generation he drew enthusiasm from international contacts and causes. Mazzini, Lekawski, Garibaldi, William Wells Brown, Lloyd Garrison, Michael Davitt, Peter Kropotkin and many others engaged in desperate struggles were the sources of Cowen's inspiration. Moscow, Warsaw, Italy, Paris, Boston and Dublin were as much part of Cowen's firmament as London and Newcastle upon Tyne. It was from this background, often revolutionary in character, that Cowen approached the situation in Britain. And these international cornerstones kept Cowenism insulated from provincial parochialism or a simple equation with Victorian northern civic pride. In this sense, Cowen broke through the normal boundaries of mid-nineteenth century Radicalism.

Joseph Cowen nevertheless had an intense affinity with the north east of England and its culture. For Cowen the north east and his perception of "the people" of the area were intricately linked with the working classes. Cowen connected with the demands of working class communities and movements, applying principles derived from the international arena, and developing a political style which pushed reformism to its limits. The Cowenite perspective was framed around the rights of oppressed nations to manage their own affairs and the rights of "the people" to claim inalienable liberties. Where these broad ideals were concerned Cowen was uncompromising and regarded the opportunist meanderings of organised Liberalism with revulsion. "I stand by the old doctrines" he wrote in 1896,

> "and am true to the aims of earlier years. My politics are a creed and not a profession. They were adopted from conviction and not as a short road to fame or an easy means of securing social distinction or success. I cannot stoop to conquer, am too proud to canvass and too independent to become a delegate. I can only serve the opinions I believe in my own way. That is not the orthodox way." (1)

As Justin McCarthy noted: "Cowen's temper and principles would not readily recognise the necessity for compromise." (2)

Joseph Cowen's amalgam of international fraternity, association with working class movements and adhesion to principles was explosive (sometimes literally). It could be the mainspring of an astonishing creativity and dynamism. From this volcano of energy came a powerful provincial press, a major theatre, material aid for movements of liberation in Italy, Poland and Ireland, lasting achievements in the fields of trade unionism, co-operatives and education as well as the underpinning of important segments in the long fight for democracy. Yet as the world changed Cowenite Radicalism, stiff with its principles, collided dramatically with the new Liberalism. Firstly there was Ireland. People like Michael Davitt rekindled Cowen's distinctive empathy with anti-imperial nationalism. Cowen appeared to take the Irish cause to extremes for an Englishman but only because he looked at Ireland through Irish eyes, echoing his experiences of the Italian and Polish struggles. Secondly, he continued to believe in the necessity for working class political independence long after this became a disposable commodity for politicians of the Liberal caucus. Cowen wanted a plebeian democracy as a means of overthrowing the shortsighted and selfish influence of the middle-classes. Inevitably, Ireland and class were the great breaking points between Cowen's Radicalism and Liberalism.

Nothing is easier, of course, than portraying a figure from the past as a hero. There was much in Cowen's life that could be registered as heroic, not least his attempts to grapple with ill-health in order to carry on with his politics. On the other hand, Cowen's growing fixation with the British Empire came to contradict his earlier stands on racial equality. In Cowen's case, the glorification of Empire also illustrated the extent to which English Radicalism became thoroughly permeated with imperialism. By the late-1870s there was very little of the heroic in Cowen's views on the Empire, and his lurch towards becoming an imperialist, grating against his strong support for Irish nationalism, made a confusion of his politics by 1885. It was simply self-defeating to encourage the tide of imperialism, on the one hand, whilst identifying strongly with Irish issues at a time when Home Rule was portrayed in Britain as subversive to the Empire. Cowen was not alone, of course, in embracing imperialism - it was a feature of the age rather than a personal quirk - and if a plea of mitigation before a twentieth-century jury is possible then it would rest in Cowen's unshakable refusal to desert the Irish Home Rulers.

Cowen's final years look very sad in comparison with his four decades as "the Tribune of the North". His health further deteriorated and his wife, Jane, died in 1893. Retreating into seclusion Cowen continued to be obsessed by the caucus (even encouraging the Tories in an effort to break the Liberal "machine") and he regretted some of his earlier associations. "My experience of theatres and theatrical people" he wrote, "was not of an agreeable kind." (3) "I never had a good opinion of the teetotal people" he disclosed on one occasion, rejecting a life-long alliance. (4) And in a devastating criticism of the co-operative movement Cowen told the Italian newspaper *Figaro* in 1891:

> "Of all the meannesses in God's creation and the sweating practised therein, the modern co-operator is the worst living embodiment. I know of things done and being done in the North here, of dishonest dealings, of underpaying, of sweating the life's blood out of the employed, of a wanting of the littlest of the doctrines of honest commercialism, that make one despair." (5)

By now Cowen had withdrawn from public activity almost completely, telling Holyoake:

> "I have a perfect repugnance to have my name mentioned at all [in the press]. Perhaps I have got cynical, but my indifference to public opinion is so strong that I would rather just drop out of recognition altogether." (6)

But Joseph Cowen's "retirement" was not wholly marked by sourness. He aided the Socialists, standing bail for Hyndman when the Social-Democratic Federation's leaders were arrested in the aftermath of the London unemployed riots of 1886. (7) Engels found the pages of the *Chronicle* were open to him (8) and the SDF praised Cowen and his newspapers in 1889 for help in organising among labourers. (9) The Liberals criticised Cowen for giving "no small aid to the discontented labour vote." (10) Years later, when the Independent Labour Party launched a northern magazine, *The Northern Democrat*, the inspiration derived partly from Cowen's work. The first issue of the *Northern Democrat* acknowledged the *Northern Tribune* as its true political ancestor and pledged to build "upon the foundations laid by pioneers fifty years ago." (11) Nor did Cowen entirely neglect Ireland. He supported the Home Rule Bill emanating from Gladstone's overnight conversion in 1885 (produced by dependence on Parnell's Irish Party) although Cowen would not reconsider his decision to retire from Parliament despite requests to do so from the Tyneside Irish. (12) The rancour with the caucus meant Cowen withheld endorsement of the Liberals at the 1886 general election and therefore appeared to be forsaking Home Rule - drawing from the *Irish Tribune* only the generous comment that the Irish make "every allowance for the condition of affairs in Newcastle, and we do not complain." (13) But he spoke for Parnell before the Special Commission - an early variant of a state "show" trial - set up by the Tory government in 1889 to investigate allegations (and, as it turned out, forged letters) linking Home Rulers with "outrages" in Ireland, and he offered £10,000 towards the costs of Parnell's defence. (14) In one of his last public statements Cowen wrote to an Irish gathering commemorating the Rising of 1798:

> "I cannot attend your commemoratory meeting, but I sympathise with the purpose for which it has been called. Englishmen read history with their prejudices and not with their eyes... and [this] is one of the reasons for the unhappy estrangement of the two peoples." (15)

The Joseph Cowen whom people remembered was the Cowen of forty years of sustained agitation. He was recalled by the Italian vice-consul in 1891 at a banquet marking the twenty-first anniversary of the unification of Italy as "amongst Englishmen .... the greatest friend Italy ever possessed." (16) It was a view repeated by one of Garibaldi's former "Red Shirts" in 1909, describing Cowen as a man who "did more to make their country free than any other Englishman." (17) "Joe Cowen", said the journalist Wemyss Reid, was always the man who "would find some excuse for summoning a public meeting ... in order that we might listen to some patriot exile ... or give our detestation of the despotism which at that time weighed upon Europe." (18) "It is superfluous to explain to anybody who knew Joseph Cowen" recorded one Irish nationalist, "how intense were his wrath and detestation at everything that hurt humanity." (19) To those who knew him, Joseph Cowen was always the Cowen of the Italian, Polish and American episodes, the champion of co-operatives and trade unions, the popular educator, and campaigner for the right to vote. He was the genius behind the *Newcastle Chronicle* and the Tyne Theatre, the agitator who castigated the wasteful extravagance of the monarchy and demanded an end to poverty, and he was the epitome of "the militant democracy". Perhaps above all, Cowen was synonymous with the restless fight for Irish freedom. He had always been restless in the pursuit of liberty. "In Northumberland" mused the *New York Times* in a piece of colourful idiosyncrasy, "they say Mr. Cowen had gypsy blood." (20)

Joseph Cowen died peacefully at home in the afternoon of Sunday, 18 February 1900.

NOTES AND BIBLIOGRAPHY
(Place of publication London unless otherwise stated)

CHAPTER ONE : WHO WAS JOSEPH COWEN?

(1)   E.R. Jones, **Life and Speeches of Joseph Cowen, MP**, (Sampson Low, 1885);
        see also, Joseph Cowen to Major Jones, 2 June 1885, Cowen Papers E8 [Tyne
        and Wear County Records Office].
(2)   New York Times, 25 February 1900; Daily Telegraph, 20 February 1900.
(3)   The Echo, 3 February 1891.
(4)   K.G.E. Harris, "Joseph Cowen (1829-1900)" in Joyce M. Bellamy and John
        Saville (eds), **Dictionary of Labour Biography**, Vol. 1., (Macmillan,
        1972), pp. 81/86. See also: Joseph Kelly, "Joseph Cowen, Jun" in
        Joseph O. Baylen and Norbert J. Gossman (eds), **Biographical
        Dictionary of Modern British Radicals**, Vol. 2, 1830-1870, (Harvester
        Press, Brighton, 1984).
(5)   A. Watson, **A Great Labour Leader, being a Life of the Rt. Hon.
        Thomas Burt, MP**, (Brown, Langham & Co., 1908), p. 136.
(6)   F.W. Hirst, **Early Life and Letters of John Morley**, (Macmillan, 1927),
        Vol. 2., p. 139.
(7)   Ibid.
(8)   North of England Advertiser, 9 August 1862.
(9)   Cited in Hirst, op.cit., p. 164
(10)   W.E.Adams, **Memoirs of a Social Atom**, (Hutchinson, 1903), Vol. 2.,
        p. 536.
(11)   Newcastle upon Tyne Liberal Association, **Meeting of the General
        Committee on Thursday, February 24th, 1882**, p. 10.
(12)   Newcastle Examiner, 8 July 1881.
(13)   The Echo, 3 February 1891.
(14)   Cowen: Speech at Newcastle, 17 April 1873, Cowen Papers, B142.
(15)   H.J. Gladstone, **After Thirty Years**, (Macmillan, 1928), p. 173
(16)   John Morley, cited in E.I. Waitt, **John Morley, Joseph Cowen, and
        Robert Spence Watson: Liberal Divisions in Newcastle Politics, 1873-
        1895**, (University of Manchester, unpublished Ph.D thesis, 1972), p. 169.
(17)   Justin McCarthy, **Reminiscences**, (Chatto & Windus, 1899), Vol. 2.,
        p. 175.
(18)   Sir H.W. Lucy, **Memoirs of Eight Parliaments**, (Heinemann, 1908),
        pp. 49-50.
(19)   Waitt, op.cit., p. 53.
(20)   W. Duncan, **Life of Joseph Cowen**, (Walter Scott, 1904), pp. 222-223.
(21)   Albert Harrison, **Joseph Cowen, Orator, Patriot and Englishman: a paper
        read before the Priory Street Wesleyan Young Men's Class, York**,
        (Gazette, York, 1900), p. 13. [York Public Library]
(22)   Justice, 24 February 1900.
(23)   Cited in B. Nicolaievsky and Otto Maenchen-Helfen, **Karl Marx: Man and
        Fighter**, (Penguin Books, 1976 edn.), p. 403.
(24)   May Morris, **The Introductions to the Collected Works of William Morris**,
        (Oriole Editions, New York, 1973 edn.), Vol. 2., pp. 584/585.
(25)   Thomas Burt, MP, **Lecture on the Life and Work of Joseph Cowen**, (Andrew

Reid, Newcastle upon Tyne, 1911), p. 3.

(26)   Albert Harrison, "Joseph Cowen: A Fighter for Freedom" in <u>York Labour News</u>, No. 7, August 1904. See also: Chapter Eight, n69.

(27)   Adams. op.cit., Vol. 1., Dedication.

(28)   Joseph Parker, **Tyne Folk**, (Allenson, 1896), p. 5.

(29)   F. Lavery (ed), **Irish Heroes in the War**, (Everett & Co., 1917).

(30)   T.P. O'Connor, "The Irish in Great Britain" in F. Lavery, Ibid., p. 25.

(31)   Burt, op.cit., p. 21.

(32)   W. Robb, **Hexham Fifty Years Ago and sketches of Members of Parliament and local celebrities I have met with**, (Catherall, Hexham, 1882), p.65.

(33)   S. Gwynn and G.M. Tuckwell, **The Life of the Rt. Hon. Sir Charles Dilke**, (J. Murray, 1917), Vol. 1., p. 196.

(34)   Adams, op.cit., p. 59.

(35)   <u>Newcastle Examiner</u>, 28 January 1881.

(36)   Adams, op.cit., p. 58.

(37)   **Local Biographies**, Vol. 1., p. 352. [Newcastle upon Tyne Public Library]

(38)   Robb, op.cit.

(39)   Adams, op.cit., Vol. 2., pp 495-496.

(40)   Burt, op.cit.

(41)   Gwynn and Tuckwell, op.cit., p. 196.

(42)   S.J. Reid, **Memoirs of Sir Wemyss Reid, 1842-1885**, (Cassall, 1905), p. 44.

(43)   Burt, op.cit.

(44)   Adams. op.cit.

(45)   Burt, op.cit.

(46)   <u>North of England Advertiser</u>, 9 August 1862.

(47)   Burt, op.cit.

(48)   Albert Harrison, **Joseph Cowen, Orator** ..., op.cit., p. 10.

(49)   Sir H.W. Lucy, **Later Peeps at Parliament**, (G. Newnes, 1905), p. 49.

(50)   Duncan, op.cit., p. 245.

(51)   T.M. Healy, **Letters and Leaders of My Day, 1855-1931**, (Butterworth, 1928), Vol. 1., p. 175.

(52)   Watson, op.cit., p. 136.

(53)   Lucy, op.cit., p. 34.

(54)   Watson, op.cit.

(55)   J. McCarthy, **England Under Gladstone, 1880-1884**, (Chatto & Windus, 1884), p. 155.

(56)   Lucy, op.cit.

(57)   Jessie White Mario to Jane Cowen, 1 April 1902, Cowen Papers, A978.

(58)   J.M. Davidson, **Eminent English Radicals**, (Stewart, 1880), p. 50.

(59)   J. McCarthy, p. 175.

(60)   Burt, op.cit., p. 12.

(61)   T.P. O'Connor, **Memoirs of an Old Parliamentarian**, (E. Benn, 1929), Vol. 1., p. 297; T.P. O'Connor, "The Irish in Great Britain" in Lavery, op.cit., p. 27.

CHAPTER TWO : THE EXCURSIONISTS

(1)   John Saville (ed), **W.E. Adams: Memoirs of a Social Atom**, (Augustas M. Kelley, New York, 1968 reprint of 1903 edn.), p.13.

(2)   Adams, op.cit., p.366.

(3)   Felice Orsini, **Memoirs and Adventures**, (Hamilton, Edinburgh, 1857), p.187.

(4)   Jane Cowen, **Notes**, Vol.IX, Cowen Papers E436.

(5)   Orsini, op.cit.

(6)   Joseph Cowen cited in G.J. Holyoake, **Bygones Worth Remembering**, (Fisher Unwin, 1905), Vol.1., p.233.

(7)   D.F. MacKay, **The Influence of the Italian Risorgimento on British Public Opinion**, (Unpublished Ph.D thesis, University of Oxford, 1961), p. 83, n3.

(8)   Joseph Cowen to Major Jones, 2 June 1885, Cowen Papers E8.

(9)   Northern Daily Express, 24 and 27 April 1858; Cowen Papers A606.

(10)   The Journal, 25 September 1862; Northern Daily Express, 17 September 1862.

(11)   "Elfin" in Newcastle Daily Chronicle, 6 October 1862.

(12)   Cited in Holyoake, op.cit.

(13)   Ibid.

(14)   S.J. Reid, op.cit., p.47.

(15)   Newcastle Chronicle, 5 March 1858.

(16)   E.D. Spraggon, **The Radicalism of Joseph Cowen**, (unpublished MA thesis, Newcastle upon Tyne Polytechnic, 1985), p. 48.

(17)   Davidson, op.cit., p.43.

(18)   Holyoake, op.cit., Vol.II, p.

(19)   Jane Cowen, op.cit.

(20)   Newcastle Daily Chronicle, 1 December 1862 (refers to the 1858 public meeting).

(21)   H.M. Hyndman, **The Record of an Adventurous Life**, (Macmillan,1911), p.69.

(22)   Cowen to Holyoake, 14 March 1858 (Holyoake Collection 1007: all references to the Holyoake Collection are to the Co-operative Union holdings at Manchester unless otherwise stated); Cowen to Mrs. Hawkes, 17 January 1858 (Holyoake Collection 996).

(23)   Michael St. John Packe, **The Bombs of Orsini**, (Secker & Warburg, 1957), p.249; Joseph Kelly, "Joseph Cowen, Jun" in Baylen and Gossman, op.cit., p. 160; J.M. Kelley, **The Parliamentary Career of Joseph Cowen**, (unpublished Ph.D. thesis, Loyola University of Chicago, 1970).

(24)   Holyoake, op.cit., Vol.1., p.74.

(25)   Adams, op.cit., p. 347.

(26)   Jane Cowen, op.cit., Vol.VI., Cowen Papers E436.

(27)   Newcastle Chronicle, 26 February 1858.

(28)   Newcastle Daily Chronicle,, 18 July 1871.

(29)   Newcastle Chronicle, 2 April 1858.

(30)   Newcastle Daily Chronicle, 3 June 1858.

(31)   Ibid., 14 September 1859.

(32)   MacKay, op.cit., p.163.

(33) Saville, **W.E. Adams**, op.cit., p.22.
(34) E.Holt, **Risorgimento: Modern Italy, 1815-1870**, (Macmillan,1970), p102.
(35) MacKay, op.cit., p. 83
(36) Holt, op.cit.
(37) Newcastle Daily Chronicle, 14 September 1859.
(38) Cowen to Jones, op.cit.
(39) Cited in MacKay, op.cit.
(40) Jane Cowen, op.,cit.
(41) J. McCarthy, op.cit., p.156.
(42) Hyndman, op.cit., pp.58/59.
(43) Jasper Ridley, **Garibaldi**, (Constable, 1974), p.21.
(44) Jane Cowen, **Joseph Mazzini**, Cowen Papers E436.
(45) Newcastle Daily Chronicle, 13 March 1872.
(46) Holt, op.cit., p.86.
(47) Jane Cowen, op.cit.
(48) Ibid.
(49) MacKay, op.cit., pp. 84/85.
(50) Jane Cowen, **Mazzini**, op.cit.
(51) E.R. Jones, op.cit., pp. 2/3.
(52) Jane Cowen, **General Garibaldi**, Cowen Papers E436.
(53) MacKay, op.cit.
(54) Jane Cowen, **Mazzini**, op.cit.
(55) Newcastle Daily Chronicle, 26 August 1859.
(56) Reed to Holyoake, December 1860 (Holyoake Collection 1257).
(57) MacKay, op.cit., p.109.
(58) Jane Cowen, op.cit.
(59) MacKay, op.cit., p. 242
(60) Jane Cowen, op.cit.
(61) MacKay, op.cit.
(62) Cowen to Anon., cited in Jane Cowen, op.cit.
(63) Newcastle Daily Chronicle, 19 May 1858.
(64) Ibid., 20 May 1858.
(65) Jane Cowen, **Notes**, Vol.IX., Cowen Papers E436.
(66) Ibid.
(67) Newcastle Daily Chronicle, 13 May 1858.
(68) Newcastle Chronicle, 1 May 1857.
(69) Ibid., 9 May 1858
(70) Jane Cowen, **General Garibaldi**, Cowen Papers E436.
(71) MacKay, op.cit., pp.70/71; Ridley, op.cit., pp.382/385.
(72) Newcastle Daily Chronicle,, 14 September 1859.
(73) For example: Newcastle Daily Chronicle, 22 May 1858.
(74) MacKay, op.cit., p.197.
(75) H. Rudman, **Italian Nationalism and English Letters**, (Unwin,1940),p.303.
(76) Newcastle Daily Chronicle, 18 November 1859.
(77) Jane Cowen, op.cit.
(78) Mazzini to Cowen, 19 May 1860, Cowen Papers E436.
(79) Jane Cowen, **Joseph Mazzini**, Cowen Papers E436.
(80) Reed to Holyoake, 25 July; 7 August 1860, (Holyoake Coll. 1232/1235).
(81) Ridley, op.cit., pp.458/460.
(82) Holyoake, op.,cit., Vol.1., p.245.

(83)   Reasoner, 16 October 1852, Vol.24., p.329.
(84)   Jane Cowen, **Notes**, Cowen Papers E435.
(85)   Newcastle Daily Chronicle, 18 and 21 August 1860.
(86)   Newcastle Journal, 24 November 1860; Cowen Papers A674.
(87)   Newcastle Daily Chronicle, 21 August 1860.
(88)   Holyoake, op.cit., p.247.
(89)   Styles to Cowen, 17 August 1860, Cowen Papers A660.
(90)   Holyoake. op.cit., p. 253.
(91)   Ibid., p. 256.
(92)   Ridley, op.cit., pp. 460/461.
(93)   See: Newcastle Weekly Chronicle, 27 April-22 June 1889.
(94)   **British Legion Muster Roll**, Holyoake Papers, Bishopsgate Institute.
(95)   Cowen to Holyoake, 10 December 1860 (Holyoake Collection 1251).
(96)   Newcastle Daily Chronicle, 12, 16 and 23 January 1861.

CHAPTER THREE: A CHARTIST AND SOMETHING MORE

(1)   Thomas Burt, op.cit., p.7.
(2)   Cowen to Edwards, 22 March 1852, Cowen Papers E436.
(3)   See: E.D. Spraggon, op.cit., for discussion of Cowen's commitment
        to the "autonomy" of working class movements.
(4)   The Echo, 3 February 1891.
(5)   Jane Cowen, **MSS Life**, Cowen Papers E436/I., p.37.
(6)   The fact that father and son had the same name has occasionally proved
        a source of confusion that the Cowens sought to avoid by describing
        the son as Joseph Cowen, Junior.
(7)   R. Welford, **Men of Mark**, (Walter Scott, 1895), Vol.1., p.648;
        Newcastle Daily Chronicle, 22 December 1873.
(8)   Keith Harris, Unpublished **MSS**, pp. 5/6.
(9)   See for example: Duncan, op.cit., p.245; John Oxberry, **Mr. Joseph
        Cowen, 1829-1900**, (Oxberry, Gateshead, nd); Albert Harrison, op.cit.
(10)   Newcastle Journal, 15 April 1895.
(11)   Keith Harris, **Dictionary of Labour Biography**, op.cit., p.82.
(12)   Harris, **MSS**, op.cit., p.vi.
(13)   Northern Tribune, 1854, Vol.1., p.36.
(14)   Harris, op.cit., p.vii.
(15)   Ibid., pp. vii/viii.
(16)   **A full account of the general meeting of the inhabitants of Newcastle
        upon Tyne and its vicinity ... 11 October 1819**, (Newcastle upon Tyne,
        1819), pp. 12/15. [Newcastle upon Tyne Public Library]
(17)   See: D.J. Rowe, "Tyneside Chartism" in N. McCord (ed), **Essays in
        Tyneside Labour History**, (North East Labour History Group. Newcastle
        upon Tyne, 1977).
(18)   Dorothy Thompson, **The Chartists**, (Temple Smith, 1984), pp. 138/139.
(19)   John Latimer, **Local Records**, (Newcastle Chronicle,
        Newcastle upon Tyne, 1857), pp. 113/114.
(20)   Harris, **MSS**, op.cit.
(21)   W. Bourn, **History of the Parish of Ryton**, (Wordsworth Press, Carlisle),

pp.126/127.

(22) Harris, MSS, op.cit., p.7; **Jane Cowen**, Notes, Cowen Papers E436.

(23) Harris, MSS, op.cit. See also R. Challinor and B. Ripley, **The Miners"
      Association: a trade union in the age of the Chartists**, (Lawrence and
      Wishart, 1968; Bewick Press, Whitley Bay, 1990), p.22.

(24) Jane Cowen, MSS Life, Cowen Papers E436/II; W. Bourn, op.cit., pp.92/93.

(25) W.Bourn, Ibid., p.93.

(26) Northern Star, 21 February 1846.

(27) Joseph Cowen, **Notes; hints; observations from daily life, July 1846**,
      Cowen Papers F12.

(28) See: Angela M. Blenkinsop, **A Study of a Collection of Tracts in the
      Joseph Cowen Library**, (unpublished thesis submitted for the degree
      of Ph.D., University of Newcastle upon Tyne, 1969).

(29) Jane Cowen, MSS Life, op.cit., Cowen Papers E436/II, pp.9/10.

(30) Joseph Cowen, **Notes**, op.cit.

(31) Jane Cowen, MSS Life, op.cit., p.1.

(32) Joseph Cowen, **Notes**, January 1847, Cowen Papers F12.

(33) Cowen to Holyoake, 26 November 1855, cited in Jane Cowen, op.cit.

(34) Newcastle Examiner, 8 July 1881.

(35) Peoples Journal, 6 July 1847.

(36) Newcastle Guardian, 3 July 1847.

(37) Ibid., 12 October 1850.

(38) Gateshead Observer, 29 January 1848.

(39) Peoples Journal, 6 July 1847.

(40) A. Dobbs, **Education and Social Movements**, (Longmans, 1919), p.176n.

(41) Newcastle Chronicle, 14 July 1848.

(42) E.R. Jones, op.cit., p.96.

(43) Newcastle Chronicle, 9 February 1849; Newcastle Guardian, 20
      October 1849.

(44) Gateshead Observer, 27 November 1858.

(45) Newcastle Guardian, 28 August 1848.

(46) Newcastle Courant, 21 June 1850.

(47) Reasoner, 27 May 1855.

(48) Robert Eadie in Newcastle Evening Chronicle, 21 March 1910.

(49) Newcastle Daily Chronicle, 19 July 1859.

(50) Cowen, Address at Winlaton, 26 August 1850, Cowen Papers D42.

(51) Newcastle Chronicle, 2 November 1849.

(52) Newcastle Guardian, 5 January 1850.

(53) Newcastle Chronicle, 26 May 1848.

(54) G.J. Holyoake, **History of Co-operation in England**, (private print,
      Manchester, 1875-77), Vol.2., p.504.

(55) **Blaydon and Stella Mechnanics' Institute, Report ....of the tenth annual
      soiree**, (Joseph Makepeace, Blaydon, 1856, p.42.

(56) The Times, 12 and 19 November 1856.

(57) **Blaydon and Stella Mechanics' Institute**, op.cit.

(58) Cowen to Holyoake, 8 December 1856, Cowen Papers C78.

(59) Reasoner, 23 October 1859. See also: Susan Budd. **Varieties
      of Unbelief: Atheists and Agnostics in English Society, 1850-1860**,
      (Heinemann, 1977), pp. 86, 95/96; Edward Royle, **Victorian
      Infidels: The Origins of the British Secularist Movement 1791-1866**,

(Manchester University Press, Manchester, 1974), pp. 221/222.

(60)   Newcastle Chronicle, 28 April 1848.

(61)   Newcastle Chronicle, 2 November 1849; See - Newcastle Daily
Chronicle, 3 November 1888, report on the retirement of John
Elliott, chief constable of Gateshead (Elliott, an active Chartist
in his youth, had been the door keeper at a Chartist meeting
addressed by Cowen in 1849). Some confusion surrounds the exact
date of Cowen's first public speech in Newcastle upon Tyne. He
apparently addressed a Chartist meeting held at Martin Jude"s
inn on The Side on 26 March 1849, but may have spoken earlier
at a temperance meeting on "The Demands of the Age upon the
Young" - Newcastle Weekly Chronicle, 2, 16 January, 27 February 1886.

(62)   Cowen: Speech of Welcome to Louis Kossuth to England, Newcastle
upon Tyne, 28 October 1851, Cowen Papers A104.

(63)   M. Noble, **Short Sketches of Eminent Men in the North of England,**
(Andrew Reid, 1885), p.53.

(64)   R.N. Soffer, "Attitudes and Allegiances in the unskilled North" in
International Review of Social History, Vol. 10, 1965, p.429n.

(65)   Newcastle Courant, 13 December 1850; See also H.S. Tremenheere,
Report of the Commission into the Mining Districts, (1851),
pp.31/32, detailing the high Newcastle sales of newspapers either
"Chartist and Infidel" or "hostile to the existing state."

(66)   Cowen: MSS Notes of Speeches at Winlaton Mechanics' Institute,
18 June and 26 August 1850, Cowen Papers D42.

(67)   Newcastle Courant, 2 November 1849.

(68)   Newcastle Guardian, 5 October 1850.

(69)   Reasoner, 14 May 1851.

(70)   Newcastle Courant, 4 October, 1850.

(71)   Gateshead Observer, 3 November 1849.

(72)   Reasoner, 27 November 1850.

(73)   "Marat" in the Red Republican, 28 September 1850, p.116.

(74)   Cowen: Address to the Blaydon and Winlaton Festival,
26 August 1850, Cowen Papers D42.

(75)   Newcastle Guardian, 5 October 1850.

(76)   Joseph Cowen, **Annual Report to the Winlaton Mechanics' Institute, 18 June
1849**, Cowen Papers D31.

CHAPTER FOUR: THE VOYAGE OF THE KILINSKI

(1)   P. Brock, "Joseph Cowen and the Polish Exiles", in Slavonic and
East European Review, 1953, Vol.32., p.66.

(2)   E.R. Jones, **Heroes of Industry,** (Sampson Low, 1886), p.284.

(3)   P. Brock, op.cit., pp.65/66; I. Waitt, "Revolutionaries Friend",
North Magazine, February 1972, p.12.

(4)   W.E. Adams in Newcastle Weekly Chronicle, 16 May 1863.

(5)   See for example: Newcastle Daily Chronicle 17 February 1863;
P. Brock, op.cit., p.52.

(6)   P. Brock, op.cit., p. 65.

(7)   J.M. Davidson, op.cit., p.53.
(8)   Jane Cowen, **MSS Life VI**, Cowen Papers E436, pp.75/77.
(9)   Louis Ponlewski to Joseph Cowen, 24 April 1864, Cowen Papers A808.
(10)   Mazzini to Cowen, 23 June 1865, Cowen Papers A874.
(11)   Lekawski to Cowen,, 18 May 1863, Cowen Papers E436.
(12)   Lekawski to Cowen, 6 April 1864, Cowen Papers E436.
(13)   Ibid.
(14)   P. Brock, op.cit., p.54.
(15)   Jane Cowen, **Notes**, Cowen Papers E436.
(16)   Ibid.
(17)   Joseph Cowen to C. Dobson Collett, 24 March 1852, Cowen Papers E436.
(18)   P. Brock, op.cit., p.55, n9; see also Newcastle Weekly Chronicle 4
        July, 1874.
(19)   Newcastle Chronicle, 13 July and 23 November 1849.
(20)   Ibid., 31 January and 14 March 1851.
(21)   Northern Star, 18 May 1850.
(22)   P. Brock, op.cit., pp. 57/59; Monthly Chronicle, June, 1889,
        p. 276; A. Schoyan, **The Chartist Challenge: a Portrait of George
        Julian Harney**, (Heinemann, 1958), p. 241.
(23)   W. Hamish Fraser, **Trade Unions and Society: The Struggle for
        Acceptance, 1850-80**, (George Allen and Unwin, 1974), pp. 126/127;
        Nicolaievsky and Maenchen-Helfen, op.cit., pp. 280/281.
(24)   Jane Cowen, op.cit.
(25)   F.B. Smith, **Radical Artisan: William James Linton 1812-97**,
        (Manchester University Press, Manchester, 1973), pp.107/108.
(26)   Reasoner, 13 January 1856, p.13.
(27)   Ibid., 27 May 1855, p.67.
(28)   Northern Daily Express, 2 January 1856.
(29)   See E.D. Spraggon, op.cit., p. 10/31; Cowen Papers B31 and B27; M.
        Milne, **Newspapers of Northumberland and Durham**, (Frank Graham,
        Newcastle upon Tyne, 1971), pp.38/39.
(30)   References to The Northern Tribune draw heavily on Susan Scott,
        "The Northern Tribune: A North East Radical Magazine", in North
        East Labour History Bulletin, No.19 (1985), pp.9/17; see also
        F.B. Smith, op.cit., especially Chapter 5.
(31)   N. McCord, **North East England: The Region's Development 1760-
        1960**, (Batsford, 1979), pp.16, 111, 113, 131/132.
(32)   Benwell Community Development Project, **The Making of a Ruling Class:
        Two Centuries of Capital Development on Tyneside**, (Benwell CDP,
        Newcastle upon Tyne, 1978), p.23. See also: Kenneth Warren,
        **Armstrongs of Elswick: Growth in Engineering and Armaments to the
        Merger with Vickers**, (Macmillan, 1989).
(33)   Cowen: Speech at Winlaton Mechanics' Institute, 26 August
        1850, Cowen Papers D42.
(34)   Cowen: Speech at Newcastle Democratic Reading Room, 6 June
        1852, Cowen Papers D59.
(35)   Adams, op.cit., p.536.
(36)   Cowen: Speech at Middlesbrough Mechanics' Institute,
        9 November 1852, Cowen Papers D71.
(37)   Joseph Cowen to [anon], March 1852, Cowen Papers E436.

(38) C. Muris, **The Northern Reform Union 1858-1862**, (unpublished MA thesis, University of Durham [King's College, Newcastle], 1953), pp.1/5. See too: Gregory Clays, "Mazzini, Kossuth and British Radicalism, 1848-1854" in Journal of British Studies, Vol. 28, No. 3, July 1989, for a discussion of the influence of European Republicanism on British Radicalism as a diversion from political reform in Britain; however, Cowen's experience suggests the European influence helped to stimulate a revival of domestic interest in reform.

(39) Newcastle Chronicle, 15 January 1858.

(40) Ibid., 8 January 1858.

(41) Muris, op.cit., pp.38/39.

(42) Newcastle Chronicle, 15 January 1858.

(43) Francis Gill to Richard Reed, 16 August 1858, Cowen Papers C150.

(44) Jeanette Natham to Richard Reed, 25 August 1858, Cowen Papers C150 and C157.

(45) Newcastle Guardian, 22 January 1858.

(46) Muris, op.cit., pp.34/38.

(47) E.S. Prince, Secretary of the Parliamentary Reform Committee to Richard Reed, 29 November 1858, Cowen Papers C306.

(48) S.J. Reid, op.cit., p.46.

(49) Muris, op.cit., p.26.

(50) Newcastle Daily Chronicle, 27 September 1858.

(51) Daily News cited in Newcastle Daily Chronicle, 8 December 1859.

(52) Newcastle Daily Chronicle, 24 July 1858.

(53) Ibid., 27 September 1858.

(54) Ibid., 13 October 1858.

(55) Ibid., 25 November 1858.

(56) Ibid., 30 November 1858.

(57) Muris, op.cit., p.21.

(58) Newcastle Daily Chronicle, 24 December 1858.

(59) Muris, op.cit., pp.19/21.

(60) Newcastle Daily Chronicle, 7 November 1859.

(61) Holyoake, op.cit., p.143.

(62) Newcastle Chronicle, 27 March 1857.

(63) Muris, op.cit., p.50.

(64) Newcastle Daily Chronicle, 27 May 1858.

(65) Washington Wilkes to Cowen, 5 July 1859, Cowen Papers C671; Muris, op.cit., p.60.

(66) Ibid., pp.47/48.

(67) Northern Reform Union Council, Minutes, 2 August 1859. See also: Raymond Challinor, **A Radical Lawyer in Victorian England: W.P. Roberts and the struggle for workers' rights**, (I.B. Tauris, 1990), pp. 205/207 for former Chartists' over-optimism about the revolutionary potential of volunteer rifle corps.

(68) Cited in Muris, op.cit., p.62.

(69) Newcastle Daily Chronicle, 24 June 1859.

(70) E.I..Waitt, **John Morley**, et.al., op.cit., p.4.

(71) Muris, op.cit., pp.9, 16/17.

(72) Newcastle Daily Chronicle, 8 December 1859.

(73)   Muris, op.cit., p.22.
(74)   Ibid., pp.39/40.
(75)   Newcastle Daily Chronicle, 11 July 1862.
(76)   Ibid., 15 January 1862.

CHAPTER FIVE: "INTOLERANT AND INTOLERABLE CLIQUES"

(1)   Cited in Lyall Wilkes, **Tyneside Portraits**, (Frank Graham, Newcastle upon
        Tyne, 1971), p.115.
(2)   Ibid., p.109.
(3)   Anon., **The Corporation Annual or Recollections (not random) of
        the First Reformed Town Council of the Borough of Newcastle upon
        Tyne by a late Councillor**, (W. Boas, Newcastle upon Tyne, 1836,
        3rd edition).
(4)   Lyall Wilkes, op.cit., p.104.
(5)   Ibid., p.120.
(6)   Newcastle Daily Chronicle, 7 January 1861.
(7)   Ibid.
(8)   Ibid., 8 January 1861.
(9)   Ibid., 29 January 1861.
(10)   W.H. Maehl, "Chartism in North Eastern England" in North East
        Labour History Bulletin, No.3., 1969, p.11.
(11)   Reasoner, 27 January 1861.
(12)   Cowen to Holyoake, 18 December 1857 (Holyoake Collection 976).
(13)   Newcastle Daily Chronicle, 1 May 1858.
(14)   Ibid., 25 October 1858.
(15)   Aaron Watson, **A Newspaperman's Memories**, (Hutchinson, 1925),
        p.31.
(16)   G.J. Holyoake, **Diary**, September 1859 (Holyoake Collection,
        Bishopsgate Institute); Holyoake to Cowen, 16 December 1859;
        Cowen Papers C973.
(17)   Watson, op.cit., pp.30/31; Cowen to Holyoake, 25 March 1860,
        (Holyoake Collection 1203).
(18)   Watson, op.cit., p.39.
(19)   Cowen to Holyoake, 25 March 1860 (Holyoake Collection 1203).
(20)   Holyoake, **Bygones**, op.cit., p.67; Alan J. Lee, **The Origins of the
        Popular Press, 1855-1914**, (Croom Helm, 1976), pp.83/84.
(21)   E.I. Waitt, op.cit., p.7, n.13.
(22)   Jane Cowen, **Notes**, Cowen Papers E433/III, p.33.
(23)   Richard Reed cited in James Dellow, **Memoirs of an Old Stager**,
        (Andrew Reid, Newcastle upon Tyne, 1928), p.11.
(24)   Lucy Brown, **Victorian News and Newspapers**, (Oxford University
        Press, Oxford, 1985), p.60.
(25)   Newcastle Daily Chronicle, 24 March 1862.
(26)   Adams, op.cit., pp.494/495.
(27)   Watson, op.cit., p.39.
(28)   J. Saville (ed), **W.E. Adams**, op.cit., pp.22/23.
(29)   Adams, op.cit., p. 494.

(30) **Descriptive Account of Newcastle**, (Robinsons, Brighton, 1895) pp. 28/32.

(31) T. Burt, **Lecture**, op.cit., p. 9.

(32) Watson, op.cit., p.44.

(33) Burt, op.cit., p.9.

(34) Watson, op.cit.

(35) Burt, op.cit.

(36) W.T. Stead to J.L. McCallum in J.L. McCallum, **James Annand**, (Oliphant Anderson & Ferrier, Edinburgh, 1908), p.229.

(37) Cited in G.B.Hodgson, **From Smithy to Senate: The Life Story of James Annand**, (Cassell, 1908), pp.55/56.

(38) Watson, op.cit., pp.43/44.

(39) M. Milne, op.cit., pp. 105/106.

(40) Hansard, 10 November 1882, Col. 1220.

(41) Holyoake to Amberley, 16 May 1870 (Holyoake Collection 1941).

(42) M. Milne, op.cit., p.156.

(43) F.W. Hirst, op.cit., Vol. 2., p.141.

(44) M. Milne, op.cit., p.72.

(45) Ibid., p.64. For other similar assessments see: Owen R. Ashton, **W.E. Adams: Chartist, Radical and Journalist (1832-1906)**, (Bewick Press, Whitley Bay, 1991), p. 115.

(46) Watson, op.cit., p.29.

(47) M. Milne, op.cit.

(48) Lucy Brown, op.cit., pp.71/72; Alan Lee, op.cit., p. 49.

(49) Newcastle Examiner, 8 July 1881.

(50) Lucy Brown, op.cit., p.20.

(51) Cowen to Holyoake, 25 March 1860 (Holyoake Collection 1203)

(52) Newcastle Daily Chronicle, 27 March 1865.

(53) Ibid., 15 June 1866; Lucy Brown, op.cit.

(54) Newcastle Daily Chronicle, 24 February 1900.

(55) M. Milne, op.cit., p. 123.

(56) R.W. Martin, **Northern Worthies**, (Martin, Newcastle upon Tyne, 1932), Vol. 1., p.390; M. Milne, "Richard Bagnall Reed" in Bellamy and Saville, op.cit., Vol. IV, (1977), pp. 142/146.

(57) Newcastle Examiner, 11 February 1881; Watson, op.cit., p.27;

(58) Adams, op.cit., p.493.

(59) Watson, op.cit., p. 59.

(60) M. Milne, op.cit., p.69; Newcastle Daily Chronicle, 6 July 1868 and 13 January 1871.

(61) M. Milne, op.cit.; Lucy Brown, op.cit., pp. 52/53.

(62) See: Duncan, op.cit., p.42; M. Noble, op.cit., pp.56/57; Lucy Brown, op.cit., pp.45/46; Newcastle Daily Chronicle, 26 April 1865.

(63) Duncan, op.cit.

(64) S.J. Reid, op.cit., p.70.

(65) Newcastle Daily Chronicle, 2 August 1864.

(66) Ibid., 3 August 1864.

(67) See: Newcastle Chronicle, 30 November 1849.

(68) Newcastle Daily Chronicle, 6 August 1859; 2 May 1862.

(69) Newcastle Daily Chronicle, 27 October 1862.

(70) See for example, Newcastle Daily Chronicle, 7 August 1865.

(71)   M. Milne, op.cit., p.70 n8; Newcastle Daily Chronicle, 18 March 1872.
       Watson, op.cit., pp. 33/34.
(72)   "Elfin" in Newcastle Daily Chronicle, 21 October 1861.
(73)   M. Milne, op.cit., pp. 78/80.
(74)   See: Duncan, op.cit., p.240; John Saville, W.E. Adams, op.cit.,
       p.17; John Saville, "William Edwin Adams" in Bellamy and Saville,
       op.cit., Vol. VII, (1984), pp. 1/4; Owen R. Ashton, op.cit., pp. 84,
       103/105, 127/130.
(75)   Cited in Sir H.W. Lucy, Sixty Years in the Wildnerness, (Smith,
       Elder, 1909), p.248. See also: Co-operative News, 19 April 1873.
(76)   Watson, op.cit., pp.36/37.
(77)   Cowen to Holyoake, 6 December 1863 (Holyoake Collection 1516).
(78)   Watson, op.cit. Alan Lee, op.cit., p. 127.
(79)   Co-operative News, 10 May 1873. As an illustration of Tyneside's mid-C19
       passion for sports (in this case, rowing) see: David Clasper, Harry Clasper:
       Hero of the North, (Gateshead Books, Gateshead, 1990).
(80)   Newcastle Daily Chronicle, 18 and 20 May 1868.
(81)   Bryan Rees, "The Lost Years: Northumberland Miners 1844-1862" in
       North East Labour History Bulletin, No. 19, 1985, pp. 17/29; Raymond
       Challinor, A Radical Lawyer, op.cit., pp. 205/207.
(82)   Watson, op.cit.,, pp.37/38.
(83)   See: Duncan, op.cit., pp.30, 35/36; Cowen to Holyoake, 13 March
       1860 (Holyoake Collection 1201); Richard Fynes, The Miners of
       Northumberland and Durham, (Davis, Newcastle upon Tyne, 1986 reprint
       of 1873 edn.), pp.171/186.
(84)   See for example Newcastle Daily Chronicle, 2 November 1863.
(85)   Ibid., 17/23 October 1865.
(86)   T. Burt, op.cit., pp.9/10; Newcastle Daily Chronicle, 10 August
       1865 (for Burt's letter).
(87)   Thomas Burt, Thomas Burt, (Fisher Unwin, 1924), pp.184 and 186.
(88)   A. Watson, A Great Labour Leader, op.cit., p.136.
(89)   W.H. Fraser, op.cit., p.203.
(90)   See: Rob Colls, The Colliers' Rant: Song and Culture in the
       Industrial Village, (Croom Helm, 1977); Peter Bailey, Leisure and
       Class in Victorian England: Recreation and the Contest for Control,
       1830-1885, (Methuen & Co., 1987 edn).
(91)   Kathleen Barker, "The Performing Arts in Newcastle upon Tyne"
       in John K. Walton and James Walvin (eds), Leisure in Britain, 1780-
       1939, (Manchester University Press, Manchester, 1983), pp.65 and 68.
(92)   Newcastle Daily Chronicle, 13 September 1861.
(93)   Ibid., 13 November 1861. David Harker, Allan's Illustrated Edition
       of Tyneside Songs, (F. Graham, Newcastle upon Tyne, 1972) pp. xix/xxi
(94)   Ibid., 13 January and 25 March 1862.
(95)   Barker, op.cit., p.66; Newcastle Daily Chronicle, 19 February,
       7 and 8 April 1862.
(96)   "Elfin" in Newcastle Daily Chronicle, 21 July 1862.
(97)   Newcastle Daily Chronicle, 22 July 1862.
(98)   "Elfin" in Newcastle Daily Chronicle, 8 December 1862.
(99)   Newcastle Daily Chronicle, 24 and 26 October 1863; Barker,
       op.cit., p.65.

(100)   Newcastle Daily Chronicle, 14 January and 16 March 1864.
(101)   Adams, op.cit., Vol. I, pp.91/99; Vol. II, p.478; Eric Taylor,
        "John Kane" in Bellamy and Saville, op.cit., Vol. III, (1976), pp.
        118/126.
(102)   Watson, op.cit., p.18.
(103)   S.J. Reid, op.cit., pp.68/69.
(104)   Adams, op.cit., Vol. II, p.502.
(105)   Cited in Newcastle Daily Chronicle, 12 May 1868.
(106)   See for example Newcastle Daily Chronicle 7 January 1865;
        16 September 1867; 3 April 1868.
(107)   M. Baker, The Rise of the Victorian Actor, (Croom Helm, 1978),p.86;
        A. Reed, Bruce's School, (Walter Scott,1903), p.196; Sidney
        Middlebrook, Newcastle upon Tyne: Its Growth and Achievement,
        (S.R. Publishers, Wakefield, 1968 reprint of 1950 edn), pp.304/305.
(108)   M. Baker, op.cit.,, pp.36/37; Newcastle Daily Chronicle, 18, 24
        and 30 September 1867.
(109)   George Stanley cited in Newcastle Daily Chronicle, 8 September 1868.
(110)   Adams, op.cit., pp.500/501; Newcastle Daily Chronicle, 23
        October 1868.
(111)   K. Barker, op.cit., p.66.
(112)   Newcastle Daily Chronicle, 28 March, 6 June and 8 July 1870.

CHAPTER SIX: AGITATIONS AND EMPIRE

(1)   Robertson Davies, "Playwrights and Plays" in C. Leech and T.W.
        Craik, The "Revels" History of Drama in English, Vol. VI, 1750-1880,
        (Methuen, 1975), pp. 249 and 251.
(2)   See: Terry McDermott, "Irish Workers on Tyneside in the 19th
        Century" in N. McCord (ed), Essays, op.cit; Newcastle Daily
        Chronicle, 12 October 1867, 27 July 1868, 20 March and 14 July
        1869; John Latimer, op.cit., p.383; Paul O'Sullivan, Little
        Ireland: A Short History of the Irish in Hebburn and Jarrow,
        (O'Sullivan, Dublin, 1988); Felix Lavery, op.,cit; R.J. Cooter,
        The Irish in Co. Durham and Newcastle upon Tyne, c1840-1880,
        (unpublished MA thesis, University of Durham, 1972).
(3)   Joseph Keating, op.cit., pp. 46/47, 49/50.
(4)   Newcastle Daily Chronicle, 16 September 1865; 28 February, 14, 15,
        16 and 17 March 1866.
(5)   Ibid., 7 February, 8, 9, 10, 11 October 1867.
(6)   Ibid., 8 June, 18, 19 September 1865.
(7)   Ibid., 2 October 1867.
(8)   R.E. Martin, op.cit., p. 192.
(9)   Newcastle Daily Chronicle, 15 July and 25 October 1869.
(10)   Ibid., 11 October 1867.
(11)   Maureen Callcott, The Municipal Administration of Newcastle upon
        Tyne, 1835-1900, (unpublished Ph.D. thesis, University of Newcastle
        upon Tyne, 1988), pp. 61/68.
(12)   Scrapbook, Cowen Papers, F36; Newcastle Daily Chronicle, 22 December

1862.

(13) Newcastle Daily Chronicle, 7 April 1862.

(14) Ibid., 21, 22 November 1862.

(15) Ibid., 13, 14 October 1865; 5 February 1866; 25 September, 9 October 1868.

(16) Ibid., 11 October 1867.

(17) Ibid., 2, 6, 7 January 1868.

(18) Newcastle Courant, 7 April 1848.

(19) Latimer, op.cit., p. 167.

(20) Newcastle Daily Chronicle, 6, 19 July 1866; Monthly Chronicle, 1891, Vol. 5., p. 353.

(21) Newcastle Daily Chronicle, 27 April 1870. Mazzini had not accepted Irish claims to a separate nationality in the 1850s.

(22) Ibid.,16 February 1870.

(23) Ibid., 27 April 1870.

(24) Adams, op.cit., p. 424.

(25) Ibid., pp. 422 and 429.

(26) Bradlaugh to Richard Reed, 12 December 1859, Cowen Papers C948.

(27) See: Royden Harrison, **Before the Socialists: studies in labour and politics, 1861-1881**, (Routledge & Kegan Paul, 1965), p. 46.

(28) See: Newcastle Daily Chronicle, 5 October 1861.

(29) Duncan, op.cit., p. 18; Holyoake, op.cit., Vol. I, p. 293; Newcastle Daily Chronicle, 8 October 1862.

(30) Newcastle Daily Chronicle, 9 March, 13 May 1861.

(31) Jane Cowen, **Notes** (IX), Cowen Papers E436; William Lloyd Garrison to Joseph Cowen, 12 January 1868, Cowen papers, D218; Newcastle Daily Chronicle, 10 July 1867; Duncan, op.cit., pp. 18/19;

(32) Newcastle Daily Chronicle, 27 February 1862.

(33) Ibid., 5, 10 April; 2 September; 22 October 1862.

(34) Ibid., 17 February 1863; Schoyan, op.cit., p. 259 n1.

(35) Adams, op.cit., p. 423.

(36) Newcastle Daily Chronicle, 6 October 1864; Adams, op.cit., p. 535.

(37) Holyoake to Professor Phillips, 15 May 1863 (Holyoake Coll. 1491).

(38) Newcastle Daily Chronicle, 28, 29, 31 August, 3 September 1863; Adams, op.cit., pp. 424/427; Lary Carey, "Ellen Craft" in Edward T. James (ed), **Notable American Women 1607-1950**, (Harvard University Press, Cambridge, Mass., 1971), Vol. 1., pp. 396/398.

(39) Nigel Todd, "Black-on-Tyne: The Black Presence on Tyneside in the 1860s" in North East Labour History Bulletin, No. 21., 1987; A. Reed, op.cit.

(40) See: Newcastle Daily Chronicle, 18 July 1871; 11, 30 September 1872; Ian Lipke, "Thomas Glassey (1844-1936)" in Bede Nairn and Geoffrey Serle, **Australian Dictionary of Biography, Vol. 9., 1891-1939**, (Melbourne University Press, Melbourne, 1983), pp. 24/25.

(41) Newcastle Daily Chronicle, 15 February 1866.

(42) Ibid., 3 August 1867 (India), 20 September 1867 (Australia), 11 January 1861 and 18, 31 May 1869 (New Zealand).

(43) Ibid., 12,21 March 1869; Cowen, 6 June 1852, Cowen Papers, D59.

(44) Newcastle Daily Chronicle, 27 March 1867.

(45) Jane Cowen, **Notes**, Cowen Papers E435 and E436.

(46)   Mazzini to Cowen, 11 April 1864, Cowen Papers A764/ A729.
(47)   Christopher Hibbert, **Garibaldi and His Enemies**, (Longmans, 1965),
        p. 344.
(48)   Adams, op.cit., p. 527.
(49)   Newcastle Daily Chronicle, 9 April 1864.
(50)   Joseph Cowen, Snr., cited in Newcastle Daily Chronicle, 20 April
        1864.
(51)   Jasper Ridley, op.cit., p. 558.
(52)   J.L. and B. Hammond, **James Stansfield**, (Longmans, 1932), p. 83;
        Ridley, op.cit.
(53)   Newcastle Daily Chronicle, 21 April 1864.
(54)   Jane Cowen, **General Garibaldi**, Cowen Papers, E436.
(55)   Hibbert, op.cit., p. 342.
(56)   Ridley, op.cit., pp. 562/563.
(57)   Newcastle Daily Chronicle, 11 May 1864; Cowen to Holyoake, 31 May
        1864 (Holyoake Collection 1546).
(58)   Royden Harrison, op.cit., pp. 67/68.
(59)   John A. Davis, "Garibaldi and England" in History Today, Vol. 23.,
        December 1982, pp. 21/24.
(60)   Newcastle Daily Chronicle, 5 March 1866.

CHAPTER SEVEN: QUEEN VICTORIA DRAWS THE BLINDS

(1)   F.W. Hirst, op.cit., vol. 2., p. 142.
(2)   Proceedings of the Newcastle Council, 10 January 1872, p. 41;
        Newcastle Daily Chronicle, 11 January 1872.
(3)   Newcastle Daily Chronicle, 17 April 1871.
(4)   Cowen Papers, 7 November 1871, B112. Cowen denied any formal
        connection with the Newcastle Republican club.
(5)   The Republican, 15 May 1871.
(6)   A.D. Bell, "The Administration and Finance of the Reform League,
        1865-67" in International Review of Social History, Vol. 10,
        1965, pp. 385/489.
(7)   Cowen Papers, C1742.
(8)   Ibid., C1751; Maurice Cowling, **1867, Disraeli, Gladstone and
        Revolution: The Passing of the Second Reform Bill**, (Cambridge
        University Press, Cambridge, 1967), p. 243, for an analysis of
        the Liberal "attempt to keep control" over the reform
        agitation.
(9)   The Beehive, 8 May 1875.
(10)   Newcastle Daily Chronicle, 11, 12 December 1866.
(11)   Ibid., 9, 21 January 1867.
(12)   Cowen to Howell, 1 February 1867 (Howell Collection); Newcastle Daily
        Chronicle, 29 January 1867.
(13)   Cowen to Howell, op.cit. Newcastle Daily Chronicle, 9 August 1867.
(14)   Newcastle Daily Chronicle, 9 August 1867.
(15)   Ibid., 9 July, 20 September 1867.
(16)   See especially: Ibid., 4 April, 21 September 1868 and 1 April 1869.

(17)   Fraser, op.cit., p. 160; Newcastle Daily Chronicle, 18 July 1871.
(18)   Newcastle Daily Chronicle, 11 April 1870; 15 May, 19 August 1871.
(19)   M. Noble, op.cit., p. 55.
(20)   See: Cowen's comments to the Northern Union of Mechanics' Institutes
       in Newcastle Daily Chronicle, 3 October 1867, and a speech at the
       Newcastle Working Men's Club, 18 September 1882, in Cowen Papers,
       D299.
(21)   Newcastle Weekly Chronicle, 30 October 1869.
(22)   C.E. Whiting, The University of Durham, 1832-1932, (Sheldon Press,
       1932), p. 189.
(23)   Proceedings of the Newcastle Council, 22 December 1870, p. 105.
(24)   John Wilson, A History of the Durham Miners' Association, 1870-
       1904, (J.H. Veitch & Sons, Durham, 1907), p. 319.
(25)   Newcastle Daily Chronicle, 25 November 1869; Newcastle Weekly
       Chronicle, 11 September 1869; Harris, MSS, Chapter 2, p. 18.
(26)   Newcastle Daily Chronicle, 16 December 1869; "Elfin" in
       Newcastle Daily Chronicle, 4 September 1871. See also:
       Newcastle Daily Chronicle, 31 January 1873 for a report of a
       National Education League meeting in Newcastle chaired by Cowen
       and addressed by Joseph Chamberlain.
(27)   Proceedings of Newcastle Council, 13 April 1870, pp. 240/241.
(28)   Speech at Nelson Street Lecture Room, 13 January 1871, Cowen
       Papers, D249.
(29)   Proceedings of Newcastle Council, 22 December 1870, p. 105.
(30)   Newcastle Daily Chronicle, 21 January, 10 February 1871; Duncan,
       op.cit., pp. 56/58; Newcastle Critic, 27 December 1873.
(31)   Hansard, 5 August 1876, Col. 584.
(32)   Proceedings of Newcastle Council, 6 May 1868, p. 308.
(33)   Hansard, op.cit.
(34)   A.J. Harrison, speech at St. Thomas's Church, Newcastle upon
       Tyne, cited in Newcastle Daily Chronicle, 26 February 1900.
(35)   Newcastle Daily Chronicle, 26 November 1869.
(36)   Ibid., 25 July 1871.
(37)   Ibid., 25 January 1871.
(38)   Proceedings of Newcastle Council, 7 May 1873, p. 346.
(39)   E. Allen, The North East Engineers' Strikes of 1871, (Frank Graham
       Newcastle upon Tyne, 1971), p. 98.
(40)   Ibid. See also: John Burnett, The Nine Hours Movement, (J.W.
       Swanston, Newcastle upon Tyne, 1872).
(41)   Allen, op.cit., pp. 106, 122.
(42)   E.R. Jones, The Engineers' Strike in the north of England: appendix
       to a report to the United States Government, (J.M. Carr, Newcastle
       upon Tyne, 1873), p. 4.
(43)   Fynes, op.cit., p. 299.
(44)   Duncan, op.cit., p. 25.
(45)   Cowen to W. Longstaff, 8 January (?) 1871, in K. Harris, Notes.
(46)   Duncan, op.cit., p. 26.
(47)   Newcastle Daily Chronicle, 20 June 1871; Co-operative News,
       9 September 1871.
(48)   Duncan, op.cit., p. 27.

(49)   Albert Harrison, "Joseph Cowen: A Fighter for Freedom", op.cit.

(50)   Newcastle Daily Chronicle, 30, 31 August; 1 September 1871;
       Duncan, op.cit., pp. 28/31.

(51)   W.H.G. Armytage, **A.J. Mundella, 1825-1897,** (Ernest Benn, 1951),
       pp. 102/104; Duncan, op.cit., pp. 32/33.

(52)   Newcastle Daily Chronicle, 10 October 1871.

(53)   Thomas Cooper to A.J. Mundella, 20 September 1871, cited in
       E.I. Waitt, op.cit., p. 7, n14.

(54)   Duncan, op.cit., pp. 33/34.

(55)   Newcastle Daily Chronicle, 1 September 1871.

(56)   Ibid., 4 September 1871.

(57)   **Proceedings of Newcastle Council, 6 September 1871,** pp. 483/484.

(58)   See for example: Newcastle Daily Chronicle, 11, 12, 28 September
       1871.

(59)   Ibid., 27 September 1871.

(60)   **Proceedings of Newcastle Council,** op.cit.

(61)   Newcastle Daily Chronicle, 1 September 1871.

(62)   Ibid., 28 September 1871.

(63)   Ibid., 11, 12, 14 October; 10, 11, 17 November 1871.

(64)   Ibid., 7 September 1870; Cowen Papers, 6 September 1870, A910.

(65)   Newcastle Daily Chronicle, 21 March 1871.

(66)   Ibid., 30 March; 3 April 1871.

(67)   Ibid., 25 April 1871.

(68)   Newcastle Weekly Chronicle, 29 April 1871.

(69)   Newcastle Daily Chronicle, 4 May 1871.

(70)   Ibid., 23 May 1871.

(71)   Ibid., 31 May 1871.

(72)   Irish Tribune, 28 November 1885; Cowen Papers A922/923

(73)   Newcastle Daily Chronicle, 11 July 1871.

(74)   Ibid., 1 July; 23 October 1871.

(75)   James Dellow, op.cit., p. 41.

(76)   Newcastle Daily Chronicle, 20, 21 February 1871.

(77)   Ibid., 28 February 1871.

(78)   The Republican, February 1871.

(79)   Newcastle Daily Chronicle, 2 March 1871.

(80)   Ibid., 3 March 1871.

(81)   Ibid., 24, 30 March; 4 May; 27 June 1871. The Republican, 1, 5 May
       1871. Edward Royle, **Radicals, Secularists and Republicans: Popular
       Freethought in Britain, 1866-1915,** (Manchester University Press,
       Manchester, 1980), pp. 64/68.

(82)   See: Royden Harrison, op.cit., pp. 210/215; Kingsley Martin, **The
       Crown and the Establishment,** (Penguin Books in association with
       Hutchinson, 1965 edition), pp. 39/47.

(83)   Newcastle Daily Chronicle, 7 November 1871.

(84)   Gwynn and Tuckwell, op.cit., Vol. 1., p. 139.

(85)   "Queen Victoria presses Gladstone for a Government condemnation of
       the Republican movement, November 19, 1871" cited in S. Maccoby,
       English Radicalism 1853-1886, (George Allen & Unwin, 1938), p. 164;
       David Tribe, **President Charles Bradlaugh, MP,** (Elek Books, 1971),
       pp. 130/131.

(86)   Gladstone to the Queen, 22 November 1871, cited in Frank Hardie,
        The Political Influence of Queen Victoria 1861-1901, (Oxford
        University Press, Oxford, 1935), p. 211.
(87)   Ibid.
(88)   See Holyoake Collection: Stansfield to Holyoake, 4 October 1871
        (2028); Holyoake to Richard Reed, 6 October 1871 (2029); Holyoake
        to Stansfield, 19 October 1871 (2031); Cowen, snr., to Holyoake,
        3 November 1871 (2033).
(89)   Gladstone to Lord Halifax, 4 December 1871, in H.C.G. Matthews (ed),
        The Gladstone Diaries, Vol. III, July 1871-December 1874, (Clarendon
        Press, Oxford, 1982), p. 73.
(90)   **Proceedings of Newcastle Council, 10 January 1872,** p. 41.
(91)   Newcastle Daily Chronicle, 10 January 1872.
(92)   Ibid., 21 February; 20 March; 21 May; 13 June; 10 September;
        3 December 1872.
(93)   Ibid., 6, 25 July 1872.
(94)   Ibid., 12, 13, 14 September 1872.

CHAPTER EIGHT: "THE MILITANT DEMOCRACY"

(1)   T. Rothstein, op.cit., p. 164.
(2)   F.E. Gillespie, **Labour and Politics in England 1850-67,**
        (Frank Cass, 1966 reprint of 1927 edition), p. 14.
(3)   A.R. Schoyen, op.cit., p. 234.
(4)   John Vincent, **The Formation of the British Liberal Party 1857-68,**
        (Penguin Books, 1972 edn., first published by Constable, 1966),
        p. 13.
(5)   Maurice Cowling, op.cit., p. 244.
(6)   T. Tholfsen, **Working Class Radicalism in Mid-Victorian England,**
        (Croom Helm, 1976), p. 153.
(7)   Fraser, op.cit., pp. 222/223.
(8)   Co-operative News, 19 April 1873.
(9)   Cowen: Address to the Winlaton Mechanics' Institute, 18 June 1850,
        cited in K. Harris. **MSS,** Chapter 2, p. 26; Newcastle Guardian,
        22 June 1850.
(10)   Newcastle Weekly Chronicle, 19 April 1873.
(11)   Ibid.
(12)   See: Newcastle Daily Journal, 4 January 1874; T.A. Jenkins,
        Gladstone, Whiggery and the Liberal Party 1874-1886, (Clarendon
        Press, Oxford, 1988), p. 193.
(13)   Henry Crompton in The Beehive, 7 October 1871.
(14)   Newcastle Daily Chronicle, 18 July 1871.
(15)   Ibid., 19, 26 February 1872.
(16)   Ibid., 9, 12, 23, 26, 29 February; 5, 6, 7, 9, 11, 14, 18 March;
        4, 10, 11 April; 2, 6, 7 May; 1 July 1872.
(17)   Newcastle Weekly Chronicle, 15 March 1873.
(18)   "Elfin" in Newcastle Daily Chronicle, 18 March 1872; Newcastle Daily
        Chronicle, 4 April 1872.

(19)   E.D. Spraggon, op.cit., pp. 67/68.
(20)   Newcastle Daily Chronicle, 28 February 1871.
(21)   Ibid., 5 May 1871.
(22)   Ibid., 15, 18 June 1872.
(23)   Ibid., 18, 19, 20, 21, 22, 24 June 1872.
(24)   Ibid., 23, 24, 25, 26, 28, 29 June; 1, 2, 3, 4, 5, 7, 9, 11, 12,
       18, 19, 22, 23 July; 8, 13, 23 August; 6 September 1872.
(25)   Dorothy Thompson, op.cit., pp. 356/359; Rob Colls,
       **The Pitmen of the Northern Coalfield: Work, Culture and Protest,
       1790-1850**, (MUP, Manchester, 1987), pp. 274/275, 277/278.
(26)   See: Newcastle Daily Chronicle, 17 June, 14 August 1872.
(27)   Ibid., 15 June 1872.
(28)   Ibid., 21, 22, 29 June 1872.
(29)   See: Jean Gaffin and David Thomas, **Caring and Sharing: The Centenary
       History of the Co-operative Women's Guild**, (Co-operative Union,
       Manchester, 1983), pp. 18/19; Nigel Todd, **Roses and Revolutionists:
       The Story of the Clousden Hill Free Communist and Co-operative
       Colony, 1894-1902**, (Peoples Publications, 1986), p. 57, n19.
(30)   Newcastle Daily Chronicle, 24 June 1872.
(31)   Newcastle Weekly Chronicle, 3 August 1872.
(32)   P.A. Darvill, **The Contribution of Co-operative Retail Societies to
       Welfare within the framework of the North East Coast area**,
       (unpublished M.Litt thesis, University of Durham, 1954),p. 2.
(33)   G.D.H. Cole, **A Century of Co-operation**, (Co-operative Union,
       Manchester, 1944), p. 153.
(34)   Darvill, op.cit., p. 1.
(35)   William Douglass at the 1876 Annual Meeting of the Northern Union of
       Mechanics' Institutes, cited in Darvill, op.cit., p. 6. E.R. Jones,
       Life, op.cit., p. 97.
(36)   Darvill, op.cit., p. 6, n1; p. 8.
(37)   Rev. J. Jeffrey speaking on Cowen's views at a Felling Co-operative
       Society soiree cited in Newcastle Daily Chronicle, 15 August 1865.
(38)   Cowen cited in E.D. Spraggon, op.cit., p. 82.
(39)   Cowen at 6th Annual Soiree of the Blaydon Co-operative Society,
       Newcastle Daily Chronicle, 20 June 1865.
(40)   Cited in Darvill, op.cit., p. 7.
(41)   North of England Advertiser, 28 July 1862.
(42)   Darvill, op.cit., p. 36.
(43)   Ibid., pp. 34, 36, 39.
(44)   Newcastle Working Men's Club, Minutes, 31 August 1866.
(45)   Duncan, op.cit., p. 23.
(46)   Cole, op.cit., p. 154.
(47)   Darvill, op.cit., pp. 95/96.
(48)   P. Redfern, **The New History of the C.W.S.**, (J.M. Dent & Sons,
       1938), p. 30.
(49)   Darvill, op.cit., p. 94.
(50)   Newcastle Weekly Chronicle, 13 October 1869; Co-operative News,
       13 July 1901.
(51)   Newcastle Weekly Chronicle, 17 June 1871.
(52)   Darvill, op.cit., pp. 236/237.

(53) Cowen at Blaydon Co-operative Society Annual Soiree, Newcastle Daily Chronicle, 27 June 1869.

(54) Darvill, op.cit., p. 200, n1.

(55) Newcastle Working Men's Club, op.cit.

(56) Newcastle Daily Chronicle, 8 April, 20 May 1871; 23 July 1872.

(57) Darvill, op.cit., Chapter 3 (Appendix).

(58) Co-operative News, 9 September 1871.

(59) Cole, op.cit., p. 163.

(60) Newcastle Daily Chronicle, 8 November 1871.

(61) Darvill, op.cit., pp. 102/103.

(62) Newcastle Daily Chronicle, 8 November 1871.

(63) Newcastle Weekly Chronicle, 4 November 1871; 3 May, 7, 21, 28 June, 26 July 1873. Newcastle Daily Chronicle, 12 February, 13 May, 9 December 1872; 6 January 1873. Darvill, op.cit., Chapter 3 (Appendix). Cole, op.cit., pp. 160/165.

(64) Darvill, op.cit., pp. 98/99.

(65) Newcastle Weekly Chronicle (Supplement), 19 April 1873; Co-operative News, 26 April 1873.

(66) Darvill, op.cit., p. 8.

(67) Newcastle Weekly Chronicle, op.cit. Cowen Papers B135.

(68) Co-operative News, 19 April 1873.

(69) Newcastle Weekly Chronicle, op.cit. G.J. Holyoake, op.cit., Vol. II., p. 573. Adams, op.cit., Vol. II., p. 534/536.

(70) Newcastle Daily Chronicle, 13 January 1873.

(71) Ibid., 15 February 1873; Newcastle Weekly Chronicle 1, 15 March 1873.

(72) Newcastle Weekly Chronicle, 21 June 1873.

(73) Ibid., 28 June 1873.

(74) Newcastle Weekly Chronicle 18 October 1873.

(75) Adams, op.cit., p. 539/547; See also: W.H. Maehl, "The North East Miners' Struggle for the Franchise 1872-74" in International Review of Social History, Vol. 20, 1975, p. 2.

(76) Cowen at a Co-operative Congress meeting cited in Co-operative News, 19 April 1873.

(77) Holyoake to A.W. Peel, March 1874 (Holyoake Collection 2250).

(78) A. Watson, **A Great Labour Leader**, op.cit., p. 136; Aaron Watson cited in Hirst, op.cit., Vol. 2., p. 142.

(79) Thomas Burt, op.cit., p. 209.

(80) Lord Londonderry to Disraeli cited in T.J. Nossister, **Influences, Opinion and Political Idioms in Reformed England: case studies from the north east**, (Harvester Press, Brighton, 1975),p. 101.

(81) **Local Biographies**, Vol.1, p.169 [Newcastle upon Tyne Public Library].

(82) J. Kelly in Baylen and Gossman, op.cit., p. 160.

(82) Daily Telegraph, 16 January 1874.

(83) Ibid.

CHAPTER NINE : THROWING A BRICK AT MR. GLADSTONE

(1)   Cited in <u>Co-operative News</u>, 10 May 1873.

(2)   William D. Lawson, **Lawson's Tyneside Celebrities**, (Lawson,
         Newcastle upon Tyne, 1873), p. 372.

(3)   Holyoake to Cowen, 13 February 1860, Cowen papers C1210.

(4)   <u>The Beehive</u>, 8 May 1875.

(5)   E.I. Waitt, op.cit., pp. 8/11.

(6)   Cowen to Holyoake, 21 December 1873 (Holyoake Collection 2203).

(7)   Waitt, op.cit., p. 14.

(8)   Aaron Watson, **Newspaperman**, op.cit., pp. 48/49.

(9)   W. Maehl, "The Liberal Party and the Newcastle Elections of 1874" in
         <u>Durham University Journal</u>, Vol. 57, 1965, p. 150; Waitt, op.cit.,
         pp. 21/22.

(10)   Maehl, op.cit., p. 152; Waitt, op.cit., pp. 16/17.

(11)   <u>Newcastle Weekly Chronicle</u>, 7 January 1874.

(12)   <u>Newcastle Daily Chronicle</u>, 5 January 1874.

(13)   Ibid., 5, 13 January 1874; Maile, op.cit., p. 154.

(14)   **Havelock's Records**, (George Havelock, Newcastle upon Tyne, 1885),
         December 1884, p. 145; <u>Newcastle Critic</u>, 3 January 1874;
         <u>Liverpool Leader</u> cited in <u>Newcastle Critic</u>, 24 January 1874;
         Waitt. op.cit., p. 17.

(15)   Keith Harris, **Notes.**

(16)   <u>Newcastle Daily Journal</u>, 12, 27 January 1874.

(17)   Waitt, op.cit., p. 18.

(18)   Watson, op.cit., pp. 48/49. Alan J. Lee, op.cit., pp. 192/193.

(19)   Waitt, op.cit., p. 29.

(20)   Watson, op.cit., p. 50; F. Hirst, op.cit., p. 143; Duncan, op.cit.,
         p. 84; Waitt, op.cit., p. 30.

(21)   Waitt, op.cit., pp. 44, 48/51.

(22)   <u>Newcastle Daily Chronicle</u>, 31 January 1874.

(23)   Waitt, op.cit., pp. 53/56.

(24)   Ibid., p. 58.

(25)   <u>Newcastle Weekly Chronicle</u>, 7 February 1874.

(26)   Waitt, op.cit., p. 57.

(27)   Ibid., p. 61.

(28)   Duncan, op.cit., pp. 87/88.

(29)   Peel-Holyoake correspondence, March 1874 (Holyoake Collection 2249,
         2250).

(30)   Cowen: Speech at Blaydon Mechanics' Institute, 16 September 1874,
         Cowen Papers, B167.

(31)   <u>Newcastle Weekly Chronicle</u>, 19 September 1874; 25 September 1875.

(32)   Cited in Waitt, op.cit., p. 62, n5.

(33)   Cowen to Mawson, 14 April 1875, cited in K. Harris, **Notes.**

(34)   Holyoake, **Bygones**, op.cit., Vol. II., p. 60.

(35)   <u>Newcastle Weekly Chronicle</u>, 28 February, 4 April 1874; Waitt, op.
         cit., p. 69.

(36)   R. Spence Watson, **The National Liberal Federation 1877-1906 from its
         commencement to the general election of 1906**, (Fisher Unwin, 1906),

pp. 3/4.

(37)   Newcastle Weekly Chronicle, 4 April 1874.

(38)   Waitt, op.cit.

(39)   Cowen: Speech to the National Reform Union, Manchester,
       19 December 1877, Cowen Papers C1857.

(40)   E.P. Hennock, **Fit and Proper Persons: ideals and reality in
       nineteenth century urban government,** (Edward Arnold, 1973), pp.
       171/172.

(41)   See: Callcott, op.cit., chapter six; B. Anderton, **The Struggle for
       a Public Library,** (Library Association, 1905).

(42)   Newcastle Daily Chronicle, 17 November 1871.

(43)   Waitt, op.cit., p. 72.

(44)   The Beehive, 26 December 1874.

(45)   Newcastle Weekly Chronicle, 2 January, 19 June 1875.

(46)   See: Ibid., 1 May 1875.

(47)   Burt to Holyoake, 6 November 1877, cited in K. Harris, **Notes;**
       Newcastle Daily Chronicle, 1 January 1878.

(48)   Newcastle Daily Chronicle, 1 January 1878.

(49)   Darvill, op.cit., p. 97 and chapter three (appendix).

(50)   W. Maw, **The Story of the Rutherford Grammar School,** (Northumberland
       Press, Gateshead, 1964), pp. 48/49; F.B. Smith, op.cit., p. 150.

(51)   Burt, op.cit., pp. 213/214; Newcastle Weekly Chronicle, 30 January
       1875.

(52)   N. McCord, "Some Aspects of North East England in the Nineteenth
       Century" in Northern History, Vol. VII., (1972), p. 81.

(53)   Newcastle Weekly Chronicle, 27 February, 10 July 1875.

(54)   Hansard, 23 March 1876, Cols. 501/509.

(55)   Thomas Burt, **Lecture,** op.cit., p. 16.

(56)   T. Wemyss Reid, **Politicians of Today,** (Richmond Publishing Company,
       Richmond, Surrey, 1972 reprint of 1880 edn), p. 171.

(57)   Newcastle Weekly Chronicle, 1 April 1876.

(58)   Jenkins, op.cit., pp. 84/85. For a detailed study of Cowen"s
       parliamentary relationships see: J.M. Kelly, **The Parliamentary
       Career of Joseph Cowen,** op.cit.

(59)   T. Wemyss Reid, op.cit., p. 175.

(60)   Birmingham Gazette, 5 August 1876.

(61)   Cowen to Robert Spence Watson, 26 March 1876, cited in Percy Corder,
       The Life of Robert Spence Watson, (Hedley Bros., 1914), p. 215.

(62)   S.J. Reid, op.cit., p. 171.

(63)   Gwynn and Tuckwell, op.cit., Vol. 1., p. 196.

(64)   P. Corder, op.cit.

(65)   Burt, op.cit., p. 5.

(66)   A.D. Bell, op.cit.

(67)   Newcastle Daily Chronicle, 3 August 1864; Cowen to Holyoake, 31
       May 1864 (Holyoake Collection 1457).

(68)   Andrew Jones, **The Politics of Reform, 1884,** (Cambridge University
       Press, Cambridge, 1972), p. 249.

(69)   Sir H.W. lucy, **Memoirs,** op.cit., pp. 49/50; T.P. O'Connor, **Memoirs,**
       op.cit., p. 298.

(70)   Jane Cowen, **MSS Life,** Cowen Papers E435, p. 46.

(71)   Lucy, op.cit.
(72)   Hirst, op.cit., Vol. 2., pp. 144/145.
(73)   Gwynn and Tuckwell, op.cit., p. 223.
(74)   C.G. Macquee to Cowen, 1 September 1859, Cowen Papers C718.
(75)   Holyoake to Mrs. Gladstone, 16 October 1862, (Holyoake Collection
        1446).
(76)   Waitt, op.cit., p. 15.
(77)   Hirst, op.cit., pp. 144/145.
(78)   O'Connor, op.cit. Waitt, op.cit., pp. 75/77.
(79)   Examiner cited in Newcastle Weekly Chronicle, 29 April 1876.
(80)   T.W. Heyck, **The Dimensions of British Radicalism: the case of
        Ireland, 1874-95,** (Urbana, University of Illinois Press, 1974),
        p. 11.
(81)   Jenkins, op.cit., p. 87, n146.
(82)   Peter Fraser, **Joseph Chamberlain: Radicalism and Empire 1868-1914,**
        (Cassell, 1966), p. xii.
(83)   Cited in Waitt, op.cit., p. 85.
(84)   Jenkins, op.cit., p. 194.
(85)   Ibid., p. 86, n139.
(86)   D.A. Hamer, **John Morley: Liberal Intellectual in Politics,** (Oxford
        University Press, Oxford, 1968), pp. 50, 75.
(87)   McCarthy, op.cit., p. 156.
(88)   Waitt, op.cit., p. 78, n73.
(89)   Jenkins, op.cit., p. 87, n 146; Waitt, op.cit., p. 86.
(90)   Duncan, op.cit., p. 95.
(91)   Sir. H.W. Lucy, **Later Peeps at Parliament,** op.cit., p. 34.
(92)   Cowen: Speech at Blaydon, 16 May 1883, Cowen Papers D311.
(93)   Cowen to David Lane, n.d. 1878, Cowen Papers F43.
(94)   Hansard, 2 April 1879, Col. 222.
(95)   Waitt, op.cit., p. 80.
(96)   Healey, **Letters,** op.cit., Vol. 1., p. 35.
(97)   Newcastle Daily Chronicle, 28 October 1872.
(98)   F. Hugh O'Donnell, **A History of the Irish Parliamentary Party,**
        (Longmans, 1910), Vol. 1., p. 271.
(99)   Newcastle Weekly Chronicle, 30 May 1874.
(100)   Hansard, 1 August 1876, Cols. 292/298.
(101)   Ibid., 5 April 1877, Cols. 628/634.
(102)   Ibid., 11 June 1877, Cols. 1605/1613.
(103)   O'Donnell, op.cit., pp. 328/329.
(104)   Ibid., pp. 331/336.
(105)   Jenkins, op.cit., pp. 84/85.
(106)   S.J. Reid, op.cit., p. 223; Joseph Kelly in Baylen and Gossman,
        op.cit., pp. 161/162.
(107)   McCarthy, op.cit., p. 155; M. Ostrogorski, **Democracy and the
        Organisation of Political Parties,** (Macmillan, 1902), Vol. 1.,
        p. 234.
(108)   Waitt, op.cit., p. 91.
(109)   Newcastle Daily Chronicle, 3 February 1877.
(110)   Hansard, 14 June 1877, Col. 1792.
(111)   Cowen: Speech to the National Reform Union, Manchester, 19 December

1877, Cowen Papers C1857.

(112) Ostrogorski, op.cit., pp. 234/235.

(113) Richard Shannon, **Gladstone and The Bulgarian Agitation, 1876**, (Nelson, 1964), pp. 36/112; See too: A.J.P. Taylor, **The Troublemakers**, (Panther/Hamish Hamilton, 1969 edn), Chapter 3.

(114) Hansard, 11 February 1878, Col. 1427.

(115) Cowen: Speech at Newcastle upon Tyne, 3 January 1874, Cowen Papers B166.

(116) Hansard, op.cit., Cols. 1426/1436; 11 February 1878, Col 1221.

(117) F.B. Smith, op.cit., p. 189.

(118) Cowen to Spence Watson cited in Corder, op.cit., p. 221.

(119) Gwynn and Tuckwell, op.cit..

(120) St. James Gazette, 12 December 1885.

(121) Newcastle Daily Chronicle, 8 January 1878.

(122) Waitt, op.cit., p. 78; Gwyn and Tuckwell, op.cit., p. 215; Adams, op.cit., p. 503.

(123) See: E.P. Thompson, **William Morris: Romantic to Revolutionary**, (Merlin Press, 1976 edn), p. 208.

(124) Hansard, 11 February 1878, Col. 1436.

(125) Ibid., Cols. 1221; 1429.

(126) Newcastle Daily Chronicle, 14 February 1872.

(127) Ibid., 31 January 1880.

(128) Waitt, op.cit., suggests Annand as the author although M. Milne, **Newspapers**, op.cit., p. 113, believes Stead inspired the pamphlet; for Bright's "treason" remark see R.A.J. Walling, **The Diaries of John Bright**, (Cassall, 1930), pp. 433/434.

(129) Owen R. Ashton, op.cit., pp. 103, 133/135; G.B. Hodgson, op.cit., p. 73; M. Milne, op.cit., p 105.

(130) Frederick Whyte, **The Life of W.T. Stead**, (J. Cape, 1925), pp. 47/50; W.T. Stead, **The M.P. for Russia**, (Andrew Melrose, 1909), Vol. 2., p. 280.

(131) Newcastle Daily Chronicle, 15 January 1878; Daily News, 17 March 1880.

(132) Hansard, 11 February 1878, Col. 1447; Duncan, op.cit., p. 230.

(133) Waitt, op.cit., p. 110.

(134) Manchester Guardian, 20 September 1879; Newcastle Daily Chronicle, 20 September 1879.

(135) Newcastle Daily Chronicle, 10 November 1879.

(136) Ibid., 12 November 1879.

(137) Ibid., 4 December 1879.

(138) Jenkins, op.cit., p. 108; Waitt, op.cit., p. 97.

(139) T. Lloyd, **The General Election of 1880**, (Oxford University Press, 1968), p. 25; Waitt, op.cit., pp. 132/134, 151; Duncan, op.cit., pp. 113/115. The election result was: Cowen - 11, 766; Dilke - 10, 159; Hamond - 5, 271.

CHAPTER TEN: "THE MINISTRY OF COERCION"

(1)   Hansard, 30 August 1880, Cols. 718/723.
(2)   Cowen to Charles Bradlaugh, 24 June 1880 (Bradlaugh Collection)
(3)   Cowen to C.H.A. Bille, June 1880, Cowen Papers F43.
(4)   Hansard, op.cit.
(5)   Ibid., 3 February 1881, Col. 68.
(6)   Fergus D'Arcy, "Charles Bradlaugh" in Art Cosgrove and Donal
       McCartney, **Studies in Irish History**, (University College, Dublin,
       1979), pp. 249/251.
(7)   Cowen to George Mitchell, n.d. 1881, Cowen Papers F43.
(8)   T.W. Heyck, op.cit., p. 65.
(9)   F.H. O'Donnell, op.cit., Vol. 2., p. 15.
(10)   See for example: Thomas Burt, **Address at Bedlington [on the Land
       League]**, (Local Tracts, Newcastle upon Tyne Public Library, 1881),
       pp. 1/12; and exchange of letters between Burt and Lloyd Jones in
       Newcastle Daily Chronicle, 18 November 1881.
(11)   T.M. Healey, op.cit., Vol. 1., p. 40; Hansard, 2 February 1881,
       Col. 20.
(12)   The Radical, 15 January 1881; Hansard, 8 February 1881, Cols. 356/
       371.
(13)   T.P. O'Connor, **Gladstone's House of Commons**, (Ward and Downey,
       1885), p. 391.
(14)   Hansard, op.cit.
(15)   The Radical, 29 June 1881.
(16)   Ibid., 12 February 1881.
(17)   Hansard, 25 February 1881, Cols. 1802/1813.
(18)   Ibid., 17 February 1881, Col. 1089; 18 February 1881, Col. 1294.
(19)   Ibid., 25 February 1881, Cols. 1802/1813.
(20)   F.H. O'Donnell, op.cit., p. 108; Morley to Chamberlain, 26
       November 1881 (cited in E.I. Waitt, op.cit., p. 169).
(21)   Healey, op.cit., p. 35.
(22)   Hansard, 3 June 1881, Cols. 69/81.
(23)   Ibid., 10 May 1881, Cols. 192/198.
(24)   Ibid., 29 July 1881, Cols. 181/185.
(25)   Ibid., 24 May 1881, Cols. 1238.
(26)   Ibid., 4 August 1881, Col. 842; Duncan, op.cit., pp. 183/184;
       Albert Harrison, "Joseph Cowen: Fighter for Freedom", op.cit.
(27)   Waitt, op.cit., p. 159.
(28)   Joseph Keating, op.cit., p. 55; Newcastle Daily Chronicle, 20
       March 1880.
(29)   Waitt, op.cit., p. 142.
(30)   Newcastle Daily Chronicle, 19 February 1900.
(31)   Cowen to Longstaff, 5 September 1892, Cowen Papers D430.
(32)   Cowen to Holyoake, 10 May 1880, (Holyoake Collection 2590).
(33)   W.H. James to Holyoake, 11 May 1880 (Holyoake Collection 2591).
(34)   H.M. Hyndman, op.cit., p. 204.
(35)   T.P. O'Connor, "The Irish in Great Britain" in Lavery. op.cit.,
       p. 22; Joseph Keating, op.cit., p. 51; T.M. Healey, op.cit.,

pp. 30/32, 55, 111.
(36) O'Connor, op.cit., pp. 22/23.
(37) R.B. O'Brien, **The Life of Charles Stewart Parnell,1846-1891**, (Smith, Elder, 1899), Vol. 1., p. 124; R.J. Cooter, op.cit., p. 258.
(38) Irish Tribune, 31 October 1885.
(39) Cowen to Bernard Cracroft, 29 June 1883, Cowen Papers F47; Cowen to T.W. Reid, n.d., Cowen Papers F51.
(40) Hansard, 24 February 1882, Cols. 1614/1615.
(41) Ibid., 28 February 1882, Cols. 1845/1846.
(42) Cowen to Kropotkin, 16 June 1883, Cowen Papers, F43; Waitt, op.cit., p. 174.
(43) Joseph Keating, op.cit., p. 62; Newcastle Daily Chronicle, 13 February 1884.
(44) McCarthy, op.cit., p. 157; Newcastle Daily Chronicle, 30 August 1881; Newcastle Weekly Chronicle, 3 September 1881.
(45) McCarthy, op.cit., pp. 208/209.
(46) H.J. Gladstone, op.cit., p. 173.
(47) Hansard, 23 May 1882, Cols. 1448/1467.
(48) Ibid., 11 May 1882, Cols. 502/521.
(49) McCarthy, op.cit., p. 217.
(50) James Annand, **A Plain Letter to Joseph Cowen, Esq., M.P., by a Gladstonian Radical,, 1882**, (Local Tracts, Newcastle upon Tyne Public Library) p. 15.
(51) Cowen to J. Boyd Kinnear, 6 June 1882, Cowen Papers F43.
(52) Cowen to Kropotkin, 16 June 1882, Cowen Papers F46.
(53) S. Maccoby, op.cit., p. 266.
(54) Cowen to H.S. Fagan, 13 June 1882, Cowen Papers, F47(4).
(55) Cowen to Thomas W. Miller, 6 July 1882, Cowen Papers F46.
(56) Cowen to the Newry branch of the Irish Land League, June 1882, Cowen Papers F44.
(57) Cowen: 31 January 1880 in Jane Cowen (ed), **Joseph Cowen's Speeches**, (Longmans, Green & Co., 1909), p. 72.
(58) The Times, 23 September 1880.
(59) Jane Cowen, **MSS Life**, pp. 41/42, Cowen Papers E435.
(60) Waitt, op.cit., p. 158.
(61) Newcastle Daily Chronicle, 4 January 1881.
(62) Cited in Duncan, op.cit., pp. 123/124.
(63) Freeman's Journal, 2 November 1881.
(64) Newcastle Daily Chronicle, 23 November 1881.
(65) Yvonne Kapp, **Eleanor Marx**, (Lawrence and Wishart, 1972), Vol. 1., p. 212.
(66) R. Challinor, "Dear Dr. Marx" in North East Labour History Bulletin, No. 18, 1984, pp. 26/27.
(67) Nicolaievsky and Maechen-Helfen, op.cit., p. 403.
(68) The Radical, 15 January 1881. See too: Paul Thompson, **Socialists, Liberals and Labour: The Struggle for London, 1885-1914**, (Routledge and Kegan Paul, 1967), p. 112.
(69) The Radical, 5 March 1881.
(70) M.S. Wilkins, "The Non-Socialist Origins of England's First Important Socialist Organisation" in International Review of Social History,

(1959), Vol. 4, p. 205.

(71) Challinor, op.cit., p. 26; The Radical, 12 March 1881; Newcastle Daily Chronicle, 7 March 1881.

(72) Cited in Challinor, op.cit., p. 24.

(73) Newcastle Daily Chronicle, 30 August, 3 October 1881.

(74) Hansard, 24 February 1880, Col. 1333.

(75) E.J. Hobsbawn, **Labouring Men: Studies in the History of Labour**, (Weidenfeld and Nicolson, 1968 edn), p. 233.

(76) Challinor, op.cit., p. 24.

(77) Newcastle Daily Chronicle, 7 March 1881. See too: C. Tsuzuki, **H.M. Hyndman and British Socialism**, (Oxford University Press, 1961), pp. 37/43.

(78) Edward Royle, **Radical Politics 1790-1900: Religion and Unbelief**, (Longmans, 1971), pp. 73/74.

(79) Jane Cowen (ed), **Joseph Cowen's Speeches**, op.cit., p. 168; E.D. Spraggon, op.cit., p. 73.

(80) Ibid., p. 75.

(81) Hansard, 3 March 1881, Col. 345; 5 May 1881, Col. 1840.

(82) Peter Kropotkin, **Memoirs of a Revolutionist**, (Dover Publications, New York, 1971 edn), p. 437.

(83) Cowen to Bernard Cracroft, n.d. 1882, Cowen Papers F45.

(84) Newcastle Daily Chronicle, 3 July 1882.

(85) Newcastle Weekly Chronicle, 8 July 1882.

(86) Ibid.

(87) H.M. Hyndman, op.cit., p. 262.

(88) Cowen to Westall, 23 February 1883, Cowen Papers F46.

(89) G. Woodcock and I. Avakumovic, **The Anarchist Prince: A Biographical Study of Peter Kropotkin**, (Boardman, 1950), p. 189.

(90) Cowen to Kropotkin, 31 October 1884, Cowen Papers F54(1)

(91) E. Anderson, **Record of the Tyneside Sunday Lecture Society**, (TSLS, Newcastle upon Tyne, 1907), see especially p. 155 for reference to Cowen as a vice-president of the Society "aiding ... in securing the Tyne Theatre" for lectures.

(92) Nigel Todd, **Roses and Revolutionists**, op.cit., pp. 16/19.

(93) Cowen to William Morris, 15 November 1886, British Museum Additional MS, 45, 345, f123-4.

(94) Newcastle Daily Chronicle, 17 June 1882; H.W. Lee and E. Archbold, **Social-Democracy in Britain: Fifty Years of the Socialist Movement**, (Social-Democratic Federation, 1935), pp. 46/47.

(95) Joseph Kelly in Baylen and Gossman, op.cit., p. 163.

(96) A.J. Mundella to H.J. Wilson, 14 February 1881 cited in W.S. Fowler, **A Study in Radicalism and Dissent: The Life and Times of Henry Joseph Wilson, 1833-1914**, (Epworth Press, 1961), pp. 71/72.

(97) Cowen to George Mitchell, n.d. 1881, Cowen Papers F43(5).

(98) Cowen to James Runciman, 18 May 1882, Cowen Papers F43(18).

(99) Cowen to John Ferguson, n.d. 1882, Cowen Papers F44(12).

(100) R.J. Cooter, op.cit., pp. 259/260.

(101) Ibid., pp. 264/265.

(102) Cowen to W.H. Patterson, Durham Miners' Association, 1 August 1882, Cowen Papers, F46(11); Cowen: Speech to the Society of Stonemasons,

22 September 1882, Cowen Papers B266.

(103) Newcastle Weekly Chronicle, 24 February 1883; The Echo, 2 March 1883.

(104) Cowen: Speech at Newcastle teachers' conference, 27 March 1883, Cowen Papers B290.

(105) Cowen to R.J. Burn, 26 May 1883, Cowen Papers F47(9); Newcastle Daily Chronicle, 24 and 30 May, 1883.

(106) Cowen: 22 December 1883 cited in Jane Cowen (ed), op.cit., p. 172.

(107) Cowen: Speech at North of England Commercial Travellers Association, 11 January 1884, Cowen Papers B300.

(108) Cowen: Speech at Northern Union of Mechanics' Institutes Annual Meeting, Blaydon, 17 September 1884, Cowen Papers D318.

(109) Northern Union of Mechanics' Institutes, **Annual Report, 1884**, pp. 10/17.

(110) W. Robb, op.cit., p. 80.

(111) M. Ostrogorski, op.cit., p. 233.

(112) Joseph Keating, op.cit., p. 55.

(113) Waitt. op.cit., p. 160; Newcastle upon Tyne Liberal Association, **Annual Report 1881**, p. 14;

(114) Ibid., p. 16.

(115) Waitt, op.cit., p. 154.

(116) Cowen: 3 January 1881 cited in Jane Cowen (ed), op.cit., p. 91.

(117) Hansard, 3 June 1881, Col. 81.

(118) Ibid., 28 June 1881, Cols. 1503/1508.

(119) Cowen to Ashton Dilke, n.d. 1882, Cowen Papers F44.

(120) Cowen: 28 January 1882 cited in Jane Cowen (ed), op.cit., pp. 25/32.

(121) Newcastle upon Tyne Liberal Association, **Meeting of the General Committee on Thursday, February 24th, 1882**, p. 2.

(122) Cowen to James Runciman, 18 May 1882, Cowen Papers F43.

(123) Cowen to J. Boyd Kinnear, 6 June 1882, Cowen Papers F43.

(124) Cowen to H. Byron Reed, 11 July 1882, Cowen Papers F46.

(125) M. Ostrogorski, op.cit., p. 235.

(126) Waitt, op.cit., pp. 95/96, 102, 220/222.

(127) Morley to Sir Charles Dilke, 31 January 1883, British Museum Additional MS; Ostrogorski, op.cit., pp. 235/236.

(128) Ibid.

(129) Northern Echo cited in F.W. Hirst, op.cit., Vol. 2., p. 164.

(130) Hansard, 13 May 1884, Col. 255.

(131) T.P. O'Connor, Memoirs, op.cit., Vol. 1., p. 298.

(132) Morley to Spence Watson, 10 August 1883 cited in Waitt, op.cit., p. 205.

(133) Morley to Albert Grey, n.d. December 1881 cited in Waitt, op.cit., p. 169.

(134) Morley to Spence Watson 28 May 1884 cited in Waitt, op. cit., p. 216.

(135) Ostrogorski, op.cit., pp. 236/237; F.W. Hirst, op.cit., p. 162.

(136) Cowen to Thomas Herdman, 23 February 1883, Cowen Papers F46.

(137) T.H.S. Escott, **The Future of the Radical Party**, (Harvester Press, Brighton, 1971 reprint of 1885 edn), p. lv.

(138) Hansard, 12 June 1884, Cols. 160/166.

(139) Waitt, op.cit., p. 219; Hansard, op.cit., Cols. 198/199.

(140) J. Wilson, op.cit., p. 197.
(141) Cowen to James Stainsthorpe, 28 May 1885, Cowen Papers F54(18).
(142) Cowen to Thomas Walton, 1 May 1885, Cowen Papers F54 (15).
(143) A. Watson, op.cit., p. 183.
(144) <u>Northumbrian,</u> 10 October 1885, p. 233.
(145) O.D. Edwards and P.J. Storey, "The Irish Press in Victorian Britain"
       in Roger Swift and Sheridan Gilley (eds), **The Irish in the**
       Victorian City, (Croom Helm, 1985), pp. 173/174.
(146) <u>Irish Tribune,</u> 17 January, 14 and 28 March, 11 April, 30 May,
       13 June 1885.
(147) Cowen to M. Johnson, 15 June 1884, Cowen Papers F51(1).
(148) Cowen to Kropotkin, 5 August 1885, Cowen Papers F45(17) and F46(1).
(149) <u>Irish Tribune,</u> 6 June 1885.
(150) Ibid., 31 October 1885.
(151) Ibid., 28 February, 13 June, 8 August 1885.
(152) Ibid., 21 November 1885.
(153) Ibid., 28 November 1885.
(154) Ibid., 10 October 1885.
(155) Ibid., 14 March 1885.
(156) Ibid., 14 February 1885.
(157) Ibid., 29 August 1885.
(158) Ibid., 14 February 1885.
(159) Ibid., 5 December 1885.
(160) Waitt, op.cit., pp. 236/237.
(161) Ostrogorski, op.cit., p. 237; <u>Newcastle Daily Leader,</u> 27 November
       1885; <u>Irish Tribune,</u> 12 September 1885.
(162) Ostrogorski, op.cit., p. 239.
(163) Holyoake, **Bygones,** op.cit., Vol. 2, p. 65.
(164) <u>Newcastle Daily Chronicle,</u> 17 and 24 August 1885.
(165) Ibid., 16, 17, 18, 19 November 1885.
(166) Waitt, op.cit., p. 281.
(167) Cowen cited in <u>The Times,</u> 2 July 1886.
(168) Cowen cited in Duncan, op.cit., pp. 151/152, 160/165.
(169) Cowen to Thomas Galway, 10 June 1886, Cowen Papers F93.
(170) Ostrogorski, pp. 240, 242.

CHAPTER ELEVEN: EPILOGUE

(1) Cowen to Joseph W. Pearse, 19 December 1896, Cowen Papers D503.
(2) J. McCarthy, **Reminscences**, Vol. 2., op.cit., p. 175.
(3) Cowen to F.A. Scuden, 5 June 1882, Cowen Papers F43.
(4) Cowen to Dr. Lees, 16 March 1883, Cowen Papers F47.
(5) <u>Figaro,</u> November 1891, cited by K. Harris in Bellamy and
     Saville, op.cit., p. 83, and a full translation of the
     interview may be found in P. Darvill, op.cit., Chapter 1,
     (appendix).
(6) Cowen to Holyoake, 21 June 1891, cited in K. Harris, **Notes.**
(7) May Morris, op.cit., p. 560.

(8)　　Julian Harney to Engels, 11 July 1887, in F.G. Black and
　　　　R.M. Black, **The Harney Papers**, (Van Gorcum, Assen, Netherlands,
　　　　1969), p. 321.
(9)　　Newcastle Weekly Chronicle, 8 June 1889.
(10)　 The Echo, 3 February 1891.
(11)　 Northern Democrat, No. 1, August 1906.
(12)　 T.W. Heyck, op.cit., p. 183; Hansard, 7 June 1886, Cols. 1193/1194;
　　　　Irish Tribune, 19 June 1886.
(13)　 Irish Tribune, 10 July 1886.
(14)　 E.I. Waitt, op.cit., p. 319; T.A. Jackson, **Ireland Her Own**,
　　　　(Cobbett Press, 1947), pp. 331/336.
(15)　 Cowen, 10 May 1898 cited in Duncan, op.cit., p. 185.
(16)　 Monthly Chronicle, Vol. 5., 1891, p. 526.
(17)　 Newcastle Daily Chronicle, 12 June 1909.
(18)　 Sir T.W. Reid, **Memoirs**, op.cit., pp. 45/46.
(19)　 F.H. O'Donnell, op.cit., Vol. 1., p. 332.
(20)　 New York Times, 25 February 1900.

INDEX